AH 121054

W9-CZM-121

YPT e/os 75.00

DATE DUE

OCT 0 5 2010	
NOV 0 1 2010	

GAYLORD   PRINTED IN U.S.A.

Handbook of
Chinese Mythology

TITLES IN ABC-CLIO's
Handbooks of World Mythology

HANDBOOKS OF WORLD MYTHOLOGY

Handbook of
Chinese Mythology

Lihui Yang and Deming An,

with Jessica Anderson Turner

A B C ☷ C L I O

Santa Barbara, California • Denver, Colorado • Oxford, England

Library of Congress Cataloging-in-Publication Data
Yang, Lihui.
    Handbook of Chinese mythology / Lihui Yang and Deming An, with Jessica
Anderson Turner.
        p.   cm. — (World mythology)
    Includes bibliographical references and index.
    ISBN 1-57607-806-X (hardcover : alk. paper) — ISBN 1-57607-807-8 (eBook)
1. Mythology, Chinese—Handbooks, Manuals, etc.   I. An, Deming.   II. Title.
III. Series.

    BL1825.Y355 2005
    299.5'1113—dc22

                                                                2005013851

This book is also available on the World Wide Web as an eBook. Visit
abc-clio.com for details.

ABC-CLIO, Inc.
130 Cremona Drive, P.O. Box 1911
Santa Barbara, California 93116–1911

This book is printed on acid-free paper.
Manufactured in the United States of America

CONTENTS

PREFACE AND ACKNOWLEDGMENTS

On October 30, 2000, I received an e-mail from William Hansen, a mythologist in classical studies at Indiana University. At the time my husband, Deming, and I were visiting research fellows in the Department of Folklore and Ethnomusicology at Indiana University in Bloomington. Professor Hansen told me that an editor at ABC-CLIO was looking for someone to write a handbook on Chinese mythology as part of its World Mythology series. He wondered if I could write this volume. I was pleased to hear the news of this opportunity. I responded to him swiftly: "Yes, I want to try." In fact, I had long hoped that someday I could introduce Chinese mythology to the West. I was encouraged to accept this great challenge.

I have studied Chinese myths for more than ten years. My PhD dissertation and my postdoctoral research focused on Nüwa myths. I have been conducting fieldwork on myths and relevant folk religion in Henan, Hebei, Gansu, and Shaanxi provinces since 1992, and I currently direct three research projects on mythology. For these reasons, I am familiar with ancient Chinese myths recorded in written accounts and living myths transmitted orally in China today. Additionally, I have learned how most Chinese mythologists think of myths and what they have accomplished in the field.

Since 1996 I have been teaching mythology to undergraduate and graduate students at Beijing Normal University. In this setting I have discussed mythology with students and addressed their questions about Chinese myths. I also frequently discussed Chinese mythology with American scholars and students in classroom and colloquium settings while a research fellow at Indiana University. These experiences have given me an understanding of what nonspecialists are interested in, and what might be the common misunderstandings of and biases toward Chinese myths.

To my knowledge, there are no Chinese mythology books written in English by Chinese mythologists. Although I am aware of several Chinese mythology texts that were originally written in Chinese and then translated into English, these books are quite limited. Among them, perhaps the most notable is *Dragons and Dynasties: An Introduction to Chinese Mythology* (Penguin Books, 1993), which was written in the 1960s by Chinese mythologist Yuan Ke (1916–2001). Because this book and others like it were written many years ago, they do not reflect new achievements in Chinese mythology, especially those occurring in the past twenty years.

Western scholars have made great contributions to the field of Chinese mythology from as early as the middle of the nineteenth century. Among numerous eminent books and papers, there are some that are exemplary, and thus cited in this book. Derk Bodde's article "Myths of Ancient China," a short but serious article, discusses many important issues pertaining to ancient Chinese myth studies. Anne Birrell's studies of Chinese mythology have been published in several books and are cited within this volume. Her *Chinese Mythology: An Introduction* is a valuable book that provides concise and insightful interpretations and reliable accounts that are translated from primary sources in ancient Chinese writings into English. Anthony Christie's book, *Chinese Mythology*, presents many primary classical Chinese myths and numerous beautiful illustrations. Many of the illustrations are rarely seen in mainland China.

In spite of the important contributions that Western scholars have offered, however, I have found problems with many of the English books on Chinese mythology written by Western researchers. First, the Chinese myths discussed in many of these books are usually limited to the ones recorded in ancient Chinese writings. They seldom, if at all, mention the myths that are spread orally among Han people (the majority of the country's population) and other ethnic groups in contemporary China.

Second, these books usually view Chinese myths from Western values and cultural tradition by nature of being written within Western scholarly circles. For example, these scholars often compare Chinese myths with the classical mythology of Greece and Rome, using the latter as the criterion for comparison and analysis. They sometimes ignore how myths are transmitted and function within Chinese society and culture. Additionally, these scholars often overlook how native Chinese mythologists view myth and what has been accomplished in current research and collection.

Third, their entries and sources are less selective, often including legends, folktales, historical anecdotes, and mythical figures of classical novels. Frequently the sources used in these books are an indiscriminate mix of different (and often historicized) classical documents. Two popular books about Chinese myths, for instance, *Myths and Legends of China* and *A Dictionary of Chinese Mythology*, both written by the English sinologist E. T. C. Werner (1864–1954), found their sources by mixing heterogeneous texts from ancient classics, mythical novels written by novelists in sixteenth-century Buddhist sutras, and classical Taoist texts. Unfortunately, though these two books have been sharply criticized by Chinese mythologists and other sinologists, they continue to be reprinted.

Fourth, an additional problem with many texts written by Westerners simply has to do with the difficulty of translating Chinese myths into English. Sometimes the original meanings of myths are misunderstood or are translated too literally by Western scholars. For example, in one case, the water god Gong-gong's name is translated simply and literally as "Common Work." A similar literal translation might be to interpret Confucius's name ("Kongzi" in Chinese) as "Hole Son," which clearly does not make sense.

For these reasons, it is reasonable to believe that these books provide readers more or less with noncomprehensive, confusing, or even misleading knowledge about Chinese mythology.

This book is a contribution to the many books written by Western scholars on Chinese mythology. It has some special characteristics among English-language books, which include:

1. **Native mythologists' standpoint.** This book makes the most of Western scholars' achievements in Chinese mythology, but it also pays attention to how Chinese people and Chinese mythologists perceive Chinese myths, and what they have done, or are doing, in the field of Chinese myth study, especially in the past twenty years. For example, this book introduces the enormous national project San Tao Jicheng, or the Three Collections of Folk Literature, which formally started in 1984 and is nearly completed. This book, and current Chinese scholarship on mythology, greatly benefit from this project. We also try to represent in this book the recent interpretations some Chinese mythologists and historians make about "the historicizing of Chinese myths."

2. **A more comprehensive picture of Chinese mythology.** This book not only presents the myths from ancient Chinese documents but also introduces living myths that are orally transmitted in contemporary China. Additionally, though this book focuses on the myths of Han Chinese people, it also details many myths of various ethnic groups living in China to illustrate the diversity of myths and people within China. The purpose of this is to give readers an idea of the whole picture of Chinese mythology, and to explain Han myths in a more interrelated background of Chinese mythology and culture.

3. **Emphasis on the relationship between Chinese myths and their social and cultural contexts.** This book not only illustrates myth as texts, it also pays much attention to the relationship between Chinese myths and the social, cultural, and historical contexts in which myths are created, transmitted, and reshaped. Special consideration is paid to questions that have rarely been discussed before: How are myths' existence and transmission influenced by their social and cultural contexts? How were myths thought about, recorded, and changed in different periods of Chinese history? How were myths used and reconstructed as an important cultural resource to

serve people's current needs? And how have myths influenced Chinese culture and society? Thus, this book does not take myths as isolated ancient "dead" stories but tries to show their living forces and interconnections with social and cultural contexts in many ways.

4. **More selected entries and sources.** This book exhibits myths that are often discussed by Chinese scholars and known by Han Chinese people. The types of entries include gods, goddesses, spirits, demigods, places of importance in mythology (e.g., Kunlun Mountain), important mythical animals and plants (e.g., Crow of the Sun; Fusang tree), mythological accessories (e.g., Xirang, the self-growing soil; the elixir of immortality), and mythical themes (e.g., the Flood). Entries refer to that which most Chinese mythologists think of as "myths," excluding legends and tales about some mythical characters such as the Cowboy and Weaving Maiden or the Horse-headed Lady; anecdotes about real historical heroes, and figures of Taoism and Buddhism such as Laozi, Confucius, Guan Yu, Guanyin, and the Eight Immortals; and the like. The sources of this book mainly come from ancient written documents, archeological findings, the national sources collected from the San Tao Jicheng project (some are not published yet and only can be accessed by Chinese scholars), and also from contemporary research including the authors' field research and the research of other Chinese mythologists.

When dynasties in ancient Chinese history are mentioned, their specific time period in the text is not indicated except when necessary for understanding. In the middle of the Introduction is a chronology of Chinese history that details different eras and dynasties in Chinese history. Additionally, to save space and avoid unnecessary repetition, information about the author, the commentator, the time an ancient Chinese text was written, and so on is usually provided only at a particular writing's first mention. Many of these texts are discussed in the Introduction or are listed in the Glossary. Furthermore, all translations in this book are mine or those of my contributors. Regarding sources we cite that are written by Chinese scholars, we follow the traditional Chinese practice of placing the person's family name first, followed by the given name. For example, my family name is Yang, and my given name is Lihui. In China this would appear as Yang Lihui. This tradition is followed throughout the book, though our names appear on the cover in the Western order.

To write this book I organized a team of authors. An Deming is an associate professor of Chinese folklore who works at the Institute of Literature at the Chinese Academy of Social Sciences in Beijing. His research interest is Chinese folk religion, which are closely connected to Chinese myths. He has conducted fieldwork on living myths in villages in northwest China. In this book, about one-fourth of the entries are written by him. Jessica Anderson Turner is a PhD candidate of the Department of Folklore and Ethnomusicology of Indiana University. She has visited China multiple times and continues to focus her research there. As a 2003–2004 Fulbright Fellow she did field research in southern China. Her current research focuses on revivals of tradition and music in China's developing tourism industry. In this book, her work has been to organize and edit our writing.

Writing this book has been a great challenge for Deming and me. Though both of us have published several books, this is our first written in English. Chinese myths and the ancient classics are familiar to us, but it is hard to translate them properly into a foreign language. Sometimes I spent half a day looking for a suitable English word in various dictionaries! From time to time we had to abandon complicated and delicate ideas and tried instead to express ourselves simply but clearly.

We want to sincerely thank many people for helping us to finish this book. William Hansen not only recommended us to become involved in this myth series but also gave many helpful suggestions for the basic structure of this book and the Introduction. Our colleagues and friends, Ma Changyi, Liu Xicheng, Song Zhaolin, Lü Wei, Liu Zongdi, Bamo Qubumo, Chen Ganglong, Zhang Xia, and many others, generously provided many supportive ideas or precious photographs they took in their fieldwork. The editors at ABC-CLIO, Todd Hallman, Bob Neville, Simon Mason, Vicky Speck, Peter Westwick, Carla Roberts, Michelle Asakawa, Craig Hunt, and many others have helped us greatly with their inspiring suggestions, encouragement, and patience. Deming and I especially show gratitude to Jessica. What she has done for this book goes far beyond what we asked. She not only polished our English but also gave us many bright ideas and useful tips to produce a better English book of Chinese mythology. We also thank her husband, Steve Turner, who worked with an ancient black-and-white drawing of Nüwa and digitally added color, as it is brilliantly shown on the cover of this book. We are also grateful to Lihui's mother and Deming's sister Mingzhu. They helped us immensely by taking care of our daughter, which enabled us to spend time to write this book.

Last but not least, we want to especially thank our daughter, An Xin, for her love and understanding. An Xin came into this world just two months before we began to write this book. She grows along with our writing. During the past two years, she often patiently waited until we finished our writing for the day to play with her. We feel extremely pleased that, at last, we have finished this book and can now play with her lightheartedly!

Yang Lihui
November 15, 2004, Beijing

INTRODUCTION

WHAT IS A MYTH?

When the word *myth* is used in everyday conversations, many people think of those things or phenomena that are untrue, unimaginable, or mysterious. For example, many people feel that tales of UFO sightings or personal accounts of UFOs are contemporary myths. Others might say "there are many myths in Hong Kong cinema. One of them is that audiences only like to see martial arts films." Some Chinese people believe that China is creating a myth, a marvelous story, through its incredible progress in the development of a market-oriented economy in today's world. These popular uses of the word *myth* are quite different from the definitions of *myth* used by scholars who study mythology.

In mythology, there are also different definitions of *myth*. In fact, scholars have been arguing about the definition for more than 2,000 years. Among the most common arguments are the ones that myths are stories about gods or remote ancestors, myths are sacred stories, myths are stories that explain how the world and humans came to be in their present forms, and myths encapsulate important information about human thought, feeling, history, and social life.

In China, scholars also have conflicting ideas about the definition of *myth*. For example, Yuan Ke (1916–2001), one of the most distinguished modern mythologists, views the scope of myth in the broadest sense. According to Yuan, fables such as "A Clam Fights with a Snipe" (wherein a clam that is basking in the sunlight is pecked at by a snipe; the clam nips the snipe's bill with its shells, and they both refuse to give in, at which point a fisherman comes by and catches them both), "Fox Borrows the Tiger's Fierceness by Walking in the Latter's Company," mysterious legends of historical emperors and officials, the legend of the White Snake Lady (a white snake transforms into a beautiful lady and marries a young man but is imprisoned under a magic tower by an officious monk), stories of Guanyin (known as Avalokitesvara in Buddhism), and mythic novels like *Journey to the West* (stories about a great, powerful monkey king named Sun

A Nüwa temple fair in Longcheng Village, Qin'an County, Gansu Province, northwest China, 1996. (Courtesy of Yang Lihui)

Wukong) all belong to myth.[1] Though his argument is quite well-known, most Chinese mythologists still concentrate their work on studying myth in a more narrow sense. For instance, Lü Wei, one of the pioneering mythologists in contemporary China, insists that myths are sacred stories that are told in the form of narrative and employ symbols, such as images of gods, and try to understand the cosmos through explaining the origins of the world, humans, and culture. Myths provide sacred evidence to testify to the validity, rationality, and legitimacy of cultural and social institutions.[2] When examining these arguments about myth while looking at the actual situations in which Chinese myths are transmitted, two reminders might be necessary for understanding Chinese mythology.

The first reminder is that *a myth is not necessarily sacred.* Many scholars believe that a myth is a sacred narrative, and it is often told in rituals.[3] By contrast, other scholars argue, "it can be misleading to focus on this quality as primary," stating that myths can also be told for entertainment and have no known connections with solemn ritual.[4] When investigating classical Chinese myths recorded in ancient writings, one may find that it is often hard to discern whether the myth tellers believe their myths to be true. Similarly, the attitude a

myth teller in contemporary China has toward his myths can be very complicated, too. In her fieldwork on Nüwa myths and beliefs from 1993 to 2003, in
the Henan, Hebei, and Gansu provinces of northern China, Yang Lihui found
that though many people came to Nüwa temples to worship Nüwa, when they
were asked whether they believed the myths about Nüwa, the answers were
quite varied. Most said "yes," some directly said "no, that's impossible," and
others half-believed these stories to be true.[5] They told these myths to express
their views and beliefs about gods and ancestors, or to boastfully display their
knowledge about remote history or local places, or just for fun. In those places
that have no relevant temples, myth tellers are more likely to tell myths for entertainment or traditional education (many people believe that myths can provide knowledge about their past).

The second reminder about myths in China is that *a myth is not necessarily told in the form of prose*. It may also be chanted in the form of verse. Though
it is well-known that Homer's epics, in verse form, are a treasure of Greek
mythology, in many cultures myths are usually told in prose. Myth is thus often
mentioned by scholars as one of the three major genres of "prose narratives,"
along with legends and folktales.[6] However, in China, some myths are told in
the form of an epic or sung as a song. Among Han people in Sichuan, Hubei,
Henan, and Shaanxi provinces, for example, a myth may be sung in a brief or a
long narrative folk song. It may be sung in wedding ceremonies, funeral rituals,
shamans' theurgist rites, or during the occasions of a temple fair. Sometimes
several myths are combined together into a long narrative folk song. It may be
sung continually in rituals for days. In some other ethnic groups of China, especially groups in the south such as Miao, Yao, Yi, Naxi, Bai, Zhuang, Achang, and
Lahu, creation epics are common. Since they tell myths, they are sometimes
called "mythic epics" by Chinese folklorists. A famed Miao creation epic, "Ancient Songs of the Miao People" (*Miaozu Guge*), found in the southeast of
Guizhou Province and usually antiphonally sung by two or more singers (one
asks questions, and the other answers) on traditional festival occasions and in
special ceremonies such as weddings or funerals, describes in detail the
processes of the creation of the sky and the earth, of making and fixing the huge
pillars between sky and earth, the creation of the sun and the moon and the
plants and animals, the marriage of the brother-sister human ancestors and their
repropagation of humans in this world, and the process of the Miao people's
moving around for a better life, finally finding the place where they live today.[7]
The myths narrated in this epic are also orally transmitted in prose. Similar situations (a myth can be narrated both in prose and verse) can be found in many
other ethnic groups.[8] Therefore, there is no absolute distinction between a myth
told in prose form and one in verse.

For ordinary readers, the "minimum definition" of *myth* offered by Stith Thompson in 1955 may be useful. "Myth," he writes, "has to do with the gods and their actions, with creation, and with the general nature of the universe and of the earth."[9]

A GENERAL INTRODUCTION TO CHINESE MYTHOLOGY

By *Chinese mythology*, we mean the body of myths historically recorded and currently transmitted within the present geographic boundaries of China. It should include not only myths transmitted by people of the Han ethnic group but also those by the other fifty-five ethnic groups living in this broad area. Since almost every ethnic group has its own mythical gods and stories about their creative actions, there is not a systematic, integrated, and homogeneous "Chinese mythology" held and transmitted by all the Chinese people. Even among Han people, there is not an integrated system of myths.

Since it is impossible to include in this single volume all the myths transmitted in a total of fifty-six ethnic groups of China, this book will basically introduce those well-known myths that are recorded in ancient writings in the Chinese language and orally transmitted by the Han people (whose predecessor is historically called the "Huaxia Ethnic Group"), which now make up nearly 92 percent of the country's population. Some of these myths have been recorded in ancient writings, and some are still orally transmitted in contemporary China. At the same time, this book will also introduce some relevant myths or mythic motifs of other ethnic groups. In doing so, we aim to give readers a general idea of the whole picture of Chinese mythology with the hope that readers will understand Chinese myths in the broader context of Chinese culture.

Main Sources for the Myths of Ancient China

The earliest written records of ancient myths can be traced back to about 3,000 years ago, though other forms of designs and paintings on shells, bones, and bronzes probably relating to myth appeared earlier than this. Recently, researchers found a bronze vessel named "Suigongxu" (Suigong was a duke of the Sui State, now belonging to modern Shandong Province; "Xu" is an ancient bronze vessel that has a cover and two ears; it functions as a food container), which was dated to the ninth or eighth century BC, the middle of the Western

Map of China. (Digital Wisdom)

Zhou dynasty. The inscription on the inside bottom of the vessel consists of 98 Chinese characters, praising the achievements of the mythic hero Yu. It tells the story that heaven ordered Yu to scatter earth, so Yu went around all the mountains, cutting down the trees in the forests and deepening the seas and rivers to drain all the water on earth into the sea.[10] This inscription shows that the technique of recording myth in Chinese characters had become relatively mature nearly 3,000 years ago. Additionally, it illustrates that at least as late as the middle of the Western Zhou dynasty, the myth about Yu controlling the flood had already been spread, and it had been historicized into a legend about a great hero or a great king in the upper class of society.

But these inscriptions recorded myths very simply. Sometimes the mythological stories they illustrate are hard to understand. Therefore, Chinese scholars rely primarily on accounts of myths recorded in later ancient writings after the Western Zhou dynasty to study these myths.

In China, there is no sacred canon recording myths, beliefs, or sacred history like the Bible or the Koran, nor were there any literati, troubadours, or shamans (sorcerer or sorceress) who collected myths from oral tradition and compiled them into a systematic and integrated mythology, like the Greek collections attributed to Homer and Hesiod. Rather, myths in ancient China were usually spread in scattered and fragmented forms in various written material. These sources contain information about archaeology, literature, philosophy, geography, history, witchcraft, ethnography, religion, folklore, and so on. Many of them preserve only a few myths, but some of them hold a comparatively large number of myths and thus become treasures of ancient Chinese myths. Among them, *Shanhaijing* (*The Classic of Mountains and Seas*), *Chuci* (*The Songs of Chu*), and *Huainanzi* are thought to be the major repositories of Chinese ancient myth.

Shanhaijing

Shanhaijing is an important book in ancient Chinese mythology studies. It is even noted by some as an encyclopedia of ancient China. It describes various mountains and seas, products of the mountains such as plants or medicines, myths, witchcraft, and religion of ancient China. It also records the geography,

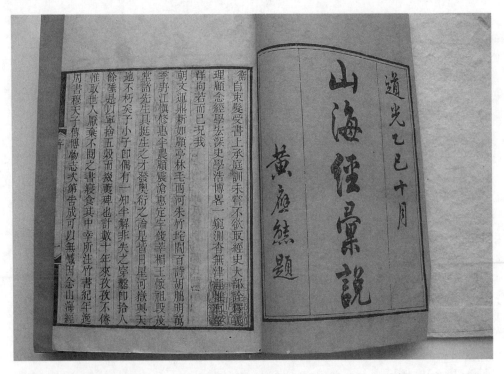

One version of Shanhaijing, *printed in 1845. Preserved in the Library of Literature Institute, Chinese Academy of Social Sciences. (Courtesy of An Deming)*

history, medicine, customs, and ethnicities in ancient times. The book contains eighteen chapters and can be divided into two main parts: the Classic of Mountains, and the Classic of Seas. The Classic of Mountains has five chapters, and the Classic of Seas has the remaining thirteen.

There is no widely accepted conclusion as to who wrote *Shanhaijing* and when it was written.[11] But most scholars believe that *Shanhaijing* was written by many different authors in different times. As for dating *Shanhaijing*, most think this book was written in the period from the middle of the Warring States era to the beginning of the Western Han era (ca. fourth century BC to the early second century BC).[12]

The focus of *Shanhaijing* is also quite controversial. Some scholars think that it is a geographic book, because there are abundant descriptions of various mountains, seas, rivers, roads, mines, and local products. Other scholars argue that *Shanhaijing* is a book about witchcraft, noting numerous descriptions in the text about gods and shamans' activities, such as how they went up and down sky ladders and communicated between gods and humans, how they produced winds and rains, and how they rescued dead gods with the elixir of immortality. This book also describes many sacrificial products and rituals, and even many shamans' names. Some scholars think *Shanhaijing* illustrates how primitive Chinese people in the Central Plain imagined the outside world.[13] Some argue that *Shanhaijing*, especially the chapters of regions beyond the seas and chapters of the great wildness, is in fact a description and interpretation of the ancient calendar system and calendric rites.[14]

Shanhaijing is commonly referred to as one of the treasures of Chinese mythology. Many well-known myths can be found in this book in their early versions, such as myths of Nüwa, Xiwangmu (the Queen Mother of the West), Gun and Yu, Jingwei, Huang Di and Chiyou, and also myths about the sky ladders, the pillars holding up the sky, the three-legged crow carrying the suns, and many others. Most of the time the plots of these myths were recorded only skeletally and fragmentally. For example, chapter 16 describes, "There are ten gods who named Nüwa's gut. Nüwa's gut turned into spirits. They took different routes and settled into the wilderness Liguan." There is no further explanation about Nüwa, the gut spirits, and the mythological event.

But sometimes *Shanhaijing* contains whole stories, written in the concise and condensed style that is common in most ancient Chinese records. For instance, in chapter 17, a text describes the battle between Huang Di, or the Yellow Emperor, and Chiyou:

> Here is Xikun Mountain, where the Gonggong Terrace is located. Archers do not dare to face it in the north. Here there is a goddess dressed in green. Her name is

the Huang Di's Daughter Ba. Chiyou made weapons and attacked Huang Di. Thus, Huang Di commanded Yinglong (Responding Dragon) to launch an attack against him in the wilderness of the Central Plain. Yinglong began by storing all the water. Chiyou asked Feng Bo (the Wind God) and Yu Shi (the Rain Master) to release a cloudburst. Then Huang Di asked the goddess Ba to descend down from the heavens and the rain was stopped. This eventually killed Chiyou.

The story recorded in this text is quite concise but complete. Besides this myth, myths about the divine bird Jingwei filling up the sea, the hero Kuafu pursuing the sun, and the cultural heroes[15] Gun and Yu controlling the flood are also found in complete forms. For this reason, it is difficult to agree with the argument that the narratives in Chinese myths are weak and that there are only a few Chinese myths narrating full stories.[16]

Chuci

Chuci is an ancient poem collection from the end of the Warring States era and the early Western Han era. It was written mainly by Qu Yuan (ca. 340–278 BC), who was the earliest celebrated poet in ancient China, as well as several other poets. *Chuci* literally means "the Songs of Chu." Originally it was widely used to refer to the songs popular in the Chu area (now Hubei and Hunan provinces in southern China) and sung by the Chu people. Because of this collection, which was compiled by the Han scholar Liu Xiang, *Chuci* became a title for a specific new poem style in the Warring States era represented by Qu Yuan. Its style is characterized by strong local flavor. It used the Chu dialect, was sung in Chu rhythm, and recorded many Chu places and local products. Besides these, differing from the folk songs of the Central Plain at that time whose style followed an orderly four-character poem, the sentences in a song of Chu were of different lengths. A more obvious characteristic of the Chu song is that in the middle of every sentence (and sometimes at the end), a syllable is always used as the mood indicator pronounced as "Xi." Apart from the folk songs of Chu, *Chuci* was also deeply influenced by Chu customs. Chu people believed in witchcraft and liked to offer sacrifices to gods and ghosts. When they offered sacrifices they often composed music and songs to amuse the gods. Qu Yuan was born in the Chu area and deeply influenced by Chu culture. He not only wrote poems by learning from folk sacrificial songs but also adopted a lot of Chu myths and legends to compose his poems. Among his poems, "Tianwen" ("Questions of Heaven") contains the most myths.

"Tianwen" was said to have been written by Qu Yuan after he was unjustly exiled from the royal palace of Chu. When he saw paintings of gods and ances-

*Qu Yuan (*Poems of Chu Yuan, *1638)*

tors on the walls of the ancestral temple of Chu, he wrote this poem on the wall to express his anger and doubt about reality and the universe. The poem asks 172 questions related to popularly spread myths, legends, and pieces of history. Among them are many myths, including myths about Gun and Yu restraining the great flood, Yi shooting down the surplus suns, Gonggong destroying the mountain that supported the heavens, Kunlun Mountain, Zhulong (literally meaning "Torch Dragon"), the eight poles supporting the sky, and the toad on the moon. "Tianwen" sometimes provides rich details about some ancient myths, such as the Gun myth:

When the sparrow hawk and turtle joined together (and offered strategies),
Why did Gun accept their suggestions?
He obeyed everyone's plea to stop the flood,
Why did the Supreme Divinity kill him?
His corpse was abandoned at Yushan,
Why did it not rot for three years?

. . .

He was blocked at Yushan and was not allowed to go west,
How did he surmount those lofty and precipitous peaks?
He metamorphosed into a yellow bear after his death,
Why did those shamans revive him?

. . .

This text contains many details of the Gun myth; some of them cannot be found in other writings. For instance, it states that when Gun began to try to control the flood, there appeared the sparrow hawk and turtle and they joined together. Scholars infer that when Gun tried to control the flood, he might have adopted suggestions and strategies of the sparrow hawk and turtle.[17] Other plots of the Gun myth recorded in this poem also are unique, such as Gun being detained at Yushan, or Yu Mountain, after his death and not allowed to go west. Taking on the image of a yellow bear, he managed to surmount those steep peaks to find shamans to help him come back to life.

However, since this poem was written in the form of questions, stories in the poem usually appear in fragments. Therefore, it is almost impossible to understand a full myth from it. Sometimes the questions were written in such a vague and succinct way that it is difficult really to understand what questions Qu Yuan was actually asking.[18] This shortcoming limits the role that "Tianwen" plays in Chinese myth studies.

Huainanzi

Huainanzi (ca. 139 BC) is a book written and compiled at the beginning of the Western Han dynasty by Liu An, the king of Huainan, and many of his aides. Liu An is said to have enjoyed reading books and playing music. He wanted to accomplish something beneficial to others and become a legacy. So he gathered thousands of literary scholars and alchemists to write *Huainanzi*, which is attributed to the Eclectics, a school of thought that combined various philosophies and flourished during the pre-Qin period.

Huainanzi preserves many ancient myths, legends, and historical accounts. The myths that it contains include the following: Nüwa repairs the broken sky; Yi shoots down the extra nine suns; Chang'e steals the elixir of immortality and flees to the moon; Yu controls the flood; Gongong butts into Mount Buzhou and destroys the sky pillar and the cords holding up the earth. Some of these myths are recorded only in *Huainanzi,* and some provide important contrasts to other ancient writings. Therefore, many of its records are often cited in studies of Chinese myths. Generally speaking, myths in *Huainanzi* are usually complete. Compared to myths recorded in *Shanhaijing* and "Tian-wen," which are usually recorded fragmentally, myths in *Huainanzi* are often written in a more complete form, with detailed story plots. For example, the myth of the goddess Nüwa in *Huainanzi* states that

in remote antiquity, the four poles supporting the sky collapsed, and the land of the nine divisions of ancient China broke up. The sky could not completely cover the earth, and the earth could not totally carry the world. Fires raged fiercely and did not go out. Floodwater ran everywhere and did not subside. The fierce beasts devoured kind people, and violent birds seized the old and the weak. Nüwa then melted stones of five different colors to patch the sky, cut the legs off of a huge tortoise and set them up to support the four extremities of the sky, slaughtered the Black Dragon to save the people, and collected ashes of reeds to stop the flood. After that the sky got renewed, the four sky pillars were set up again, the flood was stopped, and the nine divisions became peaceful.

Nüwa was mending the sky. Originally drawn in the 17th century by Xiao Yuncong. (Yang Lihui, Rethinking on the Source Area of the Cult of Nüwa, *Beijing Shifan Daxue Chubanshe, 1999)*

This text narrates a complete event: the setting, the reasons of the goddess Nüwa's actions, the process of the solution, and the result. It presents a precious record of an ancient Nüwa myth and thus is often cited by researchers.

Three Features of the Written Records

When we examine the written records of ancient myths in the Chinese language, three features seem to be obvious and often are argued by scholars: that the myths are scattered and fragmented, that they are historicized, and that they have been rewritten as literature and philosophy.

Scattered and Fragmented.   Myths in ancient China are preserved in various written accounts, usually in a fragmented form. They were not collected and organized into a single, systematic mythology of China. This phenomenon is usually taken as evidence of the scarcity and undevelopment of Chinese myths. Some scholars explain that this is because Chinese people pay more attention to real life than to the supernatural world. When criticizing the false impression that China has a deficiency of myths, Yuan Ke pointed out three major reasons that caused this characteristic. The first reason comes from the lack of gifted poets like Homer and Hesiod to collect various ancient Chinese myths from oral tradition and retell them in an eloquent style. The second reason is that in ancient times, Chinese writings were usually in "unwieldy and ideographic forms," not yet sophisticated enough to express the complexities of Chinese myths. And the third reason is the negative attitude of ancient Chinese scholars (especially the Confucians) toward the miraculous and marvelous elements in myths.[19] In contrast to the common idea that this characteristic is a disadvantage for the records of Chinese myths, Yuan Ke thinks it has some advantages. Chinese myths have not suffered what Yuan Ke describes as a complete reworking by literati and others, like Homer's and Hesiod's work, and thus remain in a more or less "pristine condition." Additionally, they are "more reliable documentary evidence of a primitive and archaic oral tradition in the world of myth."[20]

Historicized.   That early myth records were historicized has been recognized by many scholars. Zhong Jingwen and Yang Lihui have examined the history of myth study in ancient China, pointing out that the historicizing, or rationalizing, of myths is prevalent during the 2,000 years of mythology research before the fall of the Qing dynasty. If a scholar found something strange or incredible in the ancient texts, these findings would be removed or rationalized. An anecdote about Confucius (named Kong Qiu in Chinese, but is popularly respected as Kongzi or Kongfuzi, 551 BC–479 BC) states that when he was asked whether Huang Di was really four-faced as it was popularly said ("face" is pronounced *mian* in Chinese), he replied that in fact this meant that Huang Di sent four officials in four directions to administrate (*mian* also means "direction"). Another example comes from Luo Mi, a scholar in the Southern Song dynasty. When he wrote a book of history, he interpreted the myth of Nüwa repairing the broken sky as a historical event in which the ancient empress Nüwa put down a rebellion made by one of her dukes. After this rationalization, ancient scholars would then interpret these myths to be accounts of the history of China.[21]

However, recently some Chinese scholars have put forward different ideas. They think that the historicizing of ancient Chinese myths is a presumption or hypothesis made by Chinese scholars themselves. When Chinese scholars began to build a modern discipline of Chinese mythology at the beginning of the twentieth century, they were deeply influenced by Western scholarship and wanted to look for the subject of mythology in historical documents. Thus, there are arguments that these scholars changed history into myths. In the view of some scholars today, there is no such thing as the historicizing of myths. Instead, there was the mythologizing of history.[22]

Confucius (Bettman/Corbis)

Rewritten as Literature and Philosophy. Examples of myth being rewritten as literature and philosophy can be found in Taoist writings, especially in the book *Zhuangzi.* When the famous Taoist philosopher Zhuangzi (or Zhuang Zhou, ca. 369–286 BC; "Zi" is an ancient respectful address for a learned man) adopted ancient myths into his writings, he decorated them with many descriptions and filled them with his Taoist ideas. An example of this is the Hundun myth. Hundun is a god who has no openings on his body whatsoever. The gods Shu and Hu, hoping to pay a debt of gratitude to Hundun, tried to chisel openings into Hundun's body. They chiseled one hole each day. After seven days of their work, Hundun died. Like many other myths or legends appearing in *Zhuangzi,* the Hundun story has clearly been reshaped by Zhuangzi to illustrate his Taoist philosophy. The two meddling gods Shu and Hu are used to symbolize the artificial order (time and direction), while Hundun symbolizes the primeval chaos, which is a natural, unspecified, unified whole. In the story the artificial order destroyed the natural and harmonic whole. In this example, Zhuangzi used a very simple story to express his idea that one should respect nature and should not insist on doing something that is not natural. He stressed that politicians should let events take their own course, and they should not intervene in this natural order without understanding it completely.

Myths Orally Transmitted among Contemporary Han People

Textual analysis of ancient written recordings has long been the traditional method of Chinese mythologists. Though this method of literary text research is necessary and beneficial to Chinese mythology, it can be abused and cause misleading conclusions about Chinese mythology.[23] Today more and more Chinese mythologists consciously use a synthesis of methods by combining ancient written texts with material from archeological findings and oral tradition.

Concern for myths collected from oral tradition can be traced back to the early decades of the twentieth century.[24] The first large-scale collection of living myths in China occurred during the 1950s and 1960s.[25] But as noted previously, the largest collection of living myths from oral tradition in modern China is the national project San Tao Jicheng, or the Three Collections of Folk Literature.

The San Tao Jicheng Project

Formally begun in 1984 and near completion, San Tao Jicheng aims to be a general investigation of Chinese oral tradition. Managed by the Ministry of Culture, the State Ethnic Affairs Commission, and the China Federation of Literary and Art Circles, the project was carried out by the Society for the Study of Folk Literature and Art, which is now called the Chinese Folk Literature and Art Society. The project does not aim to collect only myths, though. Rather, it consists of three collections: stories (including myths, legends, fairy tales, jokes, and other prose narrative forms), folk songs and rhymes, and proverbs. The participants of this project first collected these stories, folk songs, and proverbs in villages, then chose part of the material and compiled it into a county collection. These county collections were then compiled into volumes for each province. As of 1990, over 4 million proverbs, 3 million folk songs and rhymes, and nearly 2 million stories had been collected. More than 2 million people were involved in this collection project.[26]

In the process of conducting this research, many orally transmitted myths have been collected and published. These myths were mainly gathered from the Han people, but some also spread in the vast areas inhabited by other ethnic

Zhong Jingwen (1903–2002), one of the founders and pioneers of Chinese folkloristics, the former executive deputy chief of the editing board of the San Tao Jicheng project, 1982. (An Deming, A Biography of Zhong Jingwen, *Shandong Jiaoyu Chubanshe, 2003)*

groups living in China. For example, as a result of the project, in Huzhou District, Zhejiang Province, more than twenty myths, all from Han people, were selected for the district's volume of stories.[27] In Sichuan Province, a book titled *Selected Myths from Sichuan Province* was published in 1992. This book contains more than 120 living myths and various versions that are spread among ten ethnic groups in contemporary Sichuan Province. Among them, over ninety myths and versions are collected from the Han, and others are gathered from Tibetan, Yi, Lisu, Qiang, Tujia, Miao, Hui, Naxi, and Mongol peoples.[28]

Some Chinese mythologists pay much attention to these living myths collected from oral tradition, especially from San Tao Jicheng, to study Chinese myths. For example, Zhong Jingwen studied the brother-sister marriage myth using material collected for San Tao Jicheng.[29] Zhang Zhenli, using data that he and his research team collected from Han people in the Central Plain area[30] as well as myths from this area collected in San Tao Jicheng, compared these recently collected myths with ancient ones. He conducted this research to discover relationships between classical myths and modern ones in order to understand how classical myths in this area changed over time, and how they exist in contemporary Henan Province.[31] Yang Lihui used more than 500 myths about Nüwa and the brother-sister marriage, mainly from the San Tao Jicheng project and from her own fieldwork in Han communities in modern Hebei, Henan, and Gansu provinces, in her book, *The Cult of Nüwa: Myths and Beliefs in China*. Stressing a more synthetic approach and the significance of context, she not only discusses the transformation of Nüwa myths during the past 2,000 years but also examines the social and cultural contexts in which myths are told today. She further looks into the functions of Nüwa myths and beliefs and the reasons why they are of great vitality today. Yang indicates several characteristics of the transformation of myths in modern Chinese society, comparing them to their ancient versions. These characteristics mainly include adhesion and the combination of various myth types and motifs, localization, secularization, and the influence of religion.[32] These forms of transformation can be found in many myths that are told orally in contemporary China.

A Myth-telling Performance in Renzu Temple

In 1993, mythologist Yang Lihui did a field study in Huaiyang County, Henan Province, to investigate how myths continue to be told in situational contexts[33] in contemporary Han communities, how classical myths are transformed and in what ways, and how and why people reconstruct them in their social and cultural lives.[34] Huaiyang County is located in the eastern part of Henan Province, 32 kilometers (20 miles) northeast of Zhoukou City. It has an area of 1,469 square kilometers (588 square miles) and a population of 1.24 million. Under its administration are six towns and fourteen villages.[35] Huaiyang is said to be the legendary capital of the god Fuxi's mythic kingdom. In the northern part of the county is the Renzu Temple complex (Temple of the Ancestors of Humans). According to a 1936 report, many temples were intact at the Renzu complex at that time, including several to Fuxi and one to Nüwa. During the Cultural Revolution (1966–1976), many of the temples—including Nüwa's—were destroyed because they were thought to be "feudal superstitions." Yet in 1993, the local government was planning to reconstruct the Nüwa temple because the government now believes that the worship of human ancestors (Fuxi and Nüwa) can be a cultural resource and can attract tourists and donations. This has encouraged folk beliefs and caused a folk-culture revival.

During the lunar cycle from February 2 to March 3, a festival now is held at the Renzu Temple complex to celebrate Fuxi's birthday. The festival draws tens of thousands of pilgrims daily from nearby villages, counties, and provinces. They come to Renzu for many different purposes: to make supplications to the ancestors; to thank the ancestors for fulfilling their supplications; and to pray for children, happiness, health, wealth, going to college, and many other things. Most of the pilgrims are women. Many of them travel here together in pilgrim associations usually led by women. Some stay for the full month of the celebration.

It is a genuine festival of local community. Outside the temples, business stalls extend for miles, selling local snacks, local handicrafts (such as "mud dogs" and cloth tigers), farm tools, and spiritual statues (Fuxi and Nüwa, Buddha, and even Chairman Mao Zedong). In the temples, there are more lively and exciting scenes. Besides the many vendors' stalls, the area is full of pilgrims: they may dance *danjingtiao* (a folk dance meaning "Carrying Pole Dance"), sing songs praising the ancestors, tell fortunes, and play local operas to please the ancestors. Among them, some women will bring shoes to Nüwa that they embroidered. They sacrifice the shoes to Nüwa by displaying them in the Renzu Temple complex or burning them with incense, paper money, or paper buildings (intended as ancestors' dwellings). By doing these things, they believe the ancestors will receive their tributes and be pleased, and thus will grant them what they hope for.

There are many customs specific to the Renzu Festival. Two that relate to Nüwa's myths and beliefs are *ninigou* and *jingge*. *Ninigou* ("mud dog") is a general name for toys made of mud. These toys are usually monkeys, swallows, turtles, tigers, or a combination of monkeys riding a tiger or a horse. The craftsmen who make the mud dogs explain their origin with a myth that the ancestors created humans by mud. The ancestors' children want to imitate their mythical activity and thus to remember them. These kinds of festival crafts illustrate how myths exist in local communities, even as toys, therefore making their place in nearly every level of society from ritual to play.

Jingge is a type of folk song that usually is sung to express people's folk beliefs, but sometimes people use the melodies to make fun and sing about their ordinary life. During the Renzu Festival, many pilgrims (especially women) will sing jingge to commemorate and praise the ancestors, simultaneously believing they can obtain the ancestors' blessings by doing so. As for the content, many jingge not only tell the myths of the ancestors but also often end with moral education or propagation—for example, this jingge song:

Remember the beginning of the world is chaos,
Without sky, without earth, without human beings.
Then the deity of sky created the sun, the moon, and the stars,
Then the deity of earth created the grain and grass.
Having the sky and earth, the chaos separated,
Thus appeared Renzu, the brother and sister.
They climbed to the high mountain Kunlun,
To throw the millstone and get married.
They gave birth to hundreds of children,
That's the origin of Baijiaxing (human beings).
Therefore, though people in this world look different,
In fact they belong to the same family.
How wrong it is to struggle for wealth and fame,
Because you can't bring them with you when you go into the grave.
I urge you to be a good person,
Because a good person can be blessed by the Renzu in earth.

A widespread myth at this festival is that of the brother-sister marriage. When Yang and her colleagues met a fifty-year-old woman (an illiterate peasant) who was selling local snacks in the Renzu Temple complex, they asked her if she knew something about the source of the Renzu Temple. She related a legend of why the Renzu Temple was reconstructed during the Ming dynasty. After that, when she was asked why people worshiped the ancestors, she told the brother-sister marriage myth: Once upon a time, there were a brother and his sister. Every day, when they went to school, they fed a stone turtle. One day when they fed the turtle, the turtle told them there would be a great flood. Only the two of them survived the deluge by hiding in the belly of the turtle. They wanted to marry each other in order to re-create human beings. Wondering whether this was proper, they decided to divine by throwing the two pieces of a millstone from two different mountains. The two pieces landed on top of one another, so they got married.

While this myth was being told to Yang, several others surrounded them, listening while the woman spoke. Upon hearing that the ancestors married, an older woman suddenly interrupted, "How can a brother marry his sister?! The two pieces of the millstone did not fall on top of each other, so they did not get married. That's why today brothers and sisters can't marry each other." The younger myth teller looked embarrassed and hesitated to continue. With encouragement from Yang and her colleagues, she concluded the story quickly and roughly: after the marriage, the brother and sister decided to create humans by molding mud. They placed the mud-humans outside to let them dry. But there

A group of pilgrims in the Renzu Temple complex during the temple fair. The leading woman was chanting jingge, 1993. (Courtesy of Yang Lihui)

came a rain. So they hurried to sweep the mud-humans back into their cave. During the process, some people lost their arms, some lost their legs, and some were blinded. That is why today there are some disabled people in this world.

Later Yang and her group caught up with the older lady and asked her to tell what she knew of the brother-sister myth. She told the same tale but in a more detailed and vivid narrative style: the brother and sister threw the two pieces of millstone from different mountains, and the two pieces separated. Therefore, the brother and sister did not get married. Then, they decided to create humans by molding mud. And when the rain came, some were disabled.

Afterward, she ended: "You literate people know human beings originated from monkeys. Why? Because when humans were created by the ancestors, they actually looked like monkeys, because they had fur on their skin. But they gradually changed, gradually changed, and then became human. Their children became more and more handsome and beautiful."

This is a myth-telling event, a moment of transmission and transformation of the myth. Many factors are interplaying in this dynamic process, including ethics, evolutionism, and belief. They interweave and shape the conduct of the myth-telling performance. This event also shows how a myth is recontextualized and transformed by a creative person. The older lady illustrated her creativity by changing the myth to solve problems of incest and evolutionism that exist in the brother-sister marriage myth. Therefore, she made it more reasonable to the modern moral system and scientific notion. While displaying to the folklorists and others her creative competence of myth telling and her authority in traditional knowledge, she also expressed her views and beliefs about ancestors, ethics, science, and human history.

Myths in Other Ethnic Groups

The Richness of Myth in China's Ethnic Minorities

Many Western readers think China is a single-ethnic country and that Chinese mythology is equally unified, integrated, and homogenous. In addition, because the Han people make up the majority of the population in China, when some Western scholars introduce Chinese myths they usually discuss only the myths of the Han people. But in fact, China has 56 ethnic groups including the Han. Since China boasts many ethnic groups, and almost every ethnic group has its own body of myths, myths spread in the modern geographic boundaries of China are rich not only in amount but also in types, themes, and motifs. For example, there are more than ten myth types explaining the origins of humans:

1. *Humans were made by gods.* Among this type, there are many subtypes, such as: (1) Gods created humans from mud. This subtype can be found in Han, Kazak, and many other ethnic groups. (2) Humans were made from carvings on wood. This type of myth can be found in Manchu, Lahu, and others. (3) Humans were made by combining many plants together. A myth told among the Tujia people states that the goddess Yiluo created humans, using bamboo as their bones, lotus leaf as the liver, cowpea as their gut, radish as their flesh, and a gourd as their head. Then she poked seven apertures into the head (two eyes, two ears, two nostrils, and one mouth) and blew air into them, and after that the human was alive. (4) Gods created humans by cutting a rein into pieces and then scattering them everywhere; these pieces transformed into human beings. This type of myth can be found in the Baima Tibetan ethnic group in Sichuan Province.
2. *Humans were sown from seeds.* A myth told by the Zou people in Taiwan states that a god sowed the seed of humans into the earth, and later humans grew.

3. *Humans were spat out from the mouths of gods and goddesses.* Among the Uighur people, it is popularly said that a goddess inhaled the dust and air of the universe and then spat out the sun, the moon, the earth, stars, and humans.

4. *Humans were made from sound.* A myth spread among the Miao people in Yunnan Province that after a huge flood, only a mother and her son were left. A god turned the mother into a girl to marry the son. When the son realized that the girl he married was none other than his mother, he ran into the wilderness and shouted. His mother followed him and also shouted. Where their voices sounded, there emerged humans.

5. *Humans came from the shadows of deities.* Humans were made by a god and a goddess projecting their shadows onto the earth. This type of myth can be found among the Miao people and other groups.

6. *Humans were created by two gods touching their knees together.* This myth, told by Yamei people in Taiwan, states that the first human couple was created this way.

7. *Humans were transformed from animals.* Among the Yao people in Guangxi Province, a popular myth explains that the great goddess Miluotuo carried a beehive home and refined the bees several times a day. After nine months, the bees were transformed into humans.

8. *Humans were transformed from plants.* A creation myth of the De'ang ethnic people in Yunnan Province describes that 102 tea leaves went around and around in the air for 30,000 years and then metamorphosed into fifty-one young men and fifty-one girls.

Besides these types of myths, there are many other types, themes, and motifs concerning the origin of humans in various ethnic groups, such as a human emerging from a cave, coming out from a huge stone or a gourd, being procreated by animals or plants, being born after a man married a goddess or an animal, being procreated by the sun, or being made from a corpse of a divine creature.[36]

Flood Myths

Most types and themes of Chinese myths are not confined to only one or two ethnic groups but are common to several ethnic groups. Flood myths have been documented among forty-three ethnic groups in China. These myths have different formal characteristics in different ethnic groups. Based on his study of over 400 versions of flood myths, Chen Jianxian, a modern Chinese mythologist, divided the flood myths in China into four principal subtypes:[37]

1. *The sibling ancestors received miraculous omens or instructions from gods.*

The main plot of this type states that a kind brother and his sister receive a prophecy from a god or goddess that there will be a destructive flood. Usually they are told to watch for omens of the flood (the eyes of a stone tortoise or a stone lion will turn red, a mortar will produce water, etc.). Because of the instruction or warning, the siblings survive the flood by hiding in the stomach of the stone tortoise or the stone lion. In order to re-create human beings, the siblings have to marry each other, but before that, they divine to decide whether they should do so (if they throw two pieces of millstone separately from two mountains but the two pieces still touch when they reach the bottom, or if they create fires on two different mountains but the smoke twists together). After their marriage, the sister gives birth to humans, or the two create humans by molding mud. Chen found that although this type of flood myth is spread in Bai, Manchu, and Hui ethnic groups, it mainly occurs in myths of the Han people. Therefore, he presumes that this type originated from Han people and was transmitted primarily by Hans.

2. *The Thunder God's revenge induced the flood.*

This subtype states that two brothers, the Thunder God and the ancestor of humans (his name differs in different texts), often quarreled with each other. One day, the human ancestor caught the Thunder God. But when he went out, his two young children (a brother and his sister; their names differ in different texts) set the god free. Before the Thunder God went back to heaven, he sent the siblings one of his teeth (or sometimes a seed of a gourd or pumpkin) and told them there would be a huge flood and they should do what they were told. When the flood came, all humans were destroyed except the brother and sister, who hid in a big gourd that grew from the seed sent by the Thunder God. In order to re-create humans, the siblings divined (their methods are various, and some are similar to the methods mentioned in the first subtype above) and then married. The sister later gave birth to a gourd. They cut the gourd into pieces, and the pieces turned into humans. Alternatively, they opened the gourd and from it came the ancestors of many ethnic groups. This type of myth can be found in fifteen ethnic groups— Miao, Yao, Buyi, Dong, Gelao, Hani, Han, Maonan, Mulao, Qiang, She, Shui, Tujia, Zhuang, and Li—but has been mainly transmitted by Miao people. Chen presumes that this type might have begun in Miao regions, especially in southeast Guizhou Province, after which it was diffused to other ethnic peoples in different regions.

3. *The only surviving man sought the Heavenly Maiden.*

This subtype states that the human ancestor plowed fields with his siblings. Every morning after they tilled, they saw that the plowed field had become uncultivated during the night. They found that a wild boar had done this. When his

Among some Han, Miao, Yao, and Tujia ethnic people, the brother-sister couple ances-tors are usually worshipped as Nuogong and Nuomu, the god and goddess who origi-nated the ritual of Nuo to drive away devils. (Yang Lihui, Rethinking on the Source Area of the Cult of Nüwa, *Beijing Shifan Daxue Chubanshe, 1999)*

siblings sought to beat or kill the boar, the human ancestor stopped them. As a reward, he received a prophecy from a god (disguised as the wild boar) that there would be a flood. He survived the flood by hiding inside a skin-covered drum (or a wooden box). He went to heaven and wanted to marry a heavenly maiden. He passed many tests and finally married the girl. They gave birth to three sons, and they became the ancestors of the Tibetan, Naxi, and Bai peoples. This type can be found among Yi, Naxi, Tibetan, Pumi, De'ang, Dulong, Lahu, and Mongol peoples but mainly is spread in the Yi and Naxi groups.

4. The brother and sister plowed the wilderness.

This subtype is a combination of the three types above. A myth of this type collected from Gelao people in western Guizhou Province in southwest China states that two brothers plowed a wild field with their sister. Every morning they saw that the plowed field had become uncultivated during the night. They found that an old man, who in fact was a god, had done this. The god told them that there would be a flood and instructed the elder brother (who was unkind) to take refuge in a stone boat, and the kind young brother and sister to hide in a huge gourd. As a result, the younger brother and the sister were the only survivors of the flood. They divined to learn whether they should marry to re-create humans (by the similar ways mentioned above). After the verification, they got married and later gave birth to a son. The son married a heavenly maiden and they became the ancestors of humans. This type is spread mainly among Yi and Miao peoples; therefore, Chen has deduced that it may have been formed from a mix of the different types of flood myths of the Yi and Miao peoples.

Among his conclusions, Chen writes that flood myths in China are quite rich not only in amount but also in their forms and types. These subtypes show different social lives and cultural characteristics of different ethnic groups, reflect ethnic identity, and illustrate the cultural communication and fusion between ethnic groups in China.[38] Though his classification and denomination of the subtypes need further analysis,[39] Chen's research provides a good example of how a type of myth is spread in many ethnic groups in China, how these myths relate to or differ from each other in different ethnic groups, and how they are transformed to fit into different ethnic cultures and social life.

Contexts of Myth Telling in Ethnic Minorities

Similar to the contexts of myth telling among the Han people, myths in other ethnic groups also are told on common occasions and in rituals. In the Maonan and Li ethnic groups in southern China, for example, myths are told like other ordinary spoken arts and are not necessarily told in rituals or special occasions. Anyone can tell myths, and there is no strict method for myth tellers to learn the art of telling myths.[40] Nevertheless, in her inspirational book about living myths in Chinese ethnic minorities, Meng Huiying, a folklorist who specializes in the oral tradition and folk belief of Chinese ethnic minorities, points out that the typical living myths rely on rituals and other special occasions when myths are told in heightened performances. Meng divided the rituals in which myths are told into four types according to their different functions: rituals offering sacrifices to heaven or ancestors, funeral rites, weddings, and rituals for daily activities such as rites of passage, praying for children, and building a new house. Examples for the first type of ritual come from the Naxi and Achang peoples. When people in the Naxi ethnic group offer sacrifices to the sky, according to tradition they will invite a *dongba* (shaman) to preside over the ritual. In the ritual, the dongba will chant classic texts (*jing*), which tell about the origin of their ethnic group and how this world was created by their ancestor, Renli'en. The Achang people divide their ancestors' souls into two types: *dajiagui* (literally meaning "big family ghost") and x*iaojiagui* ("little family ghost"). When offering sacrifices to dajiagui, the shaman will chant a creation epic that lasts one day and one night. The epic is "Zhepama and Zhemima." Zhepama and Zhemima were the first human couple in Achang mythology and belief. The epic describes how the sky and earth were created by these two ancestors, and how they created humans and cultural artifacts in this world. By chanting the creation epic in this ritual, people ask for blessings from their divine ancestors. At the same time, this epic reminds everyone in the community that they are children of the same ancestors. Thus, the mythic epic can be used to maintain the tradition and bring together the members of this ethnic community.[41]

In some ethnic groups, myths are told as part of funeral rites. In the Achang ethnic group, for example, a person is believed to have three souls. After a person dies, one soul will be sent into the grave and one soul will be sent to the ancestors. The third soul will remain in the home to be worshiped. The Achang people believe that only a shaman can properly arrange the three souls. After someone dies, the family will invite all members of the community to attend a funeral and will request that a shaman come and chant the classic texts. Before the shaman arranges for the souls, he will chant for an entire day. The first part of what he chants is the creation epic "Zhepama and Zhemima." Through telling the story of the first couple and how they created this world and humans, the ritual instructs the souls and audience who they are and who their ancestors are. The second part of this ritual is a chant of the history of the nomadic movement of the ancestors, which aims to tell the soul how to travel to meet the ancestors. So the creation epic chanted in funeral rites functions to direct the dead soul toward the ancestors and remind the living that death is not terrible but is a way to leave this world and live in another land with the divine ancestors. In this way the creation epic consoles the dead and the living, and builds a bridge to communicate between the dead and the living.[42]

A third ritual in which myths appear is the wedding. Lan Ke reported how creation myths were told in a wedding ceremony in 1974 in a Jingpo village in Yunnan Province of southwest China. The ceremony continued from morning to night with feasting, music, and dance. When evening came, the singing and dancing stopped, and guests went into the host's bamboo house. In the center of the house, people gathered and sat around a fire pit; then in a very solemn atmosphere, the *jaiwa* (shaman) chanted an epic named "Munau Jaiwa."[43] The main content of this epic is the creation myths and flood myths. It tells that in remote antiquity a flood destroyed the world. Only a girl and her young brother survived by hiding in a wooden drum. They were married following the sugges-

Khesigbuyan, a Mongolian epic singer, chanting "Manggus-yi darsan Üliger" (The hero conquered Manggus, a monster) in front of Oboo, while playing the khuur instrument. Balin You County, Zhaowuda Prefecture, Inner Mongolia, 2000. (Courtesy of Chen Ganglong)

tions of the Mountain God. Then they gave birth to a baby that could not eat or sleep and cried all day. The Mountain God cut the baby into eight parts. Four of the parts became four men, and the others became four women. Later they became the ancestors of some ethnic groups. Among them, the fourth one became the ancestor of the Jingpo people, and he then made a rule that from then on Jingpo people should not marry a sibling or a person with the same family name, and they should choose husbands and wives from certain other clans. This kind of myth told in rituals serves to confirm traditional history and remind people of the rules for marriage.[44]

Other instances in which myths appear include rituals such as praying for children, rituals when building a new house, rites of passage, and offering sacrifices to gods. For example, before the middle of the twentieth century, Wa people in Yunnan Province hunted for human heads to offer to a great god, Muyiji, who created the sky and earth, and to Xi'aobu (Corn God). Every March and April before the sowing of crops, people of the same clan went out to hunt for heads. The heads they found would be placed on altars, and the shaman would lead the clan in worshiping them, chanting the creation myth *Sigangli:* In the remote past the great god and human ancestor Muyiji ordered one god to create the earth and another to create the sky, the sun, and the moon. Muyiji created animals, plants, and humans. He put humans into a stone cave and led a small bird to peck the stone cave until it opened. The first human to come out was of the Wa people, followed by Han, Lahu, Dai, and Dan. Gradually the Wa people learned to settle down, to speak, and to build houses. They asked for seeds from Muyiji, and Muyiji ordered Xi'aobu to be the corn god. But when the Wa people planted the seeds they did not sprout, and when the harvesttime came, a flood destroyed the village. And then Muyiji told the Wa that they should offer human heads as sacrifices to the gods, and after they did this it would always rain during planting and growing, and there would be no flood during harvest. Later the Wa moved to where they live today in Yunnan Province, and their custom of using heads to offer sacrifices to Muyiji and the corn god was transmitted over time.[45]

Myth Tellers in Ethnic Minorities

Myth tellers play significant roles in maintaining myth traditions. By obtaining relevant knowledge and telling myths to others, they pass on myths from generation to generation and spread myths to many places. Myth tellers endow meaning and life to myths. When discussing myth tellers, scholars usually emphasize the importance of professional shamans. This is true to some degree, but there are others as well. Three kinds of myth tellers in ethnic groups are discussed here: shamans, storytellers or singers, and common persons. It should be noted that these three kinds of myth tellers can be found among the Han people, too.

Shamans.   Shamans play an extremely important part in preserving and transmitting traditional knowledge. Myth telling is often part of the work that a shaman does. In many places, shamans are known as the individuals who know the most about myths. In the postscript of his book *Mythological Stories of the Manchu People*, Fu Yingren, a Manchu folklore collector and formerly a shaman himself in Heilongjiang Province of northeast China, introduces the sources of the myths and sacred stories about gods that he gathered, and also the importance of the shaman in transmitting knowledge about gods. He writes that years ago, when shamanism was still popular, shamans were not allowed to tell others at will their knowledge about gods' origins and achievements. This could only be done when a shaman was very old, and he/she then told these sacred stories to his/her favorite students. When the old shaman taught these stories, he/she and the students had to burn incense, wash their hands, and gargle. The students had to kneel down to listen. During the era of the Republic of China, this strict rule gradually was broken, and Manchu myths were learned by more and more people. Fu himself became a shaman when he was fifteen years old, but he did not succeed at this. Afterward he was able to inquire into many myths and mythological stories because of his former shaman status. Eventually he knew so much about these stories that even older shamans often learned from him. The stories he compiled into his book were all told by shamans who were his relatives.[46]

A talented Yi folklorist, Bamo Qubumo, has written about the learning experience and performance development of a skilled epic performer of Nuosu people, a subgroup of the Yi ethnic people in southeast China's Sichuan Province. Qumo Yynuo was born into a professional *Bimo* (shaman) family in 1977. He began to learn to perform rituals from his father when he was seven years old. When he was fourteen he achieved expert status and began to be a master of ceremonies by himself. At age fifteen he formally began to study the *kenre* (a kind of verbal dueling) tradition. He attended many ceremonies where he chanted epics in the kenre form, and gradually he became a famous and skilled epic performer. Among his knowledge about Yi epics, the *Hnewo* epic tradition is significant. Hnewo can be chanted at weddings, funerals, and during soul-sending ceremonies in the specific narrative form of kenre. It has two forms, female and male. The male parts are all about heaven, and the female parts are all about the earth. There are twelve acts in the female part, which are used especially in wedding ceremonies. There are seven acts in the male part, generally used in funerals and in ceremonies one or two years after a funeral to send the ghost away to the ancestors. The male part tells how the gods were summoned by the god of heaven and how they created the sky and the earth; how one of the gods called the sun and moon, and they appeared; and how the hero Zhyge Alu shot down the surplus suns and moons. The female part explains why the gods in heaven wanted to create humans, how the snow on earth came into being, and how it changed. With his extensive knowledge of Yi culture, Qumo has achieved a wide reputation. He not only inherits the shaman tradition but inherits the epic tradition as well.[47]

Storytellers and Singers. Talented singers or storytellers can also be important bearers of mythological tradition. When the Dong people in southern China offer sacrifices to their ancestors, they gather together to sing songs and dance to entertain the gods. The ritual can be presided over by a shaman or sometimes by a middle-aged singer. People who attend will be divided into groups according to gender. They join hands and make two circles, one inside the other. One circle is male, the other female. In these circles they will sing and dance. Several people

The talented Yi epic singer, Qumo Yynuo, chanting an epic during a wedding ceremony, 2001. (Courtesy of Bamo Qubumo)

will lead the singing and others will follow. The content of the songs includes the creation myths of the Dong people.[48]

In Xiuyan County, Liaoning Province, in northeast China, there are many Manchu people. In the 1980s, researchers collected 115 stories from a distinguished female Manchu storyteller named Li Chengming (1914–). Among the forty-six stories that were published, there are five myths. These myths explain how humans were created by the first brother-and-sister couple after the cosmos was destroyed; why humans lost the paradise of harvesting endless grains because they took these grains for granted; how the sun and the moon were created, and why people could not look at the sun directly with their eyes; how the divine maiden Hailun repaired the broken sky; and how the ancestor of the Manchu people was born after his mother consumed a hawthorn fruit and miraculously became pregnant. Li's repertoire of stories came mainly from her father and grandfather. As an ordinary Chinese farmer, she often told stories to her neighbors and children during the slow seasons in farming, occasions of working with other people, or during the relaxed long winter nights on her warm *kang* (a brick bed that is warmed by a fire built underneath, popular in northern China).⁴⁹ The two collectors of her stories state that in these contexts, the storytellers in Xiuyan County transmit the wealth of stories they inherit from previous generations.⁵⁰

Common People as Bearers of Mythological Tradition.   Ordinary people also bear some traditional mythical knowledge though they are not specifically connected to professional or highlighted myth-telling activities. Since their possessions of myth are usually fragmented and scarce and they are often reluctant to tell myths in their daily lives, these people can be called "passive bearers of myth tradition."⁵¹ When Yang Lihui asked some ordinary pilgrims in the Renzu Temple complex whether they knew any stories about Fuxi and Nüwa, most of them could not relate the full myth but did know that humans were created by the ancestors in the remote past. In another small village in Gansu Province, northwest China, when Yang asked several old men and women chatting beside a country road about the flood myth, two of them knew only that there was indeed a flood in remote antiquity that destroyed almost the whole world. And then they sighed deeply about the complicated development of this world and the hardship of their lives. So, though these common people are passive bearers of myth tradition, they also use mythological material to create their own ways to express their views and attitudes about history, the world, and their lives.

MYTHS WITHIN CHINESE HISTORY AND SOCIETY

Myths are neither static nor separate from society. Rather, their existence and transmission are deeply influenced by their social and cultural contexts. In this section, myths in the Chinese language will be put into the context of Chinese history and society. The purpose of this is to illustrate how Chinese myths have continually been transmitted and shaped during the past thousands of years. This section will pay special attention to these questions: How were myths thought about, recorded, and changed in different periods of Chinese history? Who was involved in this? Why did people record myths? And how were myths used and reconstructed as an important cultural resource to serve people's needs?

It may be important to remind readers that the examples used in this section are chosen from the authors' standpoint. Others may select different examples and find different aspects of Chinese history and society to relate to myths. Additionally, since information in written documents about how common Chinese people thought about and told myths in ancient China is limited, the description in this section, especially the parts about myths in ancient China, will primarily rely on texts written during those periods by intellectuals. A more comprehensive and synthetic study about this topic needs to appear in the future based on more complete data, including analysis not only of written accounts but also of silk paintings, funerary stone carvings, cliff paintings, inscriptions on stone tablets, and other historical materials.

Before continuing on, the reader may wish to peruse the following table for a review of the dynasties and other ruling powers and coordinate dates throughout Chinese history.

A Brief Chronology of Chinese History

Five August Emperors (legendary)	ca. 30th century BC–ca. 21st century BC
Xia dynasty	2070 BC–1600 BC
Shang dynasty	1600 BC–1046 BC
Early Shang dynasty	1600 BC–1300 BC
Later Shang dynasty (Shang/Yin)	1300 BC–1046 BC
Zhou dynasty	1046 BC–256 BC
Western Zhou dynasty	1046 BC–771 BC
Eastern Zhou dynasty	770 BC–256 BC
Spring and Autumn era	(770 BC–476 BC)
Warring States era	(475 BC–221 BC)
Qin dynasty	221 BC–206 BC
Han dynasty	206 BC–AD 220
Western/Former Han dynasty	206 BC–AD 25
Eastern/Later Han dynasty	25–220
Three Kingdoms	220–280
Jin dynasty	265–420
Western Jin dynasty	265–317
Eastern Jin dynasty	317–420
Southern and Northern dynasties	420–589
Sui dynasty	581–618
Tang dynasty	618–907
Five dynasties	907–960
Song dynasty	960–1279
Yuan dynasty	1206–1368
Ming dynasty	1368–1644
Qing dynasty	1616–1911
Republic of China	1912–1949
People's Republic of China	1949–

The Pre–Qin Dynasty Period (before 256 BC)

Many Chinese scholars believe that the emergence of myth is intimately related to the beginning of clan societies. They deduce that Chinese myths might have been created at least 10,000 years ago with the advent of clan societies, flourishing when clan societies were well developed in the middle to late Neolithic era. This hypothesis has been partially confirmed by archeological data. In 1930, for example, Shandingdong Man, dating to about 18,000 years ago, was found at Zhoukoudian, in the Fangshan district of Beijing. Many Chinese archeologists think that Shandingdong Man shows that the social organization of the people had already changed from primitive society to a clan community. Some believe that Shandingdong people had a belief in the existence of the soul. Some scholars even assume that Shandingdong Man might have known some basic and simple myths to accompany those beliefs.[52]

In the middle to late Neolithic era of 3,500–7,000 years ago, prehistoric people within the modern boundaries of China had some complicated ideas related to myths. The patterns and decorations molded or carved on stone, jade, bone, wood, and pottery tell mythical stories. Comparing these relics with ancient writings, we may get an idea about the myths of that time. In Hemudu village in Yuyao County, Zhejiang Province, a bone dagger was found in 1973 that dated back to 7,000 years ago. On the handle of the dagger was a carved pattern depicting two symmetrical birds carrying the sun.[53] This motif of a bird carrying the sun can also be widely found on pottery in many cultural relics from modern Gansu, Shaanxi, Henan, and Shanxi provinces. Classified as the Miaodigou Type of Yangshao Culture (a Neolithic culture of central China), these relics are usually dated to 6,000 years ago. In these relics the bird carrying the sun is sometimes depicted with three legs. This same motif can be found in myths recorded in ancient writings, such as *Shanhaijing, Huainanzi,* and *Lunheng* (*Critical Essays,* written by Wang Chong, 27–ca. 100 CE). According to these texts, there was a crow settling on the sun (some versions say there were ten crows settling on ten suns). The crow functions as the spirit of the sun or, variously, the one who carries the sun across the sky. Sometimes the bird is said to be three-legged. According to an account in *Shanhaijing* (chapter 14), there was a huge tree named *Fusang* (Leaning Mulberry) in the eastern Tang Valley. In its branches rested the ten suns. As soon as one sun came back from its journey crossing the sky, another sun started forth. Each of the ten suns was carried by a crow. An earlier text, "Tianwen," ambiguously mentions the crow of the sun in the story of Yi, asking: "Why did Yi shoot down the suns? Why did the crows shed their feathers?" Wang Yi (ca. second century CE), the commentator of "Tianwen," cited a paragraph from *Huainanzi* to explain these questions, stating that at the time of Yao (a demigod of the three sage kings), the ten suns rose together and burned up the woods and grass. Yao then ordered the hero Yi to shoot down the ten suns in the sky, and Yi shot down nine of them. The nine crows settling on these suns died, and their feathers fell out. In later versions, the crow of the sun is sometimes said to be three-legged. So it can be concluded to some degree that in the middle to late Neolithic era, the mythical motif of a bird carrying the sun or a bird settling on the sun (the number may be interpreted as plural) is already quite developed. Those written myths are not just single occurrences of such mythical ideas. Instead, they receive support from artifacts found by archaeologists. It may be further assumed that the designs carved on bone or other materials were telling the sun myth in another way, not in spoken language, but in drawings and engravings.

During the Zhou dynasty (1046 BC–256 BC), written records about ancient myths in the Chinese language became more and more visible. An obvious reason for this is the mature writing system of the Zhou. From these records and comments on myths, we can see that Zhou culture and society had an impact on people's views about myth, and thus influenced the transmission and transformation of ancient myths.

The first example demonstrating this relates to the rationalism during the Eastern Zhou dynasty (770 BC–256 BC) and Confucius's historicizing interpretation of the Kui myth. Chinese intellectuals began to rationalize and historicize myths at a very early time.[54] During the Eastern Zhou dynasty this became more popular.[55] Many intellectuals doubted the reality and authenticity of myths (such as the great poet Qu Yuan), and some of them further interpreted myths by rationalizing or historicizing them. A typical example is Confucius's historicizing interpretation of the Kui myth. Kui is a one-legged mythical monster. According to *Shanhaijing* (chapter 14), Kui was said to be a divine beast who lived on Mount Liubo (*liubo* literally means "flowing wave") in the East Sea. It looked like an ox but was gray, hornless, and one-legged. Whenever it came out or dived into the sea, a storm would follow. Its light was like the sunlight and moonlight, and its sound was like thunder. Later it was caught and killed by Huang Di, who made a drum by using its hide as the cover. When struck with the bone of the Thunder God, the drum made a great sound that could be heard over five hundred miles away. Huang Di used the drum to show his power to the whole world. In some versions, this drum made of Kui's skin played an important role in the battle between Huang Di and Chiyou, the god of war and the inventor of military weapons. Huang Di beat the drum many times during the war. The sound it made was so great that it prevented Chiyou from flying away; thus Chiyou was caught and beheaded by Huang Di.

But Confucius cunningly demythologized the Kui myth and rationalized it as real history. According to a story in *Lüshi Chunqiu* (*Annals of Master Lü,*

Kui. Originally drawn in the 17th century by Jiang Yinghao. (Ma Changyi, The Classic of Mountains and Seas: Ancient Illustrations with Annotations, *Shandong Huabao Chubanshe, 2001)*

third century BC), a king of the Lu state felt strange about Kui's image, so he asked the erudite Confucius whether Kui was in fact one-legged, which is pronounced *yi zu* in Chinese. Confucius replied that the meaning of *yi zu* is actually "one is enough." In Chinese, the word *yi* means "one," and the word *zu* can be understood as both "foot" and "enough." So, *yi zu* can be interpreted as both "one leg" and "one is enough." Confucius used the term *zu* as a pun to create a fabled lesson from the Kui myth. He described Kui as an accomplished and talented official who contributed much to society. He explained that Kui was the master of music for the sage king Shun, and he adjusted musical tuning and harmonized music. People became convinced that Kui was indeed a model official. Therefore, Confucius explained, if an emperor had an excellent official like Kui, one was enough. In this way, Confucius skillfully dissolved this myth and rationalized the Kui story. He cunningly turned Kui, the one-legged mythical monster, into a virtuous and talented historical official.

Using similar methods, Confucius also rationalized myths that "Huang Di lived for three hundred years" and "Huang Di had four faces." These anecdotes were frequently cited in later years by many Confucianists. His rational attitude provides an exemplary model for pragmatically dealing with myth and legend.

As the founder and representative of Confucianism, Confucius was not interested in the supernatural realm, though he did not obviously argue against the existence of gods and ghosts. He paid attention to what he considered real in life instead of oddities, violence, disorder, and spirits. Derk Bodde asserts that Confucius's attitude toward myth relates to Confucianism. The Confucianists were, more than any other school of thought, "historically minded," and "always intensely interested in the search for historical precedents which would confirm their own social and political doctrines; on the other hand, their strong humanism tended to make them either indifferent toward supernatural matters, or to seek to explain them in purely rationalistic terms."[56] Zhong Jingwen and Yang Lihui argue that on a wider scale, rationalism was quite common throughout world mythology in certain periods of time. Its emergence also has to do with the development of rational intellect.[57] Some scholars find that the rationalism often used by Chinese scholars in ancient times is just the opposite of euhemerism in Greek studies. Coming from a novel written by a Greek writer, Euhemerus (late fourth century BC), the term *euhemerism* refers to the modification of human hero kings to gods. In contrast, Chinese scholars regularly eliminated the supernatural or marvelous elements in a myth that seemed to them improbable, and then interpreted myths as real history, and the gods as humans.

Another example from the Eastern Zhou dynasty illustrates the political struggle, the integration of ethnic groups, and the systematization of a pantheon of gods during that period. During the Spring and Autumn period (770 BC–476 BC, the first era of the Eastern Zhou), there were many clans living within the boundaries of modern China. Besides the four main ethnic groups of Xia, Shang, Ji, and Jiang, who lived in the Central Plain and formed the primary part of the Huaxia people (the predecessor of the Han people), there were more than one hundred small states and ethnic groups around the areas that now belong to Hebei, Henan, Shaanxi, Shandong, Jiangsu, and Anhui provinces. These ethnic groups all have their own divine ancestors and myths about their ancestors' miraculous birth and marvelous achievements. For example, Shang people believe that the founder of the Shang, Qi, came from a swallow that was sent down by heaven, whereas Zhou people confirm that their founder, Qi (different from the Shang's Qi), was born after his mother, Jiang Yuan, stepped into a huge footprint and became pregnant.

However, the situation began to change considerably during the Warring States era (475 BC–256 BC, the latter era of the Eastern Zhou). At that time, these states began to fight and integrate with each other. During the early part of the

Warring States era, there were just over ten states remaining. Among them, the most powerful were the seven states of Qin, Qi, Chu, Yan, Han, Zhao, and Wei. They struggled to annex other states and expand their land and power. In order to facilitate the amalgamation, to break up the substantial divide between states and ethnic groups, the formerly scattered and independent divine ancestors were connected and re-created into a new pantheon of gods. According to the brilliant historian Gu Jiegang's (1893–1980) research, the divine ancestor of the Chu people was originally Zhurong, but at this time he was changed to Zhuanxu; the ancestor of the Qin was originally born by Nüxiu after she consumed an egg dropped by a swallow, but then he also became the offspring of Zhuanxu. The northern ethnic group Hun (Xiongnu) and the south Yue were originally unrelated to each other and to Huaxia, but then they all became descendants of Yu, who was also said to be a progeny of Zhuanxu in late tradition. Since there were many unrelated gods and ancestors from different ethnic groups now in a new pantheon, scholars in the Warring States era rearranged their relationship to solve the problem: they changed their synchronic relationship to a diachronic one. The two adversary peoples, Shang and Zhou, were suddenly depicted as a brotherhood; the mothers of their founders were supposed to be the wives of the supreme god Di Ku.[58] Moreover, later both Zhuanxu and Di Ku became descendants of Huang Di. In this way, these states and ethnic groups were all attributed to the same lineage, and the amalgamation (especially the bigger states annexing the smaller ones) was thus proved reasonable.[59]

The Han Dynasty (206 BC–220 CE)

Historians consider the Qin and Han dynasties as the first Chinese empire. Though the Qin dynasty is famous in later years for the Great Wall and the Terracotta Warriors (thousands of life-size pottery warriors, horses, and weapons that were unearthed in the 1970s), it was quickly overthrown by the Han dynasty in 206 BC, only fifteen years after it unified the country. The Han dynasty not only boasted a much longer vitality (426 years) but also was very influential in Chinese society and culture long after it ended. Even today, the majority of Chinese people are called "Han," the Chinese language is called "the Han Language," and the Chinese writing system is called "Han Characters."

Written myth texts in the Han dynasty enjoy an important significance in Chinese mythology. Scholars often use the myths that appeared in Han recordings when they investigate myths in early times of ancient China. Myths in Han recordings usually are more complete and detailed, whereas recordings before the Qin dynasty (primarily the Zhou dynasty) tend to be fragmented and were frequently historicized. Even so, Han writers adopted many living myths from popular tradition into their writings, so they sometimes provided new myth versions. For this reason, although Han writings appeared later than the myths written before the Qin, it does not necessarily mean that myths in Han texts emerged later than those of earlier texts. They might have been popular in earlier times and only were recorded in later years by Han writers.

In the first general history book of China, *Shiji* (*Historical Records*), written by exemplary historian Sima Qian (ca. 145–ca. 86 BC), a number of myths, together with various legends, folktales, and popular customs, are described. Among them are myths of the Five August Emperors (names differ in different texts; in this book, they are Huang Di, Zhuanxu, Di Ku, Yao, and Shun), the remote ancestors of Shang, Zhou, Qin, and Chu peoples. These myths came from earlier written literature, but sometimes they also took their sources from popular living tradition. For instance, the myth of the Shang founder Qi says that Jiandi is a daughter of the Yousong clan and is the second concubine of Di Ku. One day, when she went out to bathe with Di Ku, she saw a swallow dropping an egg. She picked it up and swallowed it. Then she inexplicably became pregnant, and later gave birth to Qi. Compared to the earlier two texts appearing in *Shijing* (*The Classic of Poetry*, compiled in or before 500 BC) and "Tianwen," the story in *Shiji* is more complete and contains several details that cannot be found in the former two texts. Besides this, *Shiji* provides a different version of the miraculous birth story of Houji, Zhou's founder. Guo Biheng deduces in his dissertation that Sima Qian might have adopted these myth versions from living oral tradition.[60]

When discussing the reason why Sima Qian used abundant material from living popular tradition to write a historical book, Guo Biheng notes the lack of written sources in the early ages of the Western Han. After Qinshihuang (the First Emperor) of Qin unified China, he and his assistants felt that those earlier classic writings of philosophy and of histories of other sizeable states were subversive to their rule. To eliminate these potential dangers, in 213 BC they burned all books except for the ones on agriculture, medicine, and divination, as well as the ones collected by the Qin government. But soon after that, in 209 BC, when the leading rebel, Xiang Yu, overthrew the Qin, he burned the Qin palace and those books stored by the Qin government. These two fires destroyed almost all of the books written before this time. For this reason, in the Western Han dynasty, intellectuals were busy rewriting classics of earlier times by recalling them from memory, or by finding new sources from living tradition. This was the case when Sima Qian began to write his historical book. Finding the earlier

Sima Qian (Instructional Resources Corporation)

historical accounts severely deficient, he had to rely on the living popular custom and oral tradition to supplement the shortcoming.[61] What's more, he spent several years visiting places that now belong to Hubei, Hunan, Anhui, Zhejiang, Jiangsu, Shandong, and Henan provinces. He collected abundant historical materials, among them rich folk literature.

But Sima Qian did not accept all the myths he received from oral tradition and writings. Instead, he selected what he wanted and re-worked them into his book. The history in his book begins with the story of the five emperors (apparently he did not take the Three Divine Sovereigns as the start because their achievements are more implausible). When he dealt with hundreds of stories about Huang Di, he cast away those versions too vulgar and spectacular for him, and he selected what he felt to be "elegant." According to myths about the battle between Huang Di and Chiyou, when Chiyou attacked Huang Di, Huang Di commanded Yinglong to launch an attack against him in the wilderness. Yinglong began by storing all of the water. Chiyou asked the wind god and rain master to release a cloudburst. Then Huang Di asked the goddess of drought to descend from the heavens, and the rain was stopped. Eventually Huang Di killed Chiyou. Other stories state that Chiyou was able to soar into the sky and overcome the dangerous and difficult obstructions. But Huang Di made a drum from the hide of Kui and beat it many times. The sound it made was so great that it prevented Chiyou from flying away. So Chiyou was caught and killed by Huang Di. Another version states that Chiyou led many ferocious mythical animals to attack Huang Di at the Zhuolu plain. So Huang Di ordered his subjects to blow horns sounding like dragons to threaten them. Sima Qian did not put all of these myth versions into his own rendition of the Huang Di story. About this fierce battle, he says only that Chiyou was a duke under the administration of Huang Di. He did not obey Huang Di and later rebelled against him. Thus Huang Di called up an army of other dukes and fought with Chiyou. Chiyou was killed at last, and Huang Di was respected by the dukes as "the Son of Heaven." Obviously, Sima Qian abandoned these "mysterious" or "absurd" myths about this battle between gods. Furthermore, he historicized stories that he felt were relevant, as most ancient scholars did in their works.

Toward the late Han dynasty, the predominantly Confucian thought in the Western Han became weakened within society. The "Five Elements" (metal, wood, water, fire, and earth, which were thought to be the basic substances of the world and were sometimes used to explain the origin of all things in the world, or a person's fate) and divination, combined with pseudoscientific reasoning, became extremely popular. Many people believed in mystical prophecy and superstition. In this social context, a philosopher named Wang Chong (27–ca. 100 CE) wrote the book *Lunheng* (*Critical Essays*), criticizing this kind of social phenomenon. He argued that superstitions and mystical prophecies were untrue. His evidence mainly came from real-life experiences. In his book he cited plenty of myths, such as that Nüwa repaired the broken sky, Yi shot down the ten suns, Cangjie invented Chinese characters, Jiandi devoured a swallow egg and gave birth to Qi, Jiang Yuan stepped into a huge footprint and gave birth to Houji, Gonggong butted into a pillar of the sky, and many others. Wang Chong's purpose was not to record living myths, though, but to use his experiences to demonstrate that these "popular sayings" or superstitions were unfounded. For example, he argued that the myth that Nüwa repaired the broken sky was nonsense. He reasoned that the heavens could not be made of stone and that as a human, Nüwa could not reach it to repair the sky with melted stones. He recorded myths in order to criticize them using the argument of common sense. His ideas represent the belief that myths are false knowledge, which is opposite to the idea that myths are historical. His ideas found many supporters in later times as others criticized myth as superstition in other periods of history, even today.

After Han through the Qing Dynasty (220–1911 CE)

Many Chinese people feel that all of Chinese history is a series of dynastic circles, because almost every dynasty repeats a similar story: a heroic founding, an arduous establishment, a prosperous period, a long decline, revolt and rebellion, collapse, and replacement by a new dynasty. Writing about the Han dynasty in the book *China: Tradition and Transformation*, sinologist John K. Fairbank shares this impression, and he thus comments that "as a result, the tremendous growth and development of Chinese civilization has been all but hidden behind this apparent circular motion in human affairs, and the later history is made into a series of more or less successful attempts to repeat the story of the Earlier Han."[62]

Even so, every dynasty has its own characteristics and problems. After the Han dynasty, China continued to develop and change. During the 1,700 years since the end of the Han dynasty, China has experienced many dynastic changes and cultural expansions, such as the Southern and Northern dynasties (420–589), a period when many ethnic cultures integrated on a large scale; the Tang (618–907) and Song (960–1279) dynasties, in which Chinese culture flourished; and the Yuan (1206–1368) and Qing (1616–1911) dynasties, when China was taken under the rule of "Barbarians," the Mongols and Manchu. In the Qing dynasty, traditional China reached its peak.[63]

Though this period is not as prolific as the pre-Qin through Han dynasties, there are still some remarkable commentaries on classical myths found in documents and literature. These writings about myths are also directly related to the societies in which they existed. Two examples will illustrate this. The first relates to the strong interest in mysteries in the Wei (220–265) and Jin (265–420) dynasties and Gan Bao's (ca. fourth century) *Soushenji* (*In Search of the Supernatural*). The second relates to nationalism in the late Qing dynasty and comments and uses of the ancestors' miraculous birth myth.

Orthodox Confucianism was discredited by the end of the Eastern Han. During the Wei and Jin dynasties the general interest of philosophy shifted from Confucianism to Taoism and metaphysical philosophy and scriptures. Literati and scholars engaged in highly sophisticated discussions. The Buddhists also used discussion to defend their theories. Taoism had been prevalent during the Han dynasty; now, in a time of political, social, and economic instability, intellectuals became more interested in searching for an essential view of the universe. In their "pure conversations" (*qingtan*), literati and scholars tried to find out the "Great Mystery" of the world; hence the philosophical streams of the Jin period are called "The School of Mysteries" (*Xuanxue*). In correspondence to their strong interests in mystery, many literati and scholars were fond of talking about strange and miraculous phenomena: stories about gods, immortals, ghosts, and their powers. They even collected some of these mysteries and compiled them into books. Such works include Zhang Hua's *Bowuzhi* (*A Treatise on Research into Nature*), Guo Pu's commentary on *Shanhaijing*, Gan Bao's *Soushenji*, Ge Hong's *Shenxianzhuan* (*Bibliographies of Immortals*), and Wang Jia's *Shiyiji* (*Researches into Lost Records*), along with many others. Among them, Gan Bao's *Soushenji* is one of the most representative.

Gan Bao was a historian and a member of the literati during the Eastern Jin dynasty (317–420). Influenced by the prevailing interest in mystery, he liked to probe into the occult arts (generally including divination, astrology, and geomancy). Two anecdotes explain Gan Bao's motivation for writing *Soushenji*. One says that his father's servant-girl was buried with his father when he died, but after more than ten years, when the grave was opened, the servant-girl was alive and said the dead man often fetched food for her. Another story depicts that his elder brother died and several days later was revived. He said he had seen some gods and ghosts. These stories touched Gan Bao. He then examined ancient writings to seek other stories about strange and marvelous things. To enrich his compilation, he interviewed many elderly people and widely collected myths, legends, and stories from oral tradition. His purpose was to prove that strange and mystical things could happen, and that gods and ghosts really exist. The original book he wrote was lost before the Southern Song dynasty. The version that exists today was compiled by a Ming scholar named Hu Yingling.

In this book, Gan Bao recorded many myths. Some Chinese mythologists believe that *Soushenji* is the second-best book to preserve ancient myths (the one considered to be the best is *Shanhaijing*).[64] The myths recorded in this text include those of Shennong, Chisongzi (the rain master of Shennong), Feng Bo, Yu Shi, Zhuanxu's three sons, the sage king Shun, Xiwangmu, Chang'e, Panhu, and King Fuyu. Most records of these myths are sketchy in detail, though some are very thorough, such as the Panhu myth (wherein a dog married a girl and they became ancestors of some southern ethnic peoples). Sometimes it even provides different versions of the same story type. In chapter 20, for example, a kind old woman was said to have received a divine prophecy as a reward for her benevolence. She was told that her city would soon be sunk when the eyes of a stone tortoise turned red. The old lady went to see the tortoise every day. When a child learned what this lady was doing, he sneakily rubbed red color onto the tortoise's eyes. The old woman went out of the city, led by a dragon. Soon afterwards the city sunk and became a lake. A similar story can be found in chapter 13. These accounts provide valuable sources for mythology and folk narrative research.

In 1644 the Manchu people, who originally lived in the northeast area of modern China, successfully broke through the Great Wall and became the new rulers of China. The Manchu dynasty developed traditional China to its height in the eighteen century but declined in the nineteenth century. In 1912, with the last emperor's abdication, the Qing dynasty ended, marking the end of ancient Chinese empires.

In the late Qing dynasty, China faced a string of crises: the central government's corruption and disability, oppression of the rulers from another ethnic group, imperialist invasion, relinquishing of territory and compensation to other countries, the Boxer Movement, and new ideas about China's modernization. Intellectuals commonly considered these crises the Qing government's fault. Some suggested the government should reform, and others hoped the Manchu rulers would be overthrown and a new state would be established. Nationalism increased dramatically. In this atmosphere, many radical nationalists wanted to distinguish the differences among ethnic groups and tried to summon people to resist the domination of the Manchu. Their leader, Sun Yatsen (1866–1925), called on people to dispel "the barbarians" from central China and recover Han conventions. To serve their strong political purposes, many revolutionary scholars discussed myths about the origins of clans. In his book *Huangshi* (*History of the Yellow*), Huang Jie examined ancient writings of the myths of clan origins, arguing that the ancestors of all ethnic groups except Han came from nonhumans. For example, he suggested that the people from southern ethnic groups descended from a dog, and the Tubo, an ancient ethnic group, also descended from a dog. Tujue, another group, came from a female wolf. The Gaoche ethnic group came from a male wolf, and the Dangxiang and Qiang came from a monkey. Huang Jie wrote that these people who came from the marriage between man and animal were so shameful that the sun and the moon would lose their light. Through his research, he strove to show the excellence of Han Chinese in race and culture. By this means Huang wanted to propagate the idea that Han people should resist being ruled by the Manchu government. He suggested that all Han should unite together to fight for this cause.[65] Another scholar, Chen Qubing, utilized the clan origin myth of Manchu to criticize Manchu people in his book *Qing Mishi* (*The Secret History of Qing*). The Manchu origin myth states that two or three girls were bathing in a lake when a magpie carrying a red hawthorn fruit in its mouth passed by, dropping the fruit. One of the girls caught the fruit and ate it. She then became pregnant. Later she gave birth to a boy and named him Aixinjueluo. Soon after, he became the ancestor of the Manchu people. Chen compared this story to the similar origin myth of the Shang people, the Han predecessors. Chen concluded that it was disgraceful that the Manchu people only knew their mother but not their father, and they did not know the difference between man and animal since their ancestors came from a bird. He wrote that the myth showed that Manchu people wanted to deceive others to believe that they came from a divine origin. However, Chen states, the similar miraculous events in the Shang myth were not amazing in the beginning, but were later distorted by other writers. In this way, Chen tried to make the Shang myth sound reasonable and the Manchu myth sound absurd. His deeper goal was to demonstrate the superiority of the Han and the inferiority of the

Manchu. These radical nationalists used myth as a significant cultural resource to serve their political purpose of overthrowing the Manchu dynasty.

Republic of China (1912–1949)

Beginning in the middle of the nineteenth century, China suffered a series of failures and setbacks during conflicts with other foreign powers. As a result, China was forced to open itself to the world and became a semicolonial country. Even after the fall of the Manchu dynasty and the establishment of the Republic of China, China was still often oppressed and bullied by other foreign forces. Stimulated and shamed by these failures, at the end of the nineteenth century and the early part of the twentieth century, many patriotic intellectuals began to search for the reasons why China was so easily defeated by those "barbarians," and tried to uncover the "foul diseases" in Chinese politics, ethics, thought, and scholarship. They attributed one of the main reasons to Chinese traditional culture—a shackle, in their view, that suppressed humanity, creativity, and democracy. They intensely criticized traditional culture, primarily written culture created and carried by ancient nobles and intellectuals, and they hoped to build a new national, scientific, and democratic culture to educate Chinese people and, furthermore, to reconstruct a unified, independent, strong, and modernized China. In 1915 a group of professors at Peking University started a New Culture Movement to fight against Confucianism (which stressed obedience and hierarchy in social relationships), old literature, and the inflexible classical written language. These scholars were advocates for a new culture of antiimperialism and antifeudalism and a new body of literature written in vernacular Chinese. This movement culminated in the May Fourth Movement of 1919 and lasted to the 1920s. They built this new culture mainly by exploring the values of native folk culture and learning from Western and Japanese culture and scientific technology. Therefore, there arose an enthusiasm among intellectuals for studying Chinese folklore as well as foreign scholarship. Folk songs and stories were widely collected and researched, and Western concepts (such as democracy, equality, and liberty) and various social and philosophical thoughts and theories then current in the Western world and Japan (such as Marxism, realism, utilitarianism, pragmatism, and individualism) were introduced to China.

In this circumstance, myth received much academic attention. In fact, Chinese mythology as a subject in a modern sense is commonly thought to formally have begun in 1902, when the word *shenhua* (myth) was translated from Japanese into Chinese for the first time. Later, during the New Culture Movement, with opened eyes and much knowledge about Western and Japanese scholarship, many scholars began to study Chinese myths and compare them with myths of India, Greece, and northern Europe. The most popular foreign theory they applied was from the English Anthropological School, mainly from E. B. Tylor (1832–1917), J. G. Frazer (1854–1941), and especially Andrew Lang (1844–1913).[66] Maodun (whose real name is Shen Yanbin, 1896–1981), one of the forerunners of modern Chinese mythologists, began to be interested in myth in 1918. At that time he read some English books about the myths and legends of Greece, Rome, India, and Egypt, and some theoretical books about the Anthropological School. From 1925 to 1930 he utilized its theory to discuss myths with regard to meaning, classification, origin,

and preservation. He also compared Chinese myths to those of Greece and northern Europe. From today's viewpoint, many of his explanations seem superficial, merely mechanical applications of the anthropological school theory. However, he is the first Chinese mythologist to systematically study ancient Chinese myths by using Western mythological theory.

In 1937 the Japanese army invaded China, and the War of Resistance against Japan (1937–1945) broke out. To avoid the war, the central government and many institutes and universities in northern China were compelled to move to the south. The formerly isolated border area now became the cultural center. Scholars and students from different disciplines swarmed there. Because of the absence of reference books in the border area, many scholars had to pay attention to rich ethnic cultures and living oral tradition. This produced a new stage of Chinese myth study. Many scholars of literature, sociology, an-

The cover of the anniversary issue of Geyao [Folk Songs Weekly], *a journal first published in 1922. It promoted the enthusiasm of collecting and researching folk songs in China, and thus played an important role in the history of Chinese folkloristics. (Courtesy of authors)*

thropology, linguistics, and history investigated living myths, rituals, and beliefs of the ethnic minorities and then compared them to the versions recorded in ancient Chinese writings. Myth was thus probed by putting it into living social and cultural contexts. Functions and social roles of myths were emphasized. Additionally, many scholars in this period studied myth from multiple points of view of different disciplines. A representative scholar of this period is Wen Yiduo (1899–1946), a professor at Qinghua University. His study of myth began in the middle of the 1930s and flourished during the War of Resistance against Japan. He wrote several influential articles discussing myths about Jiang Yuan, Fuxi and Nüwa, dragons, immortals, and others. When examining the Fuxi myth, he analyzed various sources not only from classical written documents but also from orally told myths (from Miao, Yao, and other ethnic peoples) and from archeological relics. He examined the intrinsic relationship between myth and social life from multiple points of view. In an article, he listed forty-nine brother-sister marriage myth versions collected by other ethnographers from Miao, Yao, and other ethnic peoples to demonstrate that Fuxi and Nüwa were in fact gourds. Therefore, the gourd, according to his research, was actually the common ancestor of humans in primitive thought. Though some of his conclusions need more support, his approach of studying myth from multiple points of view still inspires today's mythological study.

The People's Republic of China (1949–Present)

In 1949 the Gongchantang (CCP, or Chinese Communist Party) defeated the Kuomintang (KMT, or National People's Party), the party in power during the Republic of China, and became the new government of the People's Republic of China (PRC). Having experienced large-scale development and demolishment (especially in "the Great Leap Forward" of 1958–1959 and "the Cultural Revolution" of 1966–1976) during the time of Mao Zedong (the highest leader of the CCP, from the 1930s to 1976), with the beginning of Deng Xiaoping's leadership in 1978 China quickened its pace toward an open, strong, and modernized country. Mao's extreme policy of encouraging "class struggle" was replaced by Deng's policy of developing the economy and improving productivity. China's current leadership has continued these policies, securing for China a more important and active role in the global political and economic realms.

These considerable social and political changes have also deeply influenced myth. Corresponding to these changes, myths in the PRC have gone through two stages. The first stage is from 1949 to 1976, when myths were deeply impacted by

Mao Zedong (Bettman/Corbis)

political ideology, especially in the period of the Cultural Revolution. The second stage is from 1978 through the present, when myths have been comparatively released from strong political influences and have been revived and reconstructed.

1949–1976

During this first period, attitudes toward myth seemed contradictory. On one hand, myths were perceived to be created by common laborers, showing the positive efforts of human beings to try to explain and control the world. Mao Zedong, for example, often cited and rewrote myths in his articles or poems. He especially enjoyed using myths related to rebel gods or demigods, such as the myth of Gonggong fighting against Zhuanxu to be the Supreme Divinity and butting Mount Buzhou in his failure. In using this story, Mao, as an outstanding revolutionist, showed his praise of the rebellion against the established order. On the other hand, however, myths were also thought to be negative and passive. This is mainly because myths were usually connected with folk belief, which was considered superstitious and harmful since it encouraged people to obey nature and gods. During the Cultural Revolution, especially in the *Po Si Jiu* (Destroy the Four Old Things) Campaign, which started in 1966, all "old thoughts, old culture, old customs, and old habits" were called on to be eliminated since these were perceived as belonging to the exploiting class and as being backward and improper for the development of socialism. Among the "olds" to be abolished, folk belief stood in obvious violation. In a short period of time, temples, statues of gods, and stories about gods were all considered to be old superstition and thus were destroyed. In the Renzu Temple complex in Henan Province, for instance, several statues including Nüwa's were demolished along with Fuxi's mausoleum, and Fuxi was dishonored by his statue being paraded through the streets. The temple fair was banned. People were prevented from openly telling myths and visiting the temple for worship, though some of them occasionally went in secret.[67] During this time, telling myths became taboo. Even in 1993, when Yang Lihui did field research at Renzu, some myth tellers were still hesitant to tell myths about Fuxi and Nüwa. When asked by acquaintances what they were doing, some myth tellers laughed at themselves and disclaimed that they were "telling old superstitions." The answer was obviously a strategy: through actively admitting their own backwardness, the myth tellers hoped to protect themselves from political pressure.

1978–Today

Since 1978, China has become more open. The central government has focused its attention on developing the national economy, and it has become more tolerant of folk tradition. Folk beliefs and myths that had been suppressed as feudal superstition have received more space to exist in society. Since the 1980s, especially since the mid-1990s, many local governments have used folk traditions (including myth) as cultural resources to build local identity and to develop the local economy through the marketing of these ideas to locals and tourists. This strategy is vividly described in the phrase "Culture builds the stage, and economy plays the opera." In many cases the central government, local governments, local communities, and tourists all come together to revive folk traditions. For example, the Renzu Festival in Huaiyang County was banned during the Cultural Revolution, but in 1993 the temple fair had not only been restored but the local government and local community were also planning to rebuild the statues that had been destroyed, including Nüwa's. In Hou village, Hongdong County, Shanxi Province, the destroyed Nüwa temple was rebuilt in 1999. The process of revival has involved many interplaying factors. It is supported by the local government, which hopes to propagate and develop the local economy by promoting a unique local culture. The temple was designed by local folk intellectuals who hope to restore the old tradition. Many villagers have engaged in the act of rebuilding the temple, hoping to get both economic benefits and the goddess's blessing.[68] With the rebuilding of these Nüwa temples, related Nüwa myths have been told again. People use relevant myths to validate their special relationship with Nüwa and to find meaning for their current activities. They also use myths to create a local identity. All in all, they utilize myths to serve their modern life.

In summary, the discussion in this section illustrates that myths are an organic part of the whole social and cultural system and are intimately connected

The new Nüwa temple at Hou village, Hongdong County, Shanxi Province, northern China, 2000. (Courtesy of Xu Fang)

with other social and cultural phenomena, such as belief, politics, economy, ethnic identity, morals, and science. Which myths are chosen to be written down, why myths are retold or reconstructed, how myths are evaluated and studied, and whether myths are praised or oppressed are often related to certain social, historical, and cultural contexts. From the relationships among myth, history, and society one can get an idea of how Chinese society and culture have continually changed and developed, and how these changes and developments deeply influence the transmission and transformation of living myths within these contexts.

INFLUENCE OF MYTH ON CHINESE CULTURE AND SOCIETY

The influence of Chinese history and society on myths is only one side of the picture. On the other side, those myths that have been handed down for thousands of years and contain Chinese people's philosophy, art, beliefs, customs, and value systems also have a great influence on Chinese society and culture.

Influence of Myth on Belief

Myths tell stories about gods. Their rise is intimately related to people's beliefs. In China, those gods who play the main roles in myths are also usually the ones worshiped as the central part of belief systems. In She County, Hebei Province, in northern China, for example, there is a large Nüwa palace said to have been built during the Ming dynasty. On every lunar March 15 to 18, there is a Nüwa palace festival. A lot of people from nearby cities and villages visit the palace to worship Nüwa. Nüwa myths are actively transmitted during this occasion, together with some belief legends that are told to prove Nüwa's power and efficacy. One legend states that a daughter-in-law had great filial piety toward her father-in-law. She was so considerate of him that every night in the winter she warmed the quilt for him to sleep with. Rumors about a sexual relationship spread in the community. This young woman felt she was seriously misunderstood, so, one year when she went to worship Nüwa during the temple fair, she jumped from the top of the temple into a large incense pot to test her innocence. She received divine protection from Nüwa, and not even a hair on her head was hurt. Thus, her innocence was confirmed for everyone to see. Another popular legend states that Nüwa protected a high Communist leader by delivering a thick fog when he was chased by Japanese invaders in the 1940s. The fog helped hide him, and he escaped from his pursuers. Such legends illustrate belief in Nüwa's protection and provide strong support for the preservation and transmission of Nüwa myths. Additionally, the fact that Nüwa myths are regularly repeated during the temple fair serves to strengthen and broaden beliefs in Nüwa.[69]

Similar to this situation occurring among Han people, many gods worshiped by other ethnic groups also exist in myths. Myths often form the basic parts of beliefs. For example, among Naxi people in Yongning County, Yunnan Province, a great goddess named Heidi Ganmu is an important presence in myths as well as in beliefs. She is believed to be the goddess who takes charge of population growth and decline, controls the growth of crops, and rules the health and production of livestock. Every lunar July 25, people offer sacrifices to this goddess. Another goddess, Zihong Jiemei, is popularly said to be a goddess in heaven who later married a man surviving a great flood, so she is considered to be the ancestress of humans and is given sacrifices every October. In the Achang ethnic group in Yunnan

Nüwa palace, She County, Hebei Province, northern China, 1993. (Courtesy of Yang Lihui)

Province, a myth mentions that a brother and sister married and created the sky and heaven, and then produced humans. For this reason, they are worshiped as two great gods and as the ancestors of the Achang people.

Influence of Myth on Literature and Art

Chinese myths have long been thought to be the root of Chinese literature and art. Myths have had a great impact on writers. During the history of Chinese literature, many eminent poets and writers, including Qu Yuan, Tao Yuanming (365–427 CE), Li Bai (701–762), Li He (790–816), Wu Cheng'en (ca. 1500–ca. 1582), Cao Xueqin (ca. 1715–1763), Lu Xun (1881–1936), and Guo Moruo (1892–1978), were all more or less nourished by Chinese myths. Some of them directly took myths as their writing material, and some further absorbed from myths stylistic techniques such as exaggeration, fantasy, and fiction. By doing this, these literary figures developed a strong romantic writing style in Chinese literature, which is thought to originate from myths.

Myths were not fixed when they were woven into literature and art. Instead, they were always rewritten and reconstructed by different writers for different goals and needs. This revives old myths with new meanings in new contexts. A popular animated TV series, *The Legend of Nezha*, provides a typical example.

Until recently, animated cartoon films and TV series in China came mostly from Japan and the United States (particularly Disney films). These programs charmed numerous Chinese children and made them much addicted to these cartoons. Adults in China began to worry about this and to call for Chinese-made animated movies and TV programs. In 2003 *The Legend of Nezha* was produced and achieved great success. The series tells the story of how Nezha, a naïve child with many shortcomings, is trained through a series of struggles with many evils, and finally becomes a virtuous hero who weeds out evil and helps people live in peace. Produced by CCTV (China Central Television), this program aims to make a high-quality show full of Chinese tradition and values while using the modern animation styles that children love to watch. The producers hope to make a nationally recognized art form to give Chinese children an education about traditional Chinese stories and morals. The series combines

Kuafu Chased the Sun. *Originally drawn in the 17th century by Jiang Yinghao. (Ma Changyi,* The Classic of Mountains and Seas: Ancient Illustrations with Annotations, *Shandong Huabao Chubanshe, 2001)*

the traditional stories about Nezha with many other myths or legends. Several famous Chinese mythological figures, such as Nüwa, Gonggong, Jingwei, and Kuafu, were adapted. Their myths were changed for the purpose of propagating values and morals for today's Chinese children to learn and follow. The myth that Kuafu pursued the sun is widely known and is used in the Nezha series. In ancient records, the reason Kuafu pursued the sun is not very clear. Sometimes it is said that he wanted to compete with the sun in a race to see who could run the fastest. Before Kuafu reaches the sun, he dies of thirst. However, in the Nezha series, Kuafu is said to be a leader of a Titan group and the representative of justice and self-devotion. The evil goddess Shiji Niangniang tied up the crow of the sun, the spirit of the sun, to a huge mountain so that the bird could not sit down and the normal order of the universe was disturbed. To save people from the disaster, Nezha asked for help from Kuafu, who at last defeated the wicked spirit of the mountain. After this, in despair because of the evil power, the sun bird wanted to fly to the far northern pole to sink itself into the dead sea, never to rise again. To stop it from doing so and to rescue humans from eternal darkness, Kuafu chased the sun. He finally stopped the crow but was so tired that he died. He was metamorphosed into a forest and continued to help people. Thus the classical Kuafu myth has been rewritten for this TV series, retold in the context of speedy globalization in contemporary China, for the current purpose of instructing children about Chinese heritage and spirit. In addition to its entertainment function, the Kuafu myth serves to help children to build values of justice and the belief that justice will overcome evil in the end.

Influence of Myth on Daily Life

As a traditional genre that was primarily created in the ancient past and has been transmitted for thousands of years, myth has deeply influenced people's ordinary lives throughout history. It often helps to shape people's attitudes toward the world, provides evidence and reasons for their behaviors, and supplies meanings and models for their current lives.

In some ethnic Chinese groups dog meat is thought to be a delicious and nutritious food. However, the Yao and She people usually are forbidden to eat it. The origin of this custom is traced back to the Panhu myth. Panhu was a dog of the divine sovereign, Di Ku. When Di Ku got into trouble during an invasion, Panhu brought the enemy general's head to Di Ku and thus helped him to win the war. As a reward, Panhu received the emperor's daughter as his wife. The dog then carried the princess to the mountains of southern China, where they had many children. Therefore, Panhu is worshiped as the ancestor of the Yao and She ethnic groups. According to an ethnography written in 1980–1981 about the Yao people of a village on Yao Mountain, Guangxi Province, Yao people worship Panhu as their first ancestor and their protector. They honor him with the title "King Pan." As a result of this belief, Yao people cannot offend a dog in their daily activities, and would not dare to eat dog meat. One of the ethnographers mentions a story that has spread among villagers: a young man in the village told people that he had eaten dog meat, and when his father heard this, as a punishment, he fiercely knocked his son's head with his tobacco pipe. In the Sanjiang and Baise districts, if any one of the Yao people was found to have eaten dog meat by mistake, he would be made to butcher a pig and take a bath in the pig's blood, then offer the pig as a sacrifice to King Pan.[70] A similar taboo against eating dog meat is prevalent among the She people.[71]

In some other ethnic groups in the south, such as the Miao, Zhuang, Tujia, Buyi, Shui, Tibetan, Hani, and Gelao, dogs do not have the benefit of the high status of a remote ancestor, but they are still commonly respected. This is attributed to the belief about the dog's contribution in helping humans obtain the first precious grain seeds. A Tibetan myth collected in Sichuan Province states that in remote antiquity, grain grew tall and produced plentiful seeds. Humans lived easily and were rich. But they did not treasure grain; instead, some of them even used cakes as toilet paper. The God of Heaven was very annoyed at learning this, so he went down to the earth to get back all the grain. While doing so, a dog ran to him. It grasped the bottom of the god's trousers and cried. The god was touched. He left a small portion of seeds from each of

Panhu married a princess and gave birth to three sons and one daughter, who later became the ancestors of She ethnic people. Part of a long cloth painting telling the whole Panhu story. Originally painted in 1759 and now preserved in the National Museum of Chinese History, Beijing. (Song Zhaolin, The Speaking Witchcraft Paintings: An Investigation into Folk Belief in Remote Antiquity, Xueyuan Chubanshe, 2004)

the different grains for the dog. Since the grains we have today were left on the earth because of the dog, humans today should give part of their food to dogs.[72] In some other ethnic groups, people say that it was a dog that stole the grain seeds from heaven and brought them to earth, which enables people today to make their living by growing grains. A Miao myth states that in the ancient past, dogs had nine tails. When a dog went to heaven to steal grain seeds, it was discovered by the divine guards. In the process of escaping from the guards and running back to the earth, eight of its tails were cut off. Fortunately, the dog brought back some grain seeds that were stuck to its surviving tail. Because of this, when Miao people celebrate the harvest festival, they feed their dogs first. In the Gelao and Zhuang ethnicities, this type of myth also serves as an etiological myth to describe the shape of a ripe grain plant. Grain plants are bushy, curled, and bent, looking just like a dog's tail.

Influence of Myth on the Chinese Spirit

Chinese scholars maintain that the rich body of Chinese myths is one of the sources of Chinese civilization; myths impact Chinese people's spirits in many ways. Many myths in the Chinese language stress that strong effort is an essential quality of the human spirit; when facing difficulty or calamity, one must rely on his own ability and make every effort to change a bad situation rather than passively obeying fate or God's will. This theme can be found in the myths that Gun and his son Yu restrained the flood, Nüwa melted five-colored stone and repaired the broken sky, Yi shot down the extra nine suns when the world was almost burned out, and others.

Flood is a worldwide mythical theme. It can be widely found in the myths told by people of East and Southeast Asia, Europe, Africa, the Indian Islands, New Guinea, Polynesia, Micronesia, the Americas, and many other places. In Chinese mythology it also appears quite often and shapes many types of stories. Among the flood myths, the Gun-Yu myth is one of the most popular. The culture hero Gun stole Xirang, the growing-soil, from the Supreme Divinity in order to stop the flood. But he failed in his mission and was killed. His son Yu was miraculously born from the belly of his corpse and continued to fight the flood until he succeeded. The Gun-Yu myth stresses how the flood is eventually controlled by great efforts from two generations.

Compared to the flood story in the Bible or other Western flood myths, the Chinese flood myth is distinctive in some ways. The basic difference, as some scholars have suggested, is that in the Chinese version what is emphasized is the conquest of the flood and the origin of civilization, rather than the flood that occurred to punish human sin.[73] This characteristic is strongly reflected in the Gun-Yu myth. The essence of this myth is not that one should obey God's will or the law of nature, or wait for God's plan. Instead, the human spirit is praised for counting on its own ability and vigorously making every effort to conquer the natural disaster. Eventually the demigod Yu stopped the flood and changed the dejected world into a livable place for humankind. He then became the founder of the first civilized state, the Xia. His achievements won him a high reputation in literature, art, and beliefs. Today, he still is frequently used as an exemplary model to encourage people to actively handle difficult situations and to strive for a better life.

The statue of Great Yu on the campus of China Agricultural University, Beijing, 2005. (Courtesy of Yang Lihui)

In Chinese mythology, another trait of the human spirit that is strongly emphasized in many stories is toughness or unyieldingness. Some stories stress that one should strive bravely and persistently, no matter how hard a task seems, even if it is impossible to succeed. Myths related to this theme include the small bird Jingwei trying to fill up the sea, the hero Kuafu chasing the sun, and Xingtian unflaggingly fighting against the Supreme God after he was beheaded, by using his breasts as his eyes and his navel as his mouth.

Jingwei was formally Yan Di's (the Flame Emperor) daughter, named Nü Wa (different from the great mother and cosmic repairer Nüwa). When Nü Wa was playing in the Eastern Sea she was drowned and never returned. She metamorphosed into a bird called Jingwei. Jingwei was determined to fill the sea, and day after day it carried a pebble or a twig in its mouth and dropped it into the Eastern Sea. It never questioned whether it was possible to fill up the vast sea with its tiny efforts. Chinese people feel sympathetic toward Jingwei's misfortune and admire the bird for its bravery, toughness, and patience. This myth has appeared in many poems, novels, and operas, combining the diverse themes of pathos, courage, and the refusal to accept defeat. "Jingwei Tries to Fill the Sea" has become an idiom, which often is used to encourage people to learn from Jingwei's spirit and to work bravely and persistently no matter how hard the task.

Similarly, "Kuafu Chased the Sun" is also often used as an idiom. It usually functions as a positive metaphor of human courage, toughness, and persistence. Tao Yuanming, a renowned Jin poet, praised Kuafu in one of his poems:

> Kuafu cherished a great ambition,
> He then competed with the sun in a race.
> At the same time they reached Yu Valley, where the sun set down,
> It seemed neither of them won.
> Because Kuafu possessed such divine power,
> How could the water in the rivers be enough for him to drink, even if they
>   were drunk up?
> His remains metamorphosed into the forest of peach trees,
> And his merit was achieved after his death.

As in Tao's poem, the Kuafu myth appears in many Chinese poems, novels, operas, and cartoon films. Kuafu is usually praised as a tragic but great hero who bravely challenges the difficult and impossible and intrepidly acts in order to realize his dream and ambition.

Endnotes

1. Yuan, Ke. "Defining Myth from a Narrow Sense to a Broad Sense" (in Chinese). *Shehui Kexue Zhanxian* 4 (1982): 256–260. See also his *A Personal Statement to Yuan Ke's Studies* (in Chinese). Hangzhou: Zhejiang Renmin Chubanshe, 1999, 25–60.

2. Lü, Wei. "History of Chinese Myths" (in Chinese). In *History of Chinese Folk Literature*, eds. Qi Lianxiu and Cheng Qiang. Shijiazhuang: Hebei Jiaoyu Chubanshe, 1999, 3.

3. Examples of this kind of argument can be found in many articles collected in the book *Sacred Narrative: Readings in the Theory of Myth*, ed. Alan Dundes. Berkeley, Los Angeles, and London: University of California Press, 1984.

4. Kirk, G. S. "On Defining Myths." In *Sacred Narrative: Readings in the Theory of Myth*, 57. See also his *Myth: Its Meaning and Functions in Ancient and Other Cultures*. Cambridge: Cambridge University Press, 1970, 252–261. Relevant argument can also be found in William Hansen's essay, "Meanings and Boundaries: Reflections on Thompson's 'Myth and Folktales.'" In *Myth: A New Symposium*, eds. Gregory Schrempp and William Hansen. Bloomington and Indianapolis: Indiana University Press, 2002, 19–28.

5. Yang, Lihui. *The Cult of Nüwa: Myths and Beliefs in China* (in Chinese). Beijing: Zhongguo Shehui Kexue Chubanshe, 1997, 144–165. See also her *Rethinking on the Source Area of the Cult of Nüwa* (in Chinese). Beijing: Beijing Shifan Daxue Chubanshe, 1999, 133–214.

6. In his often-cited article, William Bascom adopted *prose narrative* as a comprehensive term for a major category of folklore, and took myth, legend, and folktale as its three main subdivisions. He further created two tables to show the main differences among these three forms of prose narrative. William Bascom. "The Forms of Folklore: Prose Narratives." In *Sacred Narrative: Readings in the Theory of Myth*, 5–29.

7. Yan, Bao, ed. and trans. *Ancient Songs of the Miao People* (in Miao's pronunciation and Chinese-language translation). Guiyang: Guizhou Minzu Chubanshe, 1993.

8. Ma Changyi, a prolific modern Chinese mythologist, also put forward this point in her preface to *Myths and Mythic Stories in Contemporary China* (in Chinese). Several examples are provided in this book. Ma Changyi, comp. *Myths and Mythic Stories in Contemporary China*. Beijing: Zhongguo Guangbo Dianshi Chubanshe, 1996.

9. Thompson, Stith. "Myths and Folktales." In *Myth: A Symposium* (Bibliographical and Special Series of the American Folklore Society), vol. 5 (1955): 104–110.

10. Li, Xueqin. "Studies on Suigongxu and Its Significance" (in Chinese). *Zhongguo Lishi Wenwu* 6 (2002): 4–13.

11. There are more than twenty hypotheses about the author (or authors) and dates of this work. Ye Shuxian, Xiao Bing, and Zheng Zaishu. *The Cultural Explanation of Shanhaijing: Imaginary Geography and Contact and Mutual Influence between the East and the West* (in Chinese). Wuhan: Hubei Renmin Chubanshe, 2004, vol. 1, 10.

12. There are still disagreements about the time each chapter was written. Recently, a Chinese linguist named Wang Jianjun reexamined the question about the time of writing of this work, especially the time of writing of each chapter. Basing his research on pragmatics, he concludes that the *Classic of the Great Wilderness, of Regions within the Seas*, and the *Classic of Regions beyond the Seas* were written perhaps in the Warring States era. He suggests that the *Classic of Mountains* was mostly written in the Warring States era but that most of it was supplemented by people in the Qin and Han dynasties. He argues that the last chapter of *Regions within the Seas* was written in the Qin and Han dynasties. Wang Jianjun. "Rearguing the Time of Writing of *Shanhaijing* Based on Studies of Existential Sentences" (in Chinese). Nanjing Shifan Daxue Xuebao 2 (2000): 139–144.

13. Ito, Seiji. *The World of Gods and Monsters in Shanhaijing* (in Chinese). Trans. Liu Yeyuan. Beijing: Zhongguo Minjian Wenyi Chubanshe, 1990.

14. Liu, Zongdi. "Study on *Shanhaijing* from a New Perspective: Focus on the Relationship between 'The Classic of Regions beyond the Seas,' 'The Classic of the Great Wilderness,' and the Ancient Calendar System and Calendric Rites" (in Chinese). PhD diss., Beijing Normal University, 2001.

15. A culture hero is a deity to whom are attributed the early achievements of civilization, such as the discovery of fire; the invention of tools or writing; the origin of agriculture, fishing, and hunting; the domestication of animals; the development of medicine;

and the founding of ceremonies, rituals, and customs. He also acts as the mythic hero who dispels and eliminates the evil gods and monsters, clears up the chaos, and establishes the general order of social life on earth.

16. Examples of such argument can be found in Andrew H. Plaks, *Chinese Narrative* (in Chinese, Lectures in Beijing University), ed. Yue Daiyun and Zhang Wending. Beijing: Beijing Daxue Chubanshe, 1996, 40–48.

17. Yuan, Ke. *Myths of Ancient China: An Anthology with an Annotation* (in Chinese). Beijing: Renmin Wenxue Chubanshe, [1979] 1996, 297–298.

18. For example, in one part of this poem, Qu Yuan asks, "He/She ascended the throne to be the ruler,/Who guided and respected him/her?/Nüwa has her body, and whoever created her?" These two questions, especially the first one, are puzzling. Scholars wonder whether the first question relates to Nüwa, and if it relates to her they still don't know what it means.

19. Yuan, Ke. Foreword to *Chinese Mythology: An Introduction*, by Anne Birrell. Baltimore and London: Johns Hopkins University Press, 1993, xi–xii.

20. Yuan, Ke. Foreword to *Chinese Mythology: An Introduction*, xii.

21. Zhong, Jingwen, and Yang Lihui. "The Rationalism in the History of Myth Study in Ancient China" (in Chinese). In *Proceedings of the Conference on Chinese Myth and Legend*, eds. Li Yiyuan and Wang Qiugui. Taibei: Center for Chinese Studies Research, 1996, vol. 1, 33–59.

22. For example, Chang Jincang argues that the mythological heroes, such as Gun, Yu, and Yi, were heroes in ancient Chinese history. They were mythologized into demigods during the Warring States era. See his "A Basic Question of Chinese Mythology: The Historicizing of Myth or the Mythologizing of History?" (in Chinese). *Shaanxi Shifan Daxue Xuebao* 29, 3 (2000): 5–13. Another scholar, Liu Zongdi, insists that the myth about ten suns living on a tree named Fusang in the eastern sea and being carried by the three-legged crows is actually a historical fact in ancient China. The Fusang tree was a sundial, and the ten suns around it were actually the motion of the sun. So, he thinks, the myth was produced later by misinterpreting the real fact of the ancient calendar system. See his "Study on *Shanhaijing* from a New Perspective: Focus on the Relationship between 'The Classic of Regions beyond the Seas'; 'The Classic of the Great Wilderness' and the Ancient Calendar System and Calendric Rites," 33–34.

23. In his article, Bodde points out the problems that existed in ancient records of Chinese myth, and he criticizes the textual-analysis approach Chinese scholars adopted. Since myths were recorded in fragments, and the texts were full of homophones and characters easily confused with one another, Chinese scholars have committed themselves to seeking new identifications. The identification was based on these arguments: character X of text A seems to be character Y of text B; character Y seems to be character Z of text C; therefore, they concluded that character X of text A was equal to character Z of text C. Bodde suggested that if this approach is excessively used, "it can lead to quite startling results." See "Myths of Ancient China." In *Mythologies in Ancient World*, ed. Samuel Noah Kramer. Chicago: Quadrangle Books, 1961, 377. Yang Lihui also discuss the shortcoming of the tex-

tual research, and she further suggests the advantages of utilizing orally transmitted myths as the data. See her *The Cult of Nüwa: Myths and Beliefs in China*, 225–229.

24. As early as the 1920s, the eminent folklorist Zhong Jingwen gathered myths, legends, and folktales and edited them into volumes. In the 1930s Zhong wrote several articles about the living myths, the myths orally transmitted in modern China. He pointed out that except for those myths that are recorded in ancient documents, most Chinese myths are preserved in later literature and in living folk traditions through oral tellings of myths in various contexts. Studying these living myths will greatly benefit the study of sociology, folklore, religion, ethnic studies, and cultural anthropology. Instead of relying on data from ancient written documents, Zhong used the living myths he collected or that others collected from the oral tradition to study Panhu myths, flood myths, and the myths of origins of plants. See *Essays of Zhong Jingwen's Studies on Folk Literature* (in Chinese), vol. 2. Shanghai: Shanghai Wenyi Chubanshe, 1985.

25. At that time the new government of the People's Republic of China organized many scholars and officials to investigate the society and history of Chinese ethnic groups in order to understand their cultures, identify their ethnic distinctions, and benefit the government's administration of these areas. The investigation of ethnic groups was widely carried out throughout the country, with researchers collecting and compiling a large amount of data about the cultures and histories of Chinese minorities. These data include population, language, economy, social organization, political system, folk custom, trade, communication, and many others. Among them were living myths collected from the oral traditions of these people. Unfortunately, these rich collections have seldom been seriously used to study Chinese myth until recently.

26. He, Jia. "San Tao Jicheng: The Grand Construction Project of Chinese Folk Culture in the Twentieth Century" (in Chinese). http://www.cflas.com.cn/lanmu/santaojicheng/20shijizgmjwhjshongweigongcheng.htm. For general information in English about the work of the Chinese Folk Literature and Art Society, visit their Web site: http://www.cflas.com.cn/English/JianJie/jianjie.htm.

27. Editorial Committee for the Folk Literature Collections in Huzhou District, comp. *The Collection of Stories in Huzhou District* (in Chinese). Hangzhou: Zhejiang Wenyi Chubanshe, 1991.

28. Hou, Guang, and He Xianglu, comps. *Selected Myths from Sichuan Province* (in Chinese). Chengdu: Sichuan Minzu Chubanshe, 1992.

29. Zhong, Jingwen. "Studies on Three Questions of the Brother-Sister Marriage Myth" (in Chinese). In his *The Collection of Selected Essays of Zhong Jingwen*. Beijing: Shoudu Shifan Daxue Chubanshe, 1994, 223–247.

30. Zhang Zhenli, a professor at Henan University, sponsored a research team in 1983 and investigated the living myths in oral tradition and relevant customs in the Central Plain region of China (mainly Henan Province). In 1987 they compiled a sourcebook titled *The Collection of Myths Transmitting in Contemporary Central Plain* (in Chinese). Zhang Zhenli and Cheng Jianjun, comps. Zhengzhou: Zhongguo Minjian Wenyijia Xiehui Henan Fenhui, 1987. In this book are more than 100 living myths.

31. Zhang, Zhenli. *Studies on the Transformation of Classical Myths Spreading in the Central Plain* (in Chinese). Shanghai: Shanghai Wenyi Chubanshe, 1991.

32. Yang, Lihui. *The Cult of Nüwa: Myths and Beliefs in China*, 82–120.

33. Bauman, Richard. "The Field Study of Folklore in Context." In *Handbook of American Folklore*, ed. Richard M. Dorson. Bloomington: Indiana University Press, 1983, 365–366.

34. For a more general description of Yang's fieldwork on Nüwa myth, see her books *The Cult of Nüwa: Myths and Beliefs in China*, 144–161; and *Rethinking on the Source Area of the Cult of Nüwa*, 133–214.

35. http://www.chinahuaiyang.gov.cn. Updated in July 2004.

36. Ma, Changyi. Preface to *Myths and Mythological Stories in China* (in Chinese), 1–3.

37. Chen, Jianxian. "Types and Distributions of Chinese Flood Myths" (in Chinese). *Minjian Wenxue Luntan* 3 (1996): 2–10.

38. Chen, Jianxian. "Types and Distributions of Chinese Flood Myths" (in Chinese). *Minjian Wenxue Luntan* 3 (1996): 2–10.

39. A Taiwan scholar, Lu Yilu, admits that Chen's classification is the most comprehensive one up to now, but she argues that his denominations of these types are not very proper. See her *Flood Myth: Centered on the South Ethnic Groups and the Aborigines of Taiwan in China* (in Chinese). Taibei: Liren Shuju, 2002, 16–17.

40. Meng, Huiying. *Living Myths: Studies of Myths in Chinese Ethnic Minorities* (in Chinese). Nanjing: Nankai Daxue Chubanshe, 1990, 157–158.

41. Meng, 159–163.

42. Meng, 164.

43. It seems that here, *Munau Jaiwa* should be *Labau Jaiwa*. According to an ethnologist and expert in the Jingpo language and culture, Xiao Jiacheng, *Jaiwa* could mean "poem" or "creation poem," and also means "shaman" in the Jingpo language; *Labau* means history. *Labau Jaiwa* is a well-known creation epic among the Jingpo ethnic people, while *Munau Jaiwa* is a big sacrificial ritual in which the creation epic *Labau Jaiwa* is often chanted. Xiao Jiacheng, comp. and trans. *Labau Jaiwa: The Creation Epic of Jingpo Ethnic People* (in Chinese). Beijing: Minzu Chubanshe, 1992, 1–25.

44. Lan, Ke. "Using the Social Function of Creation Myths to Examine the Essential Characteristic of Myths" (in Chinese). *Yunnan Minzu Xueyuan Xuebao* 4 (1986): 29–30.

45. Lan, 27–28.

46. Fu, Yingren, comp. *Mythological Stories of the Manchu People* (in Chinese). Ha'erbing: Beifang Wenyi Chubanshe, 1985, 133–134.

47. Bamo, Qubumo. "A Field Study of Epic Tradition: Nuosu Epic *Hnewo* as a Case" (in Chinese). PhD diss., Beijing Normal University, 2004.

48. Meng, 150.

49. Zhang, Qizhuo, and Dong Ming, comps. *The Story Collection of Three Story-tellers of the Manchu Ethnic People* (in Chinese). Shenyang: Chunfeng Wenyi Chubanshe, 1984, 576–592.

50. Zhang and Dong, 589.

51. Consulting some points achieved in the study of folk narrative, here we call those people who have rich knowledge and are willing to tell myths "creative bearers of myth tradition," while those people who preserve less mythological knowledge, can only tell myths in incomplete forms, and are reluctant to tell myths are "passive bearers of myth tradition." For an example of the argument about the active and passive bearers of tradition, please see Carl Wilhelm von Sydow, *Selected Papers on Folklore*. Copenhagen: Rosenkilde and Bagger, 1948, 203–205, passim.

52. Lü, Wei. "History of Chinese Myths" (in Chinese). In *History of Chinese Folk Literature*, 7–8.

53. The sun is also interpreted as the bodies of the two birds.

54. Xie Xuanjun argues that the rationalization of myths in ancient China began during the shift from the Shang (1600 BC–1046 BC) to Zhou dynasties. See his *Myth and National Spirit* (in Chinese). Jinan: Shandong Jiaoyu Chubanshe, 1986, 342, 189.

55. Lü Wei discusses "The Tide of Rationalizing Myths in Eastern Zhou Dynasty" in his article "History of Chinese Myths" (in Chinese). In *History of Chinese Folk Literature*, 49–58.

56. Bodde, Derk. "Myths of Ancient China." In *Mythologies of the Ancient World*, 373–375.

57. Zhong, Jingwen, and Yang Lihui. "The Rationalism in the History of Myth Study in Ancient China." In *Proceedings of the Conference on Chinese Myth and Legend*, vol. 1, 35.

58. Zhou was originally one of the tribal states under the Shang suzerainty, but it finally replaced the Shang in 1027 BC or 1122 BC.

59. Gu, Jiegang. "Studies on Fabricating History in the Warring States Era, Qin, and Han Dynasties" (in Chinese). In *Critiques of Ancient Chinese History*, eds. Lü Simian and Tong Shuye, vol. 7, bk. 1. Shanghai: Kaiming Shudian, 1941, 17–21.

60. Guo, Biheng. "A Study on the Folk Customs and Folk Literature Recorded in *Shiji*" (in Chinese). PhD diss., Beijing Normal University, 2002, 19–22.

61. Guo, 5.

62. Fairbank, John K., and Edwin O. Reischauer. *China: Tradition and Transformation*, rev. ed. Boston: Houghton Mifflin Company, 1989, 70–71.

63. For a general introduction to Chinese history, please see John K. Fairbank and Edwin O. Reischauer, *China: Tradition and Transformation*; Ray Huang, *China: A Macro History* (New York: M. E. Sharpe, 1988); and Patricia Buckley Ebrey, *The Cambridge Illustrated History of China* (Cambridge University Press, 1999).

64. Yuan, Ke. *The History of Chinese Myth* (in Chinese). Shanghai: Shanghai Wenyi Chubanshe, 1988, 180.

65. Zhong, Jingwen. "Studies of the Folkloristics in Revolutionists' Works in Late Qing Dynasty" (in Chinese). In *Essays of Zhong Jingwen's Studies on Folk Literature*, vol. 1. Shanghai: Shanghai Wenyi Chubanshe, 1982, 240–243.

66. Ma, Changyi. "The Anthropological School and Modern Chinese Mythology" (in Chinese). In *The Classics of Chinese Folklore Studies in Twentieth Century*, ed. Yuan Li. Beijing: Shehui Kexue Wenxian Chubanshe, 2002, 77–114.

67. Yang, Lihui. *The Cult of Nüwa: Myths and Beliefs in China*, 220.

68. Xu, Fang. "The Reconstruction of Folk Tradition: A Study of Nüwa Myth and Belief in Hou Village, Hongdong County, Shanxi Province" (in Chinese). Master's thesis, Beijing Normal University, 2002.

69. Yang, Lihui. *The Cult of Nüwa: Myths and Beliefs in China*, 173–174.

70. Hu, Qiwang, and Fan Honggui. *Yao Ethnic People in Pan Village: From Wandering Cultivation to Settling Down* (in Chinese). Beijing: Minzu Chubanshe, 1983, 235–240.

71. Lu, Kecai, ed. *A General Introduction to Chinese Eating Customs* (in Chinese). Beijing: Shijie Zhishi Chubanshe, 1992, 197. But with the great changes in society and culture, now this taboo is less strict. Young people sometimes do not hesitate to eat dog.

72. Zhu, Guiyuan, Wu Sumin, Tao Lifan, and Zhao Guifang, eds. *A Source Book of Myths in Ethnic Minorities in China* (in Chinese). Vol. 1, *Creation Myths*. Beijing: Zhongyang Minzu Xueyuan, 1984, 3.

73. Bodde, Derk. "Myths of Ancient China." In *Mythologies of the Ancient World*, 402–403. See also Lu Yilu, *The Flood Myths: Centered on the South Ethnic Groups and the Aborigines of Taiwan in China*, 18–21.

2

A TIMELINE OF THE MYTHOLOGICAL WORLD

It is impossible to portray a clear chronology of Chinese mythology because Chinese myths are never worked into an integrated and orderly system. Rather, myths come from different cultural traditions and appear at different times, and these myths are scattered throughout diverse sources. Additionally, the relationships between mythological events and particular gods are usually unfixed and sometimes random. However, if we ignore for a moment these confusing facts and look at the mythological events that happen in these narratives, we can construct a linear timeline of the mythological world according to the content of the myths.

THE EMERGENCE OF GODS

The existence of gods usually is the prerequisite of any other facet of myth. In myths recorded and told in Chinese, there are numerous gods and spirits who take charge of various duties, such as arranging all the parts of heaven and earth, creating water and fire, ordering the directions and seasons, and arranging the underworld. Tian Di (the Supreme Heaven or the God of Heaven) or Shang Di (the Supreme God or the Supreme Divinity) sometimes assumes the position as the highest leader of the random pantheon of the gods. During the Tang or Song dynasty, the disorderly pantheon became systemized and Yu Di, the Jade Emperor who came into being when Taoism and beliefs of the Supreme God were merged together, turned out to be the supreme ruler of the comparatively ordered pantheon of gods.

Some Chinese myths (including myths in Han and other ethnic groups) do not explain where the gods and culture heroes come from and how they come into being: gods already exist when the cosmic creation begins. But some myths do explain their origins, which are rather diverse. Gods and heroes may be born by a divine father and mother, come from an egg or other object, be created from air or sound, come from another god's corpse, be made by other deities with mud, or may be transformed from a monkey. Among these possible birth stories of gods, the most popular ones in the Chinese language are those of the creator Pangu coming from an egg and the "Gansheng myths" (in which *gan* means "responding with or reacting to an outside influence" and *sheng* means "birth").

Pangu Was Born from the Cosmic Egg

Pangu often appears as the creator of the world, the first god who was born from the cosmic egg. In some versions, he is said to be born from the primeval chaotic formlessness, the contents of which were much like a chicken's egg. He grew up in the egg while shaping heaven and earth. Each day heaven rose ten feet higher, the earth grew ten feet thicker, and Pangu grew ten feet taller. This situation lasted for 18,000 years. By then heaven was extremely high, the earth was extremely deep, and Pangu was extremely tall. Since he had to twist his body in this egg, he got his name Pangu (*pan* means "coil up"; *gu* means "antiquity").

The Gansheng Myths

In Chinese mythology, considerable gods, demigods, and heroes are described as having been born after their mothers experienced a miraculous phenomenon: they became pregnant without having sexual intercourse with men. Instead, these women became pregnant because they swallowed an egg, were exposed to the sunshine in a special way, drank divine water, swallowed mythical pearls, consumed certain plants (such as red hawthorn or Job's tears), dreamed of devouring the suns, responded to a divine animal (a dragon, for example), touched a piece of wood, or reacted to the air, and so forth. Chinese scholars classify these kinds of myths as "Gansheng myths," in which the gods' mothers miraculously became pregnant after they responded to certain outside influences and incidents, which may refer to animals, plants, or astronomical phenomena. In myths in the Chinese language, many important gods, heroes, and divine ancestors boast such Gansheng myths. For example, Fuxi was said to be born after his mother trod in a huge footprint in a marshland and then became pregnant; Huang Di was born after his mother saw a great bolt of lightning one night circling one of the stars in the Great Bear and then became miraculously pregnant; Shennong or the Divine Farmer's mother got pregnant because she was touched by a divine dragon; the sage king Shun was born after his mother saw a great rainbow; the great hero Yu was born after his mother consumed Job's tears (another version says he came out from his father's belly); the founder of the Shang people, Qi, was miraculously born after his mother ingested a swallow's egg and became pregnant; Houji, the founder of the Zhou people, was born after his mother stepped into a huge footprint in the field. These myths usually function as certifications of these gods' sacred origins and their extraordinary powers and capabilities.

THE EMERGENCE OF THE UNIVERSE

Similar to the existence of gods usually being the prerequisite of any other mythical emergence, the presence of the universe often functions as the foundation for human existence and culture's invention. But sometimes a Chinese myth may start without mentioning the creation of the universe. Many myths begin with the universe already in existence. Among the various myths in Chinese about the emergence of the universe, the following types and motifs are the most well-known.

The Cosmos Came from an Egg

This type of myth is told in relation to the creator Pangu. It posits that at the beginning of time, heaven and earth were in chaotic formlessness like a chicken's egg. Pangu was born within this chaos. After 18,000 years, the egg somehow opened and unfolded. The limpid and light part of it rose and became heaven, and the turbid and heavy part of it sank down and became the earth. In some other versions orally transmitted in contemporary China, the description of the cosmos emerging from an egg is shown more clearly. A myth version collected in Zhejiang Province maintains that Pangu could not bear to be confined to the darkness and stuffiness in the cosmic egg, so he shattered the egg into pieces. The egg white was light so it became heaven whereas the yolk was heavy so it became the earth. The broken shell of it was mixed into the white and the yolk. Two bigger pieces of the shell became the sun and the moon, and the numerous smaller pieces mixed into the white to become the stars. In contrast, those pieces mixed into the yolk became stones.

The Universe Came from a Divine Corpse

This type of myth can be found among many ethnic groups. In myths in Chinese, the most famous one also connects to Pangu. According to many versions of the Pangu myth, when Pangu was dying, his body began to transform. His breath became the winds and clouds, his voice became the thunder, his left eye became the sun, his right eye became the moon, his four limbs and trunk became the four extremes of the earth and the Five Mountains, his blood became the rivers, his veins became the earth's arteries, his flesh became fields and soil, his hair and beard became the stars, his skin and body hair became plants, his teeth and bones became various metals and rocks, his semen and marrow became pearls and jade, his sweat became the rain and the dew, and the various insects on his body reacted to the wind and turned into human beings.

Parents of the Suns and the Moons

In myths in the Chinese language, it is well-known that the sun(s) and the moon(s) are born by their parents. The divine father is commonly said to be Di Jun, or Emperor Jun, one of the supreme gods in ancient time. The mothers are Di Jun's two consorts, Xihe and Changxi. Xihe gives birth to ten suns. The suns live on the Fusang tree. When one sun finishes its work and comes back home, another sun will go out in its place. Xihe often bathed the suns in the Gan Gulf beyond the East Sea. Changxi is the mother of the twelve moons. She bathed the moons at Mount Riyue (Mount Sun and Moon).

The Separation of Heaven and the Earth

The motif of separating heaven from the earth is quite popular in Chinese mythology. A cluster of myths affirms that at the very beginning of time, heaven and the earth were tightly linked with each other, or there was only a narrow crack between them. Then, by some means they were separated from each other and remained apart through today. Widely spread by people in the ethnic groups of Han, Miao, Yao, Yi, Naxi, Buyi, Dulong, Paiwan (in Taiwan), and others, these myths are quite varied in the ways that they account for the reasons for separations and the means by which this separation occurred (see the entry "Li"). Among these various myths, a prominent one in ancient Chinese writings is the myth that Zhong and Li broke off the connection between heaven and the earth. Chiyou started a revolt and brought disaster to the common people. Influenced by him, people on the earth gradually became corrupt. They began to cheat, steal, disobey their faith, and violate the oath between them and the Supreme Divinity. Many innocent people brought complaints against them to the Supreme Divinity. The Supreme Divinity thus ordered two of his subordinates, the deities Zhong and Li, to cut off the link between heaven and the earth. From then on, people could never ascend to heaven again, and, correspondingly, the deities could never descend to the earth either.

THE EMERGENCE OF HUMANS

Numerous mythological types and themes explain the origins of humans in Chinese mythology. Among them are that humans were made by gods; that they were sown from seeds; that they were spat out from the mouths of gods and goddesses; that they were made from sound; that they were created by two gods touching their knees together; that they came from an animal's metamorphosis; that a plant metamorphosed into the first human; that humans came out of a cave or emerged from a huge stone or a gourd; that they were procreated by

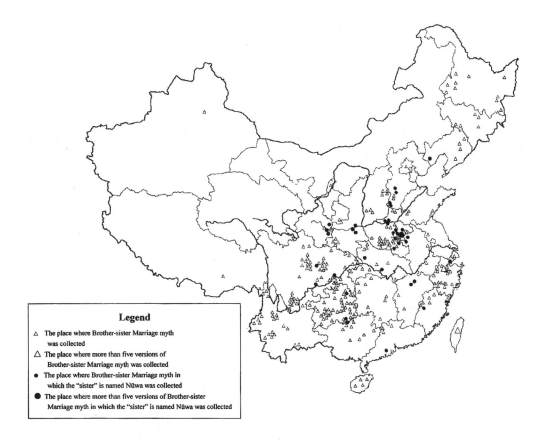

The distribution map of the brother-sister marriage myth in China. (Drawn by Yang Lihui)

animals or plants; that they were born after a man married a goddess, or after a man married an animal; that they were created by the sun; and that they were made from the corpse of a divine creature (see the Introduction to this book for more detail). Among these myths, the most celebrated in the Chinese language are as follows.

Humans Were Created by Nüwa Molding Mud

Among the Han people, the most popular story explaining the origin of humans relates to the goddess Nüwa. It holds that when heaven and the earth had been created, no humans yet existed. So Nüwa created human beings by molding them from yellow earth with her hands. The work drained her strength and took a lot of time, so after she had molded many humans she took a cord and pulled it through the mud, then lifted the cord and shook it. All of the sludge that fell down from the cord became men and women. One version of the myth explains that rich and noble people were those made by Nüwa's hands whereas poor and lowly people were those made by Nüwa dragging a cord through the mud.

Humans Were Re-created by the Brother-Sister Couple

Another widely spread type of myth explaining the origin of today's humans maintains that they were re-created by a sibling couple after their elder generations were annihilated in a big disaster. In China, this brother-sister marriage myth can be found in more than forty ethnic groups, including the Han (see the Introduction). This myth basically states that in remote antiquity, there was a great disaster (flood, fire mixed with oil, uncommon snow, etc.). All humans in the world were destroyed except for a brother and his sister. They wanted to marry each other in order to repopulate the earth but wondered whether this was proper. They agreed that if certain things happened in a test, they should get married. The test in some myth versions was to roll two pieces of a millstone down different sides of a mountain. If the stones touched at the bottom of the mountain, the siblings should marry. In other versions the brother and sister each lit a fire from a different place, and if the two lines of smoke joined each other instead of dispersing, they should marry. Usually these things all happened perfectly, so the two got married. After their marriage, some myths state that the sister gave birth to normal children. Others state that she gave birth to an abnormal fetus (such as a spherical piece of flesh, a gourd, a knife stone, and

A pair of millstones (broken) is worshipped in Fuxi Temple at Tianshui City, Gansu Province, northwest China, to commemorate the first sibling-couple ancestors, 1995. (Courtesy of Yang Lihui)

so on). In these myths Nüwa opens the abnormal fetus or cuts it into pieces, and new humans emerge (see the entry "Nüwa").

THE INVENTION OF CULTURE

China boasts abundant myths about culture heroes and their inventions. These inventions refer to the ordering of human life; acquisition of a livable environment; acquisition of a food supply for humans; creation of crafts, arts, and wisdom; establishment of customs and laws; and so on. In an ancient text in *Shi Ben* (*The Origin of Hereditary Families*, ca. third century BC), many such initial inventions made by gods, goddesses, and heroes were recorded. This text states that Fuxi invented the *qin* (a seven-stringed plucked instrument); Shennong invented the *se* (a twenty-five-stringed plucked instrument, similar to the zither); Nüwa invented the *shenghuang* (a reed-pipe wind instrument); Zhuanxu ordered Feilongshi (literally meaning "flying dragon") to make a large bell, whose sound could shock people and reach far distances; Zhurong invented the market; Goumang invented the *luo* (a net for catching birds); Huang Di asked Xihe to make the divination for the sun and Changyi to make the divination for the moon; Linglun invented music; Juyong and Cangjie made Chinese characters; Shihuang invented drawing; Boyu created cloth; Yinshou invented the mirror; Chiyou used metal to make weapons; Sorcerer Xian invented divination; Sorcerer Peng invented medicine; Sorcerer Xian (it is still disputed whether these two Sorcerers Xian are the same person) made the brass drum; Fengmeng invented shooting; Hai domesticated the cow and invented the oxcart; Xiangtu invented the horse-drawn carriage; Xizhong invented the cart; Susha first made salt by evaporation; Boyi invented the well; Yao invented the game of Go; Gun invented city walls; Gaotao invented the five chief forms of punishment in ancient China; Shun made the *xiao* (a vertical bamboo flute); Kui invented music; Keshou invented painting; Kunwu invented pottery; and so forth.

Among these numerous myths about the cultural inventions recorded in Chinese, the most prominent and characteristic ones are the stories relating to the inventions of agriculture, fire, Chinese characters, Chinese medicine, and musical instruments.

Inventing Agriculture

The myths concerning agricultural invention mainly tell how gods of agriculture, such as Houji ("Lord Millet" or "Sovereign Millet"), Shennong (the Divine Farmer), Houtu (the Divine Earth), and Shujun, started the technologies of sowing and cultivating, and invented a variety of farm tools. The most famed inventions of agriculture are attributed to Shennong. He is said to have first taught people to sow the five grains (different names are given in different explanations; they sometimes refer to rice, two kinds of millet, wheat, and beans), to examine the land, and to cultivate it according to the land's quality (dry or wet, fertile or barren, high or low, etc.). He rescued people from consuming plants and worms, and from drinking from rivers. In some versions he is said to have tasted the fruits of hundreds of plants and grasses, and recognized their sour or bitter flavors. After this process, he then taught people to take the five grains as their food. Additionally, Shennong is said to have invented numerous important farm tools such as the axe, hoe, and *leisi*, a plowlike farm tool used in ancient China. He cut wood to make the plowshare, and bent a piece of wood to make the handle of the plow. In the process of using these tools, he taught people to open up wastelands and hoe weeds. He also taught people to excavate wells and irrigate land. He invented the way of storing grain seeds. He also invented the calendar and *Jieqi*, which divided the solar year into twenty-four seasonal divisions ("twenty-four Jieqi") indicating the change of climate and timing for agricultural activities. Because of his great contributions to agriculture, he was respectfully addressed as "the Divine Farmer."

Acquisition of Fire

The most distinguished myth explaining the origin of fire in the mythological world of Chinese language is the myth about Suirenshi (in which *sui* literally means "flint," *ren* means "human," and *shi* here is a respectful address for ancient heroes), the producer of fire in remote antiquity. In a popular version he is said to be inspired by a bird that was pecking a huge tree named Sui, producing a lot of sparks. Imitating it, Suirenshi used a small branch of wood to drill into the tree and produced lots of sparks. That started the practice of making and using fire. From then on, humans began to cook food and thus differed from animals.

Discovery of Chinese Medicine

As one of the great contributions that Chinese people have made to the world, the theories of Chinese medicine claim that the human body is an integral whole and that each part of it is intimately connected and interacts with other parts. Furthermore, the human body is closely connected to nature. Disease is caused because of the internal imbalance of *Yin* and *Yang* (the two opposing principles in nature; the former represents the feminine and negative principle whereas the latter represents the masculine and positive) and therefore can be treated by balancing the two elements in the body through the use of herbal medicine, acupuncture, and moxibustion, and in other ways. Today many Chinese people believe that Chinese medicine can fundamentally put the body into a healthy and harmonious state whereas Western medicine only cures the superficial disease instead of the root cause of that disease.

The most eminent myth about the discovery of Chinese medicine relates to Shennong's contribution. Shennong is popularly said to have tasted, or in some other versions, thrashed with a magic reddish-brown whip, hundreds of herbs in order to figure out their medicinal characteristics and functions. Then he completely knew their flavors and properties of coldness, warmness, mildness, or toxicity, and thereafter used them to cure people's diseases. This work was sometimes dangerous. He once consumed seventy poisonous plants in one day. Sometimes Shennong is described not only as the primogenitor of Chinese traditional medicine but also as a general practitioner of medicine. He is depicted as the first to carefully study the pulse conditions, discern the different characteristics of medicines, and start the therapies of acupuncture and moxibustion. Shennong also wrote a medical book.

Inventing Chinese Characters

Chinese characters form the oldest writing system still most popularly used today. Compared to the phonetic systems of the West, Chinese characters may look more complex. There are four main parts of their composition, which are pictographs, simple ideographs, compound ideographs, and phonetic ideographs. The pictographic words make up the most basic part of the writing system, and the characters of the phonetic ideographs form about 90 percent of the system.

Myths explaining the mythological invention of Chinese characters are also quite famous. It is widely said that a cultural hero named Cangjie invented the Chinese character. Cangjie had four eyes and had the ability to write when he was born. He examined the constellations, observed the footprints of birds and beasts, and studied the signs visible on turtles' shells and on birds' feathers, on mountains and rivers, and on fingers and palms. From these observations he understood that natural phenomena could be differentiated and marked by pictographic signs. Relying on these signs, he created Chinese characters. This invention was such a great event that afterward the millet fell down like rain from heaven, and ghosts cried during the night.

Inventing Musical Instruments

In ancient China, especially in the Confucianism theory, music played an important role in philosophy, education, ethics, and politics. Besides its function as entertainment, it was also believed to be able to help improve people's temperament and cultivate their morals. Therefore, music was believed to help achieve the larger goal of producing a harmonious and civilized society. For this reason, musical training was usually taken as a necessary part of an intellectual's accomplishments. A talented intellectual often received compliments for his mastery of the *qin*, Chinese chess, calligraphy, and painting.

Corresponding with the important role of music in ancient Chinese culture, abundant myths in Chinese explain the origins of music, various musical instruments, and even some sacred melodies or songs composed by gods. Almost every superior god and goddess is said to have contributed something in this area. For example, it is said that Nüwa invented the *shenghuang* and the *xiao* to entertain the humans she created. Fuxi made the *se* and the *xun* (an egg-shaped clay wind instrument with finger holes) and composed the melody of "Jiabian." The divine farmer, Shennong, in some myth versions is also depicted to have invented important ancient Chinese musical instruments such as the qin and the se. He made them to help people to be calm, to keep their childlike innocence instead of being evil. He also composed a piece of music named "Fuchi" or "Xiamou." Among these myths about the invention of music, Linglun and his creations are the most famous. Linglun was the governor of music under Huang Di. He was ordered to establish music. So he went to the west of Daxia Marsh, and to the north of Ruanyu Mountain, and located a kind of bamboo from the Xiexi Valley. He made a pipe from it, the sound of which created the base of ancient Chinese musical modes. He then made twelve bamboo pipes and blew them by imitating the phoenix's singing. And that made up the twelve *lü* (a series of standard bamboo pitch pipes used in ancient music). In this way, he invented the five notes of the ancient Chinese five-tone scale (*gong, shang, jiao, zhi,* and *yu,* equivalent to 1, 2, 3, 5, and 6 in numbered musical notation or *do, re, mi, so,* and *la* in Western solfeggio) and the eight sounds made by eight musical instruments, like the *xun, sheng* (a pipe wind instrument made of gourd), drum, bamboo pipe, strings, *qing* (an ancient percussion instrument made from jade or stone), bell, and *zhu* (an ancient percussion instrument made from wood). Because of his great contribution to music, Linglun is respected in later tradition as the God of Music and the divine ancestor of actors. Because of him, musicians and actors are generally called *linglun* or *lingren* (*ren* means "human").

COSMIC DISASTERS AND RESTORATIONS

In Chinese mythology, myths about world calamities in the remote past are quite numerous. They tell how and why the former world or human race was disturbed or even destroyed during the catastrophes, which usually happened in the form of deluge, worldwide fire, rare snow, the collapse of the sky pillars, more than one sun rising in heaven, and so forth. Among some ethnic groups, the mythological world catastrophes occurred in a series and regularly. After the disasters, the stories usually continued with renewal of the world and humans. In myths relayed in Chinese, the most prominent concerning cosmic disasters and their restorations are myths about Gun and Yu controlling the flood, the brother-sister couple re-creating humans after the world deluge, Nüwa repairing the broken sky, and Yi shooting down the surplus nine suns. Since the myth about the sibling couple who became human ancestors was introduced earlier, here the other three are presented.

The Flood and Its Control

Flood myths are especially popular in Chinese mythology. Chinese flood myths usually tell how the flood imperiled the world in ancient times, and therefore how heroes or heroines tried to stop the flood and save the world from the disaster, or how human ancestors tried to re-create humans after the deluge, and how a new cosmic order was eventually rebuilt and a new civilization appeared.

Some Chinese scholars assert that there are three systems of flood myths in Chinese mythology (see the entry "the Floods"). Among them, the Gun-Yu myth is the most popular one, focusing on the theme of flood and the controlling of it. Most versions of this myth state that in the ancient era, the flood brought great damage to the world. The water was so fierce that it gushed up into heaven. Gun wanted to stop the flood. So he stole Xirang, a kind of mythical soil that was able to grow ceaselessly by itself, from the Supreme Divinity without waiting for his permission. Gun used Xirang to barricade against the overflowing water. The Supreme Divinity was angry, so he ordered the fire god Zhurong to kill Gun at the outer edge of Yushan (which literally means "feather mountain"). Gun's corpse did not rot for three years. Later, when his belly was opened with a sword, his son Yu emerged. Yu continued to fight the floodwater. He deepened the seas and lakes, dredged the rivers, and dug mountains, channeling the overflowing water to the east seas. Eventually the demigod Yu stopped the flood and changed the miserable world into a habitable place for humankind. He then became the founder of the first civilized state, Xia. According to a widespread mythological story, Yu spent thirteen years trying to control the deluge. During this period, he was so devoted to his task that he did not go to his home three times when he passed by it. In another story, he had changed into a bear to dig a mountain when his pregnant wife came to bring him food. She felt embarrassed when she saw her husband as a bear, so she ran away. Yu ran after her and she metamorphosed into a stone. When Yu shouted to the stone, "Give back my son!" the stone opened up and out came Qi (literally meaning "open up"), the first ruler of Xia.

The Repair of the Broken Sky

Though the notable myth about Nüwa mending the broken sky is sometimes attributed to flood myth systems (see the entry "the Floods"), the disaster it describes is actually not only a flood. Rather, it is a cosmic catastrophe. In some versions, this calamity was caused by the collapse of the four poles supporting heaven. In other texts, this cosmic disorder was caused by the breakdown of one of the sky poles, Mount Buzhou (literally means "not full"), in a war between the gods Gonggong and Zhuanxu (names differ in different texts). Gonggong fought with Zhuanxu to be the supreme god but failed in the war. He was so angry that he butted into Mount Buzhou. The collapse of the sky pillar(s) caused great disasters. Fires raged fiercely and could not be extinguished. Water flowed without abating. Ferocious birds and beasts seized and devoured people. At this moment, the goddess Nüwa melted stones of five different colors to patch heaven, and cut the legs off of a huge tortoise and set them up to support the four extremities of heaven. She defeated the fierce Black Dragon to save the people, and collected ashes of reeds to stop the flood. Her arduous work cleared up the terrible mess and put the world in order again. In some versions collected in the twentieth century, Nüwa not only mended the broken sky but also repaired the broken earth

that was damaged in the same disaster. Her mythical actions often serve as an etiology to explain why people today can see colorful clouds in heaven (because the goddess mended heaven with colorful stones), and why the current western land of China is high while the east is low (she used the longer legs of the tortoise to support the west, using the shorter legs to support the east).

Shooting Down the Surplus Suns

Another famous cosmic disaster and its restoration in Chinese mythology relate to shooting down the surplus suns. This type of myth can be found in many ethnic groups, such as the Han, Hani, Lahu, Luoba, Lisu, Naxi, Qiang, Tujia, Miao, Yao, Dong, Yi, Zhuang, Li, Buyi, Gelao, Mongol, Hezhe, and others. It usually tells that in ancient ages, there

Yi shooting down the surplus sun birds. Funeral stone carving of the Eastern Han dynasty, Wuliang Shrine, Jiaxiang County, Shandong Province, eastern China. (Feng Yunpeng and Feng Yunyuan, Research on Stone Carving, *1821)*

were several suns appearing in heaven (the number of the suns may be seven, ten, twelve, or another number). The weather became extremely hot, the earth was burned, and the crops all died. Humans suffered greatly from the disaster. Then a hero arrived. He shot down the surplus suns and left only one for the normal use of this world. In this way, he restored the cosmos to regular order.

In myths in the Chinese language, the hero who shot down the extra suns is Yi. He is often set in the time of the sage ruler Yao. Many versions of his myths describe that at the time of Yao, ten suns rose up together in heaven. They burned crops and dried the grasses and woods, and this resulted in the deaths of many humans. In addition, ferocious monsters took this opportunity to devour the remaining humans. So Yi shot down the additional nine suns and left one for the natural cosmic order. Thus the cosmos was renewed again.

CIRCULAR TIME

A rudimentary look at the mythological events listed above may give one an impression that the timeline of Chinese myths is linear. However, a distinguished mythologist, Wang Xiaoliang, who works at a university in Japan, suggests that the timeline in some Chinese myths, such as Nüwa repairing the broken sky and the sibling couple reproducing humans after the flood, is circular. It is different from the linear timeline in Christian mythology. He names this cluster of myths "Circularly Returning to the Original Order." He finds the basic plot structure to be like this: (1) there was a mythical paradise (the original cosmic order); (2) the original paradise was broken (because of humans' rebellion against gods, wars between gods, or the world deluge); (3) the paradise was reconstructed (resumed the initial state, or returned to the original order). Wang points out that the circular timeline in these myths shows the conception that "time is circular," held by many people in ancient times, including the Chinese. These people believed that nature and human life all experienced a circular life cycle, just like the sun rises in the morning, sets down in the evening, and rises up again in the next morning (Wang 1987, 565–572). This circular conception of time deeply influenced many famous Chinese classic novels, such as *Sanguoyanyi* (*Romance of the Three Kingdoms* by Luo Guanzhong, 1328?–1398?), *Shuihuzhuan* (*The Water Margin* by Shi Nai'an, ca. fourteenth century CE), and *Hongloumeng* (*Dream of the Red Chamber*, written by Cao Xueqin, 1715–1763). In these novels, the protagonist(s) all experience an initial order (sacred and orderly time), then go through disasters and adversities in the secular world (the original order is destroyed), and, in the end, return back to the original order again (back to the sacred and orderly time) (Wang 1987, 573–578). Though his argument needs further discussion, it provides an inspiring perspective to understand the complexity of the timeline of Chinese mythology.

Reference

Wang, Xiaoliang. *The Chinese Mythological World: A Study on the Creation Myths and Relevant Beliefs in Ethnic Groups of China* (in Chinese). Taibei: Shibao Chuban Gongsi, 1987.

3

DEITIES, THEMES, AND CONCEPTS

BA

Ba is the drought deity, the daughter of Huang Di, the Yellow Emperor. She can bring severe drought to the world by withholding water and rain. She is also called Nüba or Hanba (*nü* means "female" and *han* means "drought").

Ba is one of the most ancient goddesses in the written tradition, because her name and function are mentioned in *Shijing* (*The Classic of Poetry*, compiled in or before 500 BC), though this mention is rather simple and concise.

Ba's main function is described with more detail in *Shanhaijing*. She is said to be the daughter of Huang Di and lived on the Terrace of Gonggong, which is located on Xikun Mountain in the north. She was bald and dressed in green. Wherever she lived there always was a drought. When Chiyou attacked Huang Di, he asked Feng Bo (the Wind God) and Yu Shi (the Rain Master) to release a storm. But Huang Di asked Ba to descend from heaven and help him. The rain stopped at once, so Huang Di won the battle and then executed Chiyou. Though Ba made great contributions in the battle, somehow she could not return to heaven after the battle. Wherever she stayed there was a drought. Eventually Shujun, the Cultivation God, complained about this to Huang Di. Later the emperor instructed Ba to live north of the Red River. But Ba was unwilling to be confined; she often fled this area and wandered to other places, bringing drought with her. Therefore, if people wanted to receive rain, they needed to drive her away. The way they usually did this was to dredge the canals in advance, and then pray to her, "Goddess, go north to where you should stay!" It is said that it would rain after Ba was driven away (chapter 17 of *Shanhaijing*).

The image and character of Ba, as well as the custom of "driving Ba away," were also described in *Shenyijing* (*The Classic of Spirits and Strange Things*, which is said to have been written in the Han period, but probably was written in the Six Dynasties era, 386–589 CE). Ba was reportedly two or three *chi* (three chi equals one meter, or 3.3 feet) in height, with two eyes on her head, and she wore no clothes. She looked like a human and walked fast like the wind. Where she appeared, there was a drought. But if she was captured and plunged into excrement, the drought would be stopped.

The custom of "driving Ba away" was common in numerous variations before 1949 in some regions of Henan, Shandong, Sichuan, and other provinces. In the northern part of Henan Province, for instance, Ba was thought to be the corpse of a newly buried person. If it did not rain for a long time, the anxious farmers would open the new grave with fresh earth on top, dig the corpse out, and whip it, because they believed Ba would water the grave during the night. They called this "beating Drought Ba." They believed it would rain soon after this rite. However, in Sichuan Province in southwest China the ritual was quite different. One man would disguise himself as the Drought Ba and four men would act as warriors. Ba would escape here and there, and the warriors would run after "her" while the audience helped them by shouting or beating the drums. The ritual would last for several hours until Ba was driven away from this area.

See also Chiyou; Feng Bo; Huang Di; Shujun; Yu Shi
References and Further Reading
Birrell, Anne. *Chinese Mythology: An Introduction.* Baltimore and London: Johns Hopkins University Press, 1993, 132–134.
Ma, Changyi. *The Classic of Mountains and Seas: Ancient Illustrations with Annotations* (in Chinese). Jinan: Shandong Huabao Chubanshe, 2001, 612–613.

BOYI

Domesticator of beasts and birds, and a capable help to the hero Yu in controlling the great flood and taming all kinds of animals in the world, Boyi also appears as Yi (different from the hero Yi who shoots down the surplus suns) in different myth versions.

As the helper and minister of Yu, Boyi made many glorious contributions to the king and to ordinary people. One of his most famous deeds is helping Yu to prevent frequent floods through water control. This skill is often related to his mythical ability to tame beasts and birds. Boyi could understand the language and characteristics of animals, which enabled him to domesticate some beasts and birds and keep them from hurting human beings. Another of his important deeds is that he invented the digging of wells, one of the most vital facilities in people's lives in early times. According to some versions, because of Boyi's distinguished merits, King Yu abdicated in favor of Boyi, handing the crown over to him. But Yu's son, Qi, killed Boyi, took over as the king, and became the first ruler of Xia, the first civilized state in Chinese history.

See also Houji; Yu

References and Further Reading

Yang, Dongchen, and Yang Jianguo. "On the Historical Contribution and Position of Boyi Tribe" (in Chinese). *Zhongnan Minzu Xueyuan Xuebao* 2 (2000): 60–65.

Yuan, Ke. *Myths of Ancient China: An Anthology with Annotations* (in Chinese). Beijing: Renmin Wenxue Chubanshe, [1979] 1996, 322–327.

BUZHOU, MOUNT

A famous sky pillar, one of the mythical mountains holding up heaven; Mount Buzhou was damaged by Gonggong in a war and was partially destroyed, hence its name (*bu* means "not" or "without," and *zhou* means "complete" or "full").

The concept that heaven is supported by pillars or some other kind of foundation is found in many cultures. In China, this cosmological belief is also quite common among many ethnic groups. The sky holders can be big mountain peaks, huge trees, turtles' feet, deities' or heroes' bodies or corpses, pillars of gold or silver, or other supports. The number of the holders may be four, five, eight, or even twelve, due to variations from different ethnicities, times, and places.

Among these supports holding up heaven, Mount Buzhou is very famous. It is located at the corner of the great wilderness beyond the northwest seas. To the north it overlooks Mount Zhubi and Mount Yuechong, and to the east it overlooks the Youze Marsh, where the river runs underground and its roaring noise can be heard on the plain. Two yellow beasts guard Mount Buzhou. A mythical fruit that looks like a peach but has leaves like a jujube, with blossoms of yellow with calyx red, grows there. If one eats the fruit, one will no longer feel tired or, in one version of the myth, will not feel hungry any longer.

The most well-known myth about Mount Buzhou is that it was damaged by the water god Gonggong in his war with Zhuanxu, sometimes called Zhurong or Shennong (different names are given in different texts). This story was mentioned as early as in the late Warring States era in "Tianwen," which, similar to its other mythological recordings, put a simple and ambiguous question on the logical connection between Gonggong's rage and the tilt of the earth toward the southeast.

A much more detailed story appeared later in *Huainanzi* and *Lunheng*. Detailed accounts also exist in other written works, but with considerable variants. *Huainanzi* (chapter 3) states that Gonggong fought with Zhuanxu to be ruler in remote antiquity. In his fury he bumped against Mount Buzhou and caused this pillar of heaven to break and snap the cords of the earth. Since then, heaven tilts toward the northwest, and that is why the sun, moon, and stars continue to this day to move in that direction. The earth also had a piece missing in the southeast, and that is why the rivers of China flow toward the ocean in the east.

The same story was told in *Lunheng*, but it is connected to the Nüwa myth of repairing the broken sky. In this version Gonggong butted against Mount Buzhou in his unsuccessful war with Zhuanxu, thereby causing the pillar of the sky and the cords of the earth to break. It was then that Nüwa patched up the sky with melted colorful stones and cut off a turtle's feet to hold it up. A similar explanation was given for the variations in the Chinese topography.

In *Liezi* (which was thought to have been written in the Warring States era but probably was compiled during the Jin dynasty, 265–420 CE), though the two stories also are connected, their chronological order is opposite. Nüwa patched the broken sky first because it was defective, followed by Gonggong's damage years later.

Now more and more scholars argue that this story, "Gonggong bumps into Mount Buzhou," has no logical connection with the story that "Nüwa repaired the broken sky." They are loosely bound together with their development and change. Similar mergers of separate stories can be commonly found in Chinese oral tradition, including Chinese mythology.

No matter whom Gonggong fought with, and no matter whether the Gonggong event happened before Nüwa's repair or afterward, Mount Buzhou was damaged by Gonggong, and thereafter a new cosmological order was established.

See also Cords of the Earth; Gonggong; Nüwa; Pillars of the Sky; Shennong; Zhuanxu; Zhurong

References and Further Reading

Birrell, Anne. *Chinese Mythology: An Introduction.* Baltimore and London: Johns Hopkins University Press, 1993, 97–98.

Bodde, Derk. "Myths of Ancient China." In *Mythologies of the Ancient World,* ed. Samuel Noah Kramer. Chicago: Quadrangle Books, 1961, 386–389.

Christie, Anthony. *Chinese Mythology.* Rev. ed. New York: Peter Bedrick Books, 1985, 56–58, 69–91.

CANCONG

Cancong was the founder of the ancient Shu kingdom (modern Sichuan Province in southwest China) in mythical history, the first ancestor of Shu kings, and a mythological hero who taught the techniques of sericulture (silk production) to humans in local mythology. In his name, *can* means "silkworm" and *cong* means "cluster," which illustrates his strong affinity with sericulture.

The Cancong myth is very scattered and faint in Chinese mythological records, and therefore, we can draw only an outline of this myth from fragmental texts in some ancient Chinese literature. Cancong appeared as the first ancestor of Shu kings. His descendants were the kings Baihu and Yufu. During these three reigns the population was sparse and people did not practice writing, ritual, and music. Each of these three kings lived for several hundreds of years, and the people who followed them vanished. Like many other mythological ancestors and gods, Cancong also had an unusual appearance in that his eyes bulged in an upright position, which showed his extraordinary powers. He always wore green clothes, thus he was also called "Green God" or "God in Green Clothes." Yuan Ke, an important Chinese mythologist, deduced that the original figure of this god of sericulture is a silkworm, because the color of the silkworm is green (Yuan 1993, 367).

The most important deed Cancong did, according to the mythological record, is teaching people how to rear silkworms. According to *Xianzhuan Shiyi* (*Supplementary Material to "Biographies of Immortals" and to "Biographies of Holy Immortals,"* written in the late Tang dynasty, ca. tenth century CE, now known only in later writings that quote this work) and *Sanjiao Soushen Daquan* (*A Compendium of Information on the Gods of the Three Religions*, written in the Yuan dynasty, 1206–1368 CE), Cancong set himself up as king of Shu and taught people to breed silkworms. He made thousands of golden silkworms and gave every family one golden silkworm at the beginning of every year. The silkworms in each family multiplied prolifically, and after some time people would return the golden silkworms to their king. When Cancong toured the area of his realm to make an inspection, wherever he stopped, people would gather and form silkworm markets. Because people received great benefits from Cancong, they built many temples throughout western China to worship and offer sacrifices to him.

During the twentieth century, especially in 1986, one of the most famous primitive tribal ruins of ancient Shu was uncovered at Sanxingdui (Three Stars Mound), which is located in the northeastern corner of the Sichuan plain. Archaeological studies of the cultural relics found in the many layers of the site revealed a significant civilization existing as early as approximately 5,000 to 3,000 years ago, dating from the late Neolithic age to the Shang dynasty. Among the artifacts were pottery, jade, and gold or bronze figures, such as a gilded wooden walking stick that symbolizes the power of the king of Shu. Other artifacts include a set of bronze masks displaying characteristics of local mythological figures. These characteristics include high noses, wide mouths, and, most noticeably, bulging eyes; some even portray the eyeballs sticking out of the mask like short pillars. Though the origin and race of these Sanxingdui people remain a mystery, many scholars think the bronze masks with protruding eyes are the statues of Cancong, the founding god of the Shu tribe.

See also Leizu

References and Further Reading

Birrell, Anne. *Chinese Mythology: An Introduction*. Baltimore and London: Johns Hopkins University Press, 1993, 61–63.

Qu, Xiaoqiang, Li Dianyuan, and Duan Yu, eds. *The Culture of Sanxingdui* (in Chinese). Chengdu: Sichuan Renmin Chubanshe, 1993.

Yuan, Ke. *A Survey of Chinese Mythology* (in Chinese). Chengdu: Bashu Shushe, 1993, 365–368.

CANGJIE

Cangjie is the famous culture hero who invented Chinese characters. He is said to be an official historiographer of Huang Di in mythical history.

The records about Cangjie's invention can be found in texts of the Warring States era, and these records are quite detailed in the Han era. These accounts, like many other mythological recordings, are incomplete and sometimes conflict with each other. Cangjie is described in these writings as having remarkable vision and ability. He had four eyes and was able to write when he was born. He examined the constellations, observed the footprints of birds and beasts, and studied the signs visible on turtles' shells, birds' feathers, mountains and rivers, and fingers and palms. From these observations he understood that natural phenomena could be differentiated and marked by pictographic signs. Relying on these signs, he created Chinese characters. This invention was such a great event that afterward millet fell down like rain from heaven, and ghosts cried during the night. Some scholars interpret that such miraculous phenomena show the magical power of writing. But Gao You (third century CE), a scholar who annotated many of the classics, explained that along with the invention of writing, deceit appeared too. Humans began to neglect farming, their essential work, and attend to trifle benefits. Heaven knew they would be hungry, so it rained millet. And the ghosts were afraid that they would be accused by man's writing, so they cried.

The Cangjie myth continues to be told in contemporary China. A story collected in Shaanxi Province describes the mythic process of how Cangjie invented the characters. Cangjie was an official of Huang Di whose main duty was to record things that happened. He used knotted ropes of various sizes and colors to memorize different events and experiences. But it eventually became difficult to recall what each knot meant. Cangjie decided to find an easier way to record human history and thoughts. He visited many thoughtful people for inspiration. Then he lived in seclusion in a cave and created signs based upon pictographs. The word 日

(the sun) was created according to the round shape of the sun, the word 月 (the moon) was created according to the shape of the crescent, the word 人 (human) imitated the profile of a man, and the word 爪 (claw) imitated the footprint of birds and beasts. He called these words *zi* (characters). After this invention he began to teach people everywhere to write these characters. Since the written characters he invented were "as many in number as ten liters of rapeseed," people could not learn and remember that large amount. Even Confucius, the founder of Confucianism and one of the greatest educators in ancient China, only learned 70 percent of the original amount. Cangjie felt very disappointed and annoyed, so he threw the other 30 percent away to foreign countries. That was the origin of other characters of foreign languages.

The Cangjie statue in Qin'an County, Gansu Province, 1997. (Courtesy of An Deming)

Another modern myth spread in Sichuan Province associates Cangjie's invention with Nüwa, the goddess and creator of humans. Cangjie used 女 (meaning "woman") as a character element and combined other components, then created some words with negative meanings, such as 奸 ("wicked") and 妖 ("demon"), because he looked down on women. The great mother of humans, Nüwa, was very upset about this. She accused Cangjie of prejudice and asked him to create some good words with 女. At last, Cangjie invented the words 好 ("good") and 娘 ("mother").

Like most deities of Chinese mythology, Cangjie is part of the popular religion of many people and is respected and worshiped in rituals. During the Song dynasty he was worshiped as the ancestor who founded the professions of the Xu Li group of people, petty officials taking charge of documents and paperwork in government who therefore handled words every day. He was called "King Cang." According to *Shilin Yanyu* (*Records of History and Anecdotes*, written by a Song dynasty writer, Ye Mengde, 1077–1148 CE), every autumn, many Xu Li in the capital put their money together and held a festival to worship King Cang. They often drank all day during the festival. Today, one can also find evidence of similar worship in Shangdong, Henan, Hebei, Shaanxi, and other provinces, such as Cangjie's Tombs, Cangjie's Temples, and Cangjie's Platforms, where he is said to have invented the characters. These relics illustrate people's great respect for and remembrance of Cangjie. Among them, Cangjie Temple in Baishui County, Shaanxi Province, is the largest tribute. In local legends, Cangjie is said to have been born here, created words here, and been buried here after his death. He also is given the title of respect "The Saint Cang." Since heaven rained millet after Cangjie created words, people in Shaanxi Province hold a magnificent festival every lunar April at the *jieqi* of Gu Yu (literally means "Grain Rain," one of the twenty-four jieqi. In the traditional Chinese calendar, one solar year is divided into twenty-four terms, called "twenty-four jieqi." The word *jieqi* refers to a day marking one of the twenty-four divisions of one solar year). The festival usually lasts seven to ten days. People will offer Saint Cang steamed breads with various patterns and designs, and perform local dramas for his entertainment. They pray for his blessing. Customs relating to writing and characters are quite popular here. Paper with words on it is not allowed to be thrown away. Pillows often are embroidered with characters. Children will worship Saint Cang, instead of Confucius, before they become elementary school students. And students often touch the stone tablet in Cangjie Temple, believing that by doing so their handwriting will become good.

See also Huang Di; Nüwa

References and Further Reading

Fairbank, John K., and Edwin O. Reischauer. *China: Tradition and Transformation.* Rev. ed. Boston: Houghton Mifflin Company, 1989, 22–27.

Ning, Rui, and Wang Chengyao. "Legends and Beliefs on Cangjie in Baishui County, Northwest China" (in Chinese). *Zhonguo Minjian Wenhua* 3 (1994): 81–96.

Yuan, Ke. *Myths of Ancient China: An Anthology with Annotations* (in Chinese). Beijing: Renmin Wenxue Chubanshe, [1979] 1996, 72–78.

CHANG'E

Chang'e is the spirit of the moon, one of the most well-known goddesses in Chinese mythology. She stole the elixir of immortality from her husband, the great hero Yi, and flew to the moon.

Chang'e was originally called Heng'e, though later the name Chang'e became popularly used. Since the character *heng* in her name happened to be the same character used in a certain Han emperor's name, Heng'e's name had to be

According to Chinese tradition, at the Mid-Autumn Festival, many families will hang a painting of Chang'e and make offerings to her. In this painting, Chang'e is standing under the laurel tree with a maidservant holding a feather fan to serve her, while a rabbit is pounding the elixir of immortality. Beijing, 2004. (Courtesy of An Deming)

changed to Chang'e or to a different Chinese *heng* character due to the taboo of sharing an imperial Han name. Some scholars believe that Chang'e is originally the twelve moons' mother, Changxi, since they both have direct relationships with the moon and their names could be the same in ancient Chinese phonology (Yuan 1993, 463; Gu 1979).

Early traces of the Chang'e myth are found in the initial periods of the Warring States era (fifth century BC). In the divination book of that time, *Guizang* (*The Storehouse of All Things*, now known only through later quotation), which was written for shamans' divination, Chang'e was said to have stolen the elixir of immortality from Xiwangmu, the Queen Mother of the West. She reportedly consumed it, then flew to the moon and became the spirit of the moon. However, the story recorded here was simple and did not mention Yi, Chang'e's husband, at all.

A more complete story about Chang'e appeared in *Huainanzi* at the beginning of the Han dynasty. Yi got the elixir of immortality from Xiwangmu, but Heng'e stole it from him and consumed it. Then she flew to the moon. Yi was very disappointed but could not recover the elixir (chapter 6). Gao You, the Han annotator of many classics, added that Heng'e was Yi's wife.

In some versions, Chang'e is said to metamorphose into an ugly toad after she escapes to the moon. This is usually interpreted as a punishment for her behavior of stealing the precious elixir and forsaking her husband. In Han iconography a toad often appears in the moon, standing on its hind legs, holding a pestle and pounding the elixir of immortality in a mortar. Many scholars think this toad is none other than Chang'e herself. She has been punished and transformed into a toad, and has to pound the elixir for all time (Yuan 1993, 235). Li Shangyin (ca. 813–858 CE), a famous Tang poet, also mentioned that "Chang'e endlessly pounds the elixir of immortality in a mortar" in one of his poems.

In some other versions, however, the creature pounding the elixir in the moon is a rabbit. Since it is pure white, it is often called the "Jade Rabbit." In some later iconography or literature, Chang'e is often depicted as a beautiful goddess, holding the jade rabbit in her arms, or the jade rabbit is pounding the elixir while Chang'e is not working at all.

In fact, the belief that there is a toad or a rabbit in the moon appears quite early too. This belief also can be found in texts from the Warring States era. And it is used to explain the shadow on the surface of the bright moon. Wen Yiduo, a modern Chinese scholar, argued that the earliest mythical creature appearing in the moon was the toad; then the toad and rabbit appeared together; later only the rabbit showed in the moon (Wen 1982, 313–338). Nevertheless, it is evident that the toad and rabbit in the moon (they seem not to have pounded the elixir in the earliest accounts) were originally independent of the Chang'e myth, and they were combined into it during its development process. In Han dynasty iconography the rabbit can often be seen. Sometimes it is running on the moon, and sometimes it is pounding the elixir in a mortar in front of Xiwangmu, the owner of the elixir of immortality, and her husband, Dongwanggong. However, in as late as the Jin dynasty, the pounding rabbit has somehow changed its hostess and living place. It moves onto the moon and becomes Chang'e's companion and continues its pounding work there.

Chang'e is not the only immortal inhabiting the moon. She has a neighbor named Wu Gang, though there is no clear evidence showing any direct association between them. Wu Gang is also a person who does something wrong and therefore is punished. The theme of "living on the moon as a punishment" is clearly expressed in his story. According to *Youyang Zazu* (*A Miscellany from Youyang*, by a Tang writer, Duan Chengshi, d. 863 CE), a cassia tree and a toad were on the moon. The tree was 5,000 feet high. A man named Wu Gang was chopping at the base of the tree. Since he made a mistake in his quest for immortality, he was punished and made to chop the cassia tree. However, whenever he chopped it, the gash healed itself at once. So he had to do the same futile work forever. This punishment is comparable to that of Sisyphus, the Greek mythical hero who is forced to roll a stone up a steep hill, and whenever he reaches the top, it tumbles down and he has to roll it up again.

After the Six Dynasties era (386–589 CE), Chang'e's unfortunate destiny gradually receives more sympathy. Many poems written during this era and during the Tang dynasty showed, on the one hand, blame of Chang'e for her theft of the elixir and abandonment of her husband, and, on the other hand, sympathy for her lonely and dreary life alone on the cold and shadowy moon. In these poems she often was described as a beautiful goddess, her metamorphosis into the ugly toad gradually becoming forgotten.

Today, Chang'e symbolically represents women's beauty, gentleness, elegance, and quietness. Depictions of Chang'e as a charming and graceful figure frequently appear in oral literature, cartoons, paintings, paper-cuts, poems, operas, novels, and other creative works. In particular, at the Mid-Autumn Festival held every fifteenth of August in the lunar calendar, Chang'e's figure commonly adorns the mooncake boxes along with the bright full moon, the cassia tree, and the jade rabbit.

The Chang'e myth continues to be popularly transmitted in contemporary China. Compared to ancient written recordings, the modern Chang'e myth seems more complex and rational. The myths usually appear as combinations of many mythical fragments relating to Chang'e, Yi, or Xiwangmu; they try to give a reasonable cause for Chang'e's behavior. A common story explains the origin of the Mid-Autumn Festival. In the ancient past, there was a hero named Yi who was excellent at shooting. His wife was Chang'e. One year, the ten suns rose in the sky together, causing great disaster to people. Yi shot down nine of the suns and left only one to provide light. An immortal admired Yi and sent him the elixir of immortality. Yi did not want to leave Chang'e and be immortal without her, so he let Chang'e keep the elixir. But Fengmeng, one of his apprentices, knew this secret. So, on the fifteenth of August in the lunar calendar, when Yi went hunting, Fengmeng broke into Yi's house and forced Chang'e to give the elixir to him. Chang'e refused to do so. Instead, she swallowed it and flew into the sky. Since she loved her husband very much and hoped to live nearby, she chose the moon for her residence. When Yi came back and learned what had happened, he felt so sad that he displayed the fruits and cakes Chang'e liked in the yard and gave sacrifices to his wife. People soon learned about these activities, and since they also were sympathetic to Chang'e they participated in these sacrifices with Yi. From then on, holding a memorial ceremony on the fifteenth of August in the lunar calendar has become a tradition and has spread throughout the country.

Another common version provides different reasons why Chang'e flees to the moon. After the hero Hou Yi shot down nine of the ten suns, he was pronounced king by the thankful people. However, he soon became a conceited and tyrannical ruler. In order to live long without death, he asked for the elixir from Xiwangmu. But his wife, Chang'e, stole it on the fifteenth of August because she did not want the cruel king to live long and hurt more people. She took the magic potion to prevent her husband from becoming immortal. Hou Yi was so angry when he discovered that Chang'e took the elixir, he shot at his wife as she flew toward the moon, though he missed. Chang'e fled to the moon and became the spirit of the moon. Hou Yi died soon because he was overcome with great anger. Thereafter, people offer a sacrifice to Chang'e on every lunar fifteenth of August to commemorate Chang'e's action.

In spite of her different motivations and causes for flying into the moon, Chang'e is described as a kind, smart, and self-sacrificing lady in both of these versions.

Today during the night of the Mid-Autumn Festival, many Han Chinese families will still offer a sacrifice to the moon by laying out mooncakes (round pastries stuffed with sweet bean paste or salted egg yolk) and round fruits in their yards. They wish for their families' reunion and harmony. Then, they will eat the cakes and fruits while enjoying the beautiful sight of the bright full moon. On this occasion parents will often tell the Chang'e myth to their children. And they may say that when the moon is full, they can see Chang'e, the cassia tree, and the jade rabbit there in the moon.

See also Changxi; Xiwangmu; Yi

References and Further Reading

Birrell, Anne. *Chinese Mythology: An Introduction.* Baltimore and London: Johns Hopkins University Press, 1993, 144–145.

Gu, Jiegang. "The Development of Chang'e Story" (in Chinese). *Shulin* 2 (1979): 33–34.

Li, Zhonghua. "A Study on the Developing Process of Chang'e Myth" (in Chinese). *Sixiang Zhanxian* 3 (1997): 19–26.

Walls, Jan, and Yvonne Walls, eds. and trans. *Classical Chinese Myths.* Hong Kong: Joint Publishing Co., 1984, 74–76.

Wen, Yiduo. "An Annotation to the Heaven in *Questions of Heaven*" (in Chinese). In *The Complete Works of Wen Yiduo.* Vol. 2. Beijing: Sanlian Shudian, [1948] 1982, 313–338.

Yuan, Ke. *Myths of Ancient China: An Anthology with Annotations* (in Chinese). Beijing: Renmin Wenxue Chubanshe, [1979] 1996, 284–286.

Yuan, Ke. *A Survey of Chinese Mythology* (in Chinese). Chengdu: Bashu Shushe, 1993, 232–236.

CHANGXI

Mother of the twelve moons, Changxi is also one of Di Jun's wives.

In spite of her high status in mythology, the Changxi myth is quite sparse. Her accomplishment mainly appears in *Shanhaijing*, which states that there was a lady who spent her time bathing the moons. She was Di Jun's wife, named Changxi. Changxi gave birth to the twelve moons and was beginning to bathe them at this time (chapter 16). This text does not mention what the twelve moons did to occupy themselves. Another two chapters of the same book depict that a lady named Xihe gave birth to ten suns and bathed them in the Gan Gulf. The ten suns lived on the Fusang tree. When one sun finished its work and came back home, another sun would go out instead (chapters 14 and 15). This may suggest similarities in how the twelve moons worked.

Though the Changxi myth is not very complete, it contains certain motifs, such as "there is more than one moon in the ancient past," "the moon is born from a goddess," and "bathing (or washing) the moon." These motifs can be found in the stories of many ethnic groups in China. The number of the moons varies—it can be five, seven, nine, ten, twelve, or other numbers. The moons may be created by gods and may be born from goddesses. In *Shanhaijing*, the reason the moons needed to be bathed is unclear. Some myths that are spread in the Miao, Buyi, and Yi ethnic groups explain that the sun and the moon needed to be washed in order to cleanse them of the dust they accumulated during their work and to make them bright again.

Changxi sometimes is identified as Chang'e, who stole the elixir of immortality from her husband, Yi, and flew to the moon to become the spirit of the moon. Some Chinese scholars believe they are actually the same goddess because they both have direct relationships with the moon and their names could be the same in ancient Chinese phonology (Yuan 1993, 463; Gu 1979).

See also Chang'e; Di Jun; Fusang; Twelve Moons; Xihe; Yi

References and Further Reading

Birrell, Anne. *Chinese Mythology: An Introduction.* Baltimore and London: Johns Hopkins University Press, 1993, 123–125, 144.

Gu, Jiegang. "The Development of Chang'e Story" (in Chinese). *Shulin* 2 (1979): 33–34.

Yuan, Ke. *The Classic of Mountains and Seas: A Collation and Annotation* (in Chinese). Chengdu: Bashu Shushe, 1993, 438, 463.

CHIYOU

Chiyou was the offspring of Yan Di (the Flame Emperor), the god of war, and the inventor of military weapons. He rebelled against Huang Di but failed in the war and was killed. His shackles turned into a maple tree.

Fragmentary versions of the Chiyou myth can be found scattered throughout various ancient texts. In these narratives, Chiyou is depicted as the descendent of Yan Di. He invented military weapons such as the spear, dagger-axe, sword, and halberd. In one version, he had eighty brothers (seventy-one brothers in another version), each of them with an animal body, bronze head, and iron forehead, who spoke in a human language. They used sand and stone as their food. Other versions state that Chiyou took iron and stone as his food and that he had a human body, horned head, ox hooves, four eyes, six hands, and ears and temples like swords and spears. The main event of his life story is recorded in *Shanhaijing.* Chiyou is said to have made weapons and attacked Huang Di. Thus, Huang Di commanded Yinglong to launch an attack against him in the wilderness of the central plain. Yinglong began by storing all the water. Chiyou asked Feng Bo and Yu Shi to release a cloudburst. Then Huang Di asked the drought goddess Ba to descend from heaven and stop the rain. This eventually killed Chiyou (chapter 17).

The war between Chiyou and Huang Di is one of the fiercest battles among gods in Chinese mythology, since both sides were very powerful. There are many stories that describe the process and circumstances of the war. One story states that when Chiyou attacked Huang Di, no one was able to stop him because he butted people with his horns. In one version, Chiyou was said to be able to soar into the sky and surmount the dangerous and difficult obstructions.

But Huang Di made a drum from the hide of Kui, a one-legged mythical beast, and beat it many times. The sound it made was so great that it prevented Chiyou from flying away. So Chiyou was caught and killed by Huang Di. Another version states that Chiyou led many ferocious mythical animals to attack Huang Di at the Zhuolu plain. So Huang Di ordered his subjects to blow horns sounding like dragons to threaten them. Another version said that Chiyou could stir up clouds and mist. When he fought with Huang Di, he made heavy fog for three days. Huang Di's army was caught in it and could not figure out their direction. Huang Di then invented the compass and guided his army out of the fog. Thus, Huang Di defeated Chiyou and killed him. When Chiyou was executed, his head and body were cut off and buried in different places, and his shackles turned into a maple tree.

Even after his death, Chiyou was still considered a powerful and awful god. One version of the myth said that many years after Huang Di won the battle and killed Chiyou, the world became troubled and confused. In order to deter his people from revolting, Huang Di drew Chiyou's picture and showed it to them, after which the world became peaceful again. During the Qin and Han dynasties, Chiyou was worshiped as the god of war by the army leader and even the First Emperor of Qin (*Shiji*, chapter 8).

In addition to myths about Chiyou, he survives in customs and beliefs. According to *Shuyiji* (*A Record of Accounts of Marvels*, written by Ren Fang in the Six Dynasties era), there was a kind of drama called "Chiyou's Game" in Ji Province. When dancing it, the local people formed into groups of twos or threes. They wore horns on their heads and butted each other. This custom probably started the horn-butting game in the Han period. In the villages of Taiyuan, people did not use ox heads when offering sacrifices to Chiyou, because Chiyou was ox-headed himself.

Chiyou is worshiped as the remote ancestor of the Miao ethnic group. Beliefs about him can be found in aspects of Miao's daily life today. For example, Miao people worship oxen and maple trees. Oxen are thought to be a symbol of luck and of heroism, which can bring safety and prosperity. Designs of ox horns are embroidered on their clothes or carved on their silver decorations. In Miao mythology, Jiangyang, an ancestor of the Miao people, was born from the egg of a goddess who was born from a maple tree. In Chenbu, Hunan Province, Miao people believe that the maple god can expel evils. In Wenshan, Maguan, and other Miao areas in Yunnan Province, a traditional festival called Trembling the Flower Mountain is held once every year. It is said that this festival originated from the Chiyou mythic event. After being defeated by Huang Di, Chiyou led his tribes back into the thickly forested mountains. In order to call together the scattered people over the mountains, he planted a long trunk with a colorful red waistband on the mountain and asked the young to dance and blow reed pipes around it. On hearing the sound, people came from all directions. Chiyou gathered them, and they continued to fight against Huang Di. The custom of dancing and blowing reed pipes around a flower-wreathed pole lasted for generations and has become a traditional festival for the Miao people. The colorful cloth tied to the pole was said to be "Chiyou's flag." A song is sung when the pole is planted. The song narrates how Chiyou, the Miao ancestor, fought with Huang Di, the Han ancestor, and how he was defeated and killed in the end, and thus the Miao people had to flee from the Central Plain toward the southern mountains.

See also Ba; Feng Bo; Huang Di; Yan Di; Yinglong; Yu Shi

References and Further Reading

Birrell, Anne. *Chinese Mythology: An Introduction.* Baltimore and London: Johns Hopkins University Press, 1993, 50–53, 132–134, 192–193.

Cheng, Te-K'un. "Ch'ih Yu: The God of War in Han Art." *Oriental Art*, n.s., 4.2 (1958): 45–54.

Christie, Anthony. *Chinese Mythology.* Rev. ed. New York: Peter Bedrick Books, 1985, 96.

Duan, Baolin. "A Study of Chiyou" (in Chinese). *Minzu Wenxue Yanjiu* 4 (1998): 10–14.

Walls, Jan, and Yvonne Walls, eds. and trans. *Classical Chinese Myths.* Hong Kong: Joint Publishing Co., 1984, 43–47.

Wu, Zhengbiao. "Chi You's Mythology and the Miao Customs." Trans. Li Haixia. http://www.hmongtimes.com/displaynews.asp, 2003.

Yuan, Ke. *Myths of Ancient China: An Anthology with Annotations* (in Chinese). Beijing: Renmin Wenxue Chubanshe, [1979] 1996, 128–143.

CORDS OF THE EARTH

Cords tied to the earth supposedly prevented it from collapsing. In Chinese mythology, these cords are commonly called Di Wei (*di* means "the earth," and *wei* means, basically, "cords.")

The concept of holder(s) preventing the earth from sinking can be found among many people. In Chinese mythology, the holder could be a divine creature such as a turtle, cow, fish, dragon, or snake that supports the earth from underground. Versions of this motif include four cords tied up to the four corners of the square earth, or several pillars (four, five, eight, etc.) holding the earth in place.

In some ancient texts, the earth cords were said to have been broken off during a war in the remote past. According to *Liezi*, there were flaws in the sky and the earth when it was created; therefore, Nüwa melted stones of five different colors to repair the defective sky, and cut the legs from a huge tortoise and set them up to support the four extremities of the sky. However, sometime after this, Gonggong fought with Zhuanxu to be the Supreme Emperor and failed. Gonggong was so angry that he butted into Mount Buzhou, one of the sky pillars, and damaged it. The cords of the earth were broken off too. Thereafter, the sky tilted toward the northwest, and that is why the sun, moon, and stars move in that direction. The earth had a flaw in the southeast, and that is why the rivers and rains flow in that direction. The same story was told in *Lunheng*, but the logical connection between Gonggong's war and Nüwa's mending work is just the opposite. It states that because of Gonggong's war with Zhuanxu, the sky pillar Mount Buzhou collapsed and the cords of the earth were snapped. Therefore, Nüwa smelted colorful stones to patch the sky and cut the legs off a tortoise to support the four extremities of the sky. It is clear that these two separate myths gradually became confused and merged into a new syncretic version (Yang 1997, 46–51; Birrell 1993, 69).

Some scholars claim that Di Wei refers to the four corners of the earth, because *wei* also has the meaning of "corner" (Yuan 1985, 151).

See also Buzhou, Mount; Gonggong; Nüwa; Pillars of the Sky; Zhuanxu

References and Further Reading

Birrell, Anne. *Chinese Mythology: An Introduction.* Baltimore and London: Johns Hopkins University Press, 1993, 97–98.

Yang, Lihui. *The Cult of Nüwa: Myths and Beliefs in China* (in Chinese). Beijing: Zhongguo Shehui Kexue Chubanshe, 1997, 45–63.

Yuan, Ke. *A Dictionary of Chinese Myths and Legends* (in Chinese). Shanghai: Shanghai Cishu Chubanshe, 1985, 151.

CROW OF THE SUN

The crow of the sun functions as the spirit of the sun or, in some versions, the bearer of the sun across the sky. Sometimes it is said to be three-legged, and its number might be ten, as many as the suns in ancient times.

The belief in a crow settling in the sun (or in each individual sun) or bearing the sun across the sky appears very early in Chinese texts. According to a text in *Shanhaijing,* in the great wilderness there was a huge tree named Fusang (Leaning Mulberry) growing on the top of a mountain. Its trunk reached a height of 300 *li* (about 100 miles). Beside the mountain there was a valley named Tang Valley, in which another Fusang tree was growing. Here was the place from which the ten suns rose and set back down. As soon as one sun came back from its journey crossing the sky, another sun started forth. Each of the ten suns was carried by a crow. Another earlier text, "Tianwen," also mentioned the crow of the sun along with the story of Yi in an ambiguous way, asking: "Why did Yi shoot down the suns? Why did the crows shed their feathers?" Wang Yi, the Han commentator of

A three-legged crow in the sun. Funeral stone carving of the Eastern Han dynasty, Tanghe County, Henan Province, central China. (Reproduced for ABC-CLIO from Shan Xiushan, Wang Rulin, and Li Chenguang, eds., A Collection of Han Pictorial Stone Carvings in Henan Province, Henan Meishu Chubanshe, 1989)

"Tianwen," cited a paragraph from *Huainanzi* to explain these questions, which stated that at the time of Yao (a demigod and one of the three sage kings), the ten suns rose together and burned up the woods and grass. Yao then ordered Yi to shoot down the ten suns in the sky, and Yi shot down nine of them. The nine crows settling in these suns died, and their feathers fell out. It seems that the crows in the suns, which function as the suns' spirits, are in some degree different from those who are bearers of the suns, whose main function is to carry each sun across the sky while they are on duty.

In some versions, especially in some texts during and after the Han dynasty, the crow of the sun is sometimes said to be three-legged. For example, both *Huainanzi* and *Lunheng* mention that there was a three-legged crow in the sun (the texts could also be interpreted with a plural reading that there were three-legged crows in the suns). Another version recorded during the Six Dynasties era stated that two sorts of mythical grasses of immortality grew in the northeast and southwest: one was named Di Ri (*di* means "ground," *ri* means "sun"), and the other was named Chun Sheng (*chun* means "spring," *sheng* means "grow"). The three-legged crow liked eating these grasses very much. It descended from heaven to the earth several times in order to eat them. But Xihe, the mother of the ten suns, did not like it to do so. She wanted to control the crow, so she covered its eyes with her hands to stop it from flying down.

> **See also** Fusang; Tang Valley; Xihe; Yi
>
> ***References and Further Reading***
>
> Birrell, Anne. *Chinese Mythology: An Introduction.* Baltimore and London: Johns Hopkins University Press, 1993, 38, 234, 255.
>
> Bodde, Derk. "Myths of Ancient China." In *Mythologies of the Ancient World*, ed. Samuel Noah Kramer. Chicago: Quadrangle Books, 1961, 394–398.
>
> Yuan, Ke. *A Dictionary of Chinese Myths and Legends* (in Chinese). Shanghai: Shanghai Cishu Chubanshe, 1985, 21.

DI JUN

Di Jun, or Emperor Jun, is one of the supreme gods in ancient time. He is a companion to Xihe, mother of the suns, and a companion to Changxi, mother of the moons. Many of his descendants are famous culture heroes or demigods.

Scholars presumed that Di Jun was the supreme god of the Yin people in east China. In ancient times, Di Jun was as great to the Yin people as Huang Di was to the Xia people from west China. However, the Di Jun myth can be found in no other documents save for five chapters of *Shanhaijing*. According to Chinese mythologists such as Yuan Ke, this is because Di Jun gradually faded in popularity as a deity since the kingdom of Yin collapsed. Fewer people continued to tell the Di Jun myth during the Warring States era and the early Han period, the time when *Shanhaijing* was compiled (Yuan 1993, 179–181).

One of Di Jun's famous deeds is that he made friends with the phoenix. In the Great Wilderness lived a flock of five-colored birds. They were dancing in pairs. The god Di Jun desired to go down to the earth and make friends with them. These birds looked after his two altars on the earth. This story is recorded in chapter 14 in *Shanhaijing*; according to a text in chapter 16, the five-colored bird is a type of phoenix.

In a story from chapter 18, Di Jun is described as the god who bestowed special power on the archer Yi. He gave Yi a red bow and arrows with white feathers, placing Yi on the earth to help all the countries there. Therefore Yi started his work of saving people from hardship.

A text in chapter 17 concerns Di Jun's bamboo forest. Beyond the northeast seas, in the Great Wilderness around the river, there was a mountain named Mount Fuyu. Beside the mountain there was a mound. It was about 300 *li* (about 100 miles) in circumference. To the south of the mound lay Di Ku's bamboo forest. The bamboo here was so large that just one knot of it could be used to make a boat.

The most spectacular stories associated with Di Jun are about his two consorts, Xihe and Changxi. An account in *Shanhaijing* (chapter 15) relates that beyond the east sea and next to the Gan Gulf was the kingdom of Xihe. A lady named Xihe married Di Jun and gave birth to the ten suns. She spends her time bathing the suns in the Gan Gulf.

Changxi is depicted in chapter 16 in the same book. In the Great Wilderness there was a mountain called Mount Riyue (Mount Sun and Moon). It was in the key position of the heavens. At this mountain there was a lady, Changxi, who also was Di Jun's wife. Changxi had given birth to twelve moons. In the text, Changxi was just beginning to bathe them.

Many of Di Jun's descendants founded their own kingdoms down on the earth. These offspring, such as people in the countries of Zhongrong, Siyou,

Baimin, Heichi, and Sanshen, are also described in *Shanhaijing* (chapters 14 and 15). They all were extraordinary people who possessed special powers, especially the power to control the four beasts: tiger, panther, bear, and brown bear. This power was partly inherited from their divine ancestor, Di Jun.

Among Di Jun's descendants were many skillful craftsmen who invented fundamental items for human beings. Texts in *Shanhaijing* (chapter 18) also state that Di Jun fathered Yanlong, who invented the lute and the zither; Di Jun had eight sons who created songs and dance; and that Di Jun fathered Sanshen, and Sanshen fathered Yijun (also called Qiaorui), who created all sorts of crafts for the people on the earth. In addition, Di Jun sired Yuhao, who fathered Yinliang, who fathered Fanyu, who first invented the boat; Fanyu in turn sired Xizhong, and Xizhong fathered Jiguang, the first person to make a chariot with wood.

Di Jun's most famous and divine son is Houji. Houji brought varieties of grain to people and taught them cultivating and harvesting. He later became the ancestor of the Zhou people. Houji's younger brother, Taixi, fathered Shujun (in another version, Shujun was said to be Houji's grandson). Shujun invented the technique of plowing and took the place of his father and Houji to sow grains.

> **See also** Changxi; Houji; Shujun; Xihe; Yi
>
> **References and Further Reading**
>
> Birrell, Anne. *Chinese Mythology: An Introduction.* Baltimore and London: Johns
>   Hopkins University Press, 1993, 65–66, 77–78, 123–125.
> Birrell, Anne, translated with an introduction and notes. *The Classic of Mountains
>   and Seas.* New York: Penguin Books, 1999, 157–196.
> Yuan, Ke. *Myths of Ancient China: An Anthology with Annotations* (in Chinese).
>   Beijing: Renmin Wenxue Chubanshe, [1979] 1996, 196–202.
> Yuan, Ke. *A Survey of Chinese Mythology* (in Chinese). Chengdu: Bashu Shushe,
>   1993, 179–198.

DI KU

Di Ku, or Emperor Ku, also called Gaoxin, is a grandson of Huang Di and one of the Five August Emperors in the mythical history of China. During his reign he oversaw the composition of many Chinese traditional songs and the invention of several musical instruments. By his order, his two sons who fought every day became star gods. He is also known as the father of Houji, ancestor of the Zhou people, and the father of Qi, ancestor of the Shang people. In some accounts he is identified as the father of Yao, one of the three sage kings.

In the mythical history of China, Di Ku is given a very high status. He was identified as one of the Five August Emperors, as well as one of the earliest rulers of the country (various names are given in different contexts). However, the Di Ku myth is quite sparse in written recordings. In texts compiled in the early to mid-Han dynasty, such as *Shiji* and *Dadai Liji* (*The Elder Dai's Record of Ritual*, ca. first century BC), fragments of Di Ku's mythical deeds are recorded. When he was born, Di Ku showed a divine ability: he could utter his name, "Jun." When he grew up and became the emperor, Di Ku would ride a dragon in the spring and summer, and a horse in the fall and winter.

In a story recorded in *Lüshi Chunqiu* (*Annals of Master Lü*, third century BC), Di Ku was associated with the invention of several traditional musical instruments and songs. Following Di Ku's order, Xianhei composed music for these songs, and Yourui invented musical instruments such as the small drum, drum, bell, chime, reed pipe, pipe, clay ocarina, and flute. When those tasks were complete, Di Ku ordered them to perform. Meanwhile, he commanded a phoenix to dance.

Several other stories related to Di Ku feature his descendants. One of these stories tells of Di Ku's two sons who became star gods. Ebo and Shichen were sons of Di Ku. At first they both lived at Kuanglin, but they could not bear each other and often fought. Di Ku was so displeased with this that he moved Ebo to Shangqiu and assigned him to be in charge of the Chen star. He moved Shichen to Daxia and assigned him to be in charge of the Shen star. From then on Ebo was worshiped by the Shang people, and Shichen was worshiped by the Tang (Yao) people. That is why the Chen star is also called the Shang star. The Shen star is equivalent to stars in Orion, and the Chen star is the same as those in Antares. They never appear in the sky at the same time. This phenomenon is often depicted in literature as an image to symbolize good friends who are separated by distance or persons who are on bad terms. For instance, Du Fu (712–770 CE), the famous poet of the Tang dynasty, wrote in his poem, "It is almost as hard for friends to meet as for the Shen and Shang (Chen) stars."

In a story recorded in *Shiben* (*The Origin of Hereditary Families*, ca. third century BC), Di Ku's four consorts are mentioned. These four ladies were Jiang Yuan, Jiandi, Qingdu, and Changyi. Jiang Yuan gave birth to Houji, the god of grain and ancestor of the Zhou people. Jiandi gave birth to Qi, ancestor of the Shang people. Qingdu bore Di Yao (Emperor Yao), the first of the three sage kings in ancient China. Changyi bore Di Zhi (Emperor Zhi), who inherited Di Ku's crown but resigned and handed over the crown to his brother Yao after nine years.

Another version about Di Ku's companions is from *Shiyiji* (*Researches into Lost Records*, ca. fourth century). It tells of another of Di Ku's consorts, a lady from Zoutu who gave birth to eight sons. Each of them was born after she dreamed that she swallowed the sun. People called these sons "the Eight Gods."

As a famous god and sovereign, Di Ku is also linked with the Panhu myth, the ancestral myth of the Miao, Yao, She, and Li ethnic people in south China. Worried about an imminent invasion, Di Ku issued an imperial decree that if anyone in the world could bring back the enemy general's head, he would be rewarded with the emperor's daughter as a wife, along with many other rewards. Panhu, a mythical dog in the royal palace, accomplished the mission and received the princess as his wife. They thus became ancestors of several ethnic groups in south China.

Some scholars presume that Di Ku also is identified as Di Jun, another mythical sovereign in ancient China. The reasons for this conclusion include the evidence that Di Ku took the same name of "Jun" as Di Jun; they both had a son named Houji; Di Ku's wife, Changyi, and Di Jun's wife, Changxi, actually are the same name; and so on. However, in the scattered myth texts and in the mythological history, Di Ku and Di Jun are usually treated as different gods.

See also Di Jun; Houji; Jiandi; Jiang Yuan; Pangu

References and Further Reading

Birrell, Anne. *Chinese Mythology: An Introduction.* Baltimore and London: Johns Hopkins University Press, 1993, 53–54, 100–101, 114–118.

Yuan, Ke. *Myths of Ancient China: An Anthology with Annotations* (in Chinese). Beijing: Renmin Wenxue Chubanshe, [1979] 1996, 203–207.

Yuan, Ke. *A Survey of Chinese Mythology* (in Chinese). Chengdu: Bashu Shushe, 1993, 191–198.

DRAGON

One of the most important mythical creatures in Chinese mythology, the dragon is the controller of the rain, the river, the sea, and all other kinds of water; symbol of divine power and energy; great helper of heroes; and bearer of gods or demigods. In the imperial era it was identified as the symbol of imperial power.

The figure of the dragon appeared within the modern boundaries of China at least 6,000 years ago. In 1987, at the Xishuipo Cemetery Ruins in Puyang County, Henan Province, figures of a dragon and a tiger were unearthed in a tomb. Both of them were made from numerous shells. The dragon measured 1.78 meters (nearly 6 feet) in length and 0.67 meter (2.2 feet) in height. Dating back to over 6,400 years, it is presently the earliest image of a dragon uncovered in Chinese archeology. Thus, it is widely known by the title "the First Dragon of China." In another archeological project a jade coiled dragon was uncovered that dates to around 5,000 years ago. This dragon was discovered in the Hongshan Culture relics (which are mainly located in the area between modern Inner

In Chinese mythology and belief, the dragon often appears as a most powerful and divine creature. People believe that the dragon can fly in the sky and make clouds with its breath; wherever it appears there will be clouds. (Werner Forman/Corbis)

Mongolia, Liaoning Province, and Hebei Province). It is about 26 centimeters (10.4 inches) long and coiled like the letter C. The figure has a snake's body, a boar's head, a tight-lipped snout, and two bulging eyes.

In Chinese mythology and belief, the dragon often appears as a most powerful and divine creature. People believe that the dragon can fly in the sky and make clouds with its breath; wherever it appears there will be clouds. Among its many miraculous abilities, the power of controlling rain and the river is the most well-known. In people's imaginations, dragons usually live in water and are the controllers of rain. If there is a drought in any area, by praying to a dragon, residents hope to get rain.

In Chinese scholarship, there are mainly two hypotheses concerning the essential characteristics of the dragon. One hypothesis aims to find a real prototype of the dragon. This hypothesis often identifies the dragon with a crocodile, tornado, or lightning, or even the river. Another hypothesis states that the dragon is a joint image of different animals; scholars work to discover each of these components by studying ancient texts. This hypothesis links the dragon with the fanciful images of the snake, lizard, deer, and horse, and states that the dragon is a combination of totems that originally belonged to several main tribes that integrated with each other in ancient China. These hypotheses are only two of the many ideas about the origins of the dragon. However, although people have been probing into facts and stories about the dragon for hundreds of years, the dragon has yet elluded final interpretations.

Although the dragon is a mythological creature, there are abundant detailed descriptions about its figure in classical documents and in oral tradition. Some versions state that there are several varieties of dragons. The dragons that have scales are called Jiao Long (*long* means "dragon" in Chinese), those that have horns are called Qiu Long, and those that do not have horns are called Chi Long. In many texts, the dragon's figure is depicted in a very detailed way. Some say that dragons had hang-scales one *chi* (one third of one meter) in diameter below their jaw. Some say that dragons appear with a horse's head and snake's tail. And in another version a dragon appears with a deer's horns, an ox's ears, a camel's head, a rabbit's eyes, a snake's neck, a clam's abdomen, a fish's scales, a tiger's paws, and an eagle's claws. Some documents note that dragons have a body part on their heads shaped like overlapping hills. This part is called *Chimu.* Without it dragons cannot fly into the sky. It is also said that below a dragon's jaw grows the most valuable pearl.

Another famous attribute regarding the dragon is that dragons may give birth to nine varieties of offspring that are quite different from the dragon's species. Each kind of offspring has a specific name, and they are very dissimilar in appearance, nature, and ability. However, though this belief is well-known, there are no conclusive findings about the names of the dragon's nine varieties of offspring. According to the semantic features in traditional Chinese language, some scholars assert that in early history the Chinese word for "nine" did not mean a certain amount. It was just a word that generally referred to "many" or "a lot." In later times, people considered it to be an exact figure and tried to give names to the nine varying offspring of the dragon. Therefore, several stories about these nine offspring appeared. One of the most popular versions identifies the dragon's offspring and their abilities. Because of these abilities, they were used, and continue to be used, as decorations, and thus show people's belief in these mythical creatures. The nine offspring are the following: Bixi, which is good at bearing heavy things, and thus its figure is often sculpted as the foundation of stone monuments; Chiwen, keen on looking long distances so that its figure is often painted or sculpted on eaves; Taotie, which is good at drinking water, thus its figure is usually carved on bridges to prevent flood; Yazi, which is fond of fighting, thus its figure is often used to decorate the handles of knives and swords; Bi'an, which hates criminals and therefore its figure often ornaments the gates of prisons; Suanni, keen on smoke and fire so that its figure often appears on the lid of incense burners; Baxia, which likes water very much so that its figure is usually carved on the guardrails of bridges; Jiaotu, which dislikes others to enter its house, thus its figure often appears on the gates of houses; and Pulao, which likes music and roaring, therefore its figure often decorates bells.

The dragon myths are widely spread in China, not only among Han people but also in many other ethnic groups.

A dragon king in Dahuai Village, Tianshui City, Gansu Province. (An Deming, Averting Natural Disaster: A Study of Agricultural Rituals from Farming Villages in Tianshui, Gansu Province. *Beijing: China Social Sciences Press, 2003, 67)*

In the book *Shanhaijing,* numerous gods or demigods are associated with dragons. Most of these divine creatures are described as having a dragon's or snake's appearance. Some of them had a dragon's trunk and a human head, such as Pangu, Fuxi, Nüwa, Huang Di, Yan Di, the Thunder God living in the Thunder Marsh, and gods living in areas from Tianyu Mountain to Nanyu Mountain, from Chanhu Mountain to Qi Mountain, and from Guanling Mountain to Dunti Mountain. Some of them had a bird's head and a dragon's trunk, such as the gods living in the area from Gui Mountain to Qiwu Mountain, and from Zhaoyao Mountain to Qiwei Mountain.

One of the most famous dragons in Chinese mythology is Ying Long, or Responding Dragon. It was he who helped Huang Di overcome Chiyou. He is also said to be the god of rain. In many places people pray to him in order to receive rain. Another famous dragon recorded in *Shanhaijing* is Zhulong or Zhuyin, Torch Dragon or Torch Shadow. He is a deity who composed the universe with his body.

There are many stories in *Shanhaijing* that connect heroes with dragons to explain their miraculous births. In this cluster of myths, the hero's mother had an experience of copulating with a divine dragon before she got pregnant and then gave birth to her hero son. These heroes, including Huang Di, Shennong, Yao, and Shun, all inherited the dragon's powers and did many great deeds while they were growing up.

In *Houhanshu* (*The History of the Eastern Han Dynasty,* compiled by Fan Ye, 398–445 CE) there is a dragon myth told by the Ailaoyi people, an ethnic group of the Han dynasty. It states in detail that Ailaoyi people in southwest China are descendants of a divine dragon. According to this story, in the beginning there was a woman named Shayi who lived in the area of Lao Mountain. One day when she was fishing, she was touched by a tree trunk floating in the water. She then became pregnant and gave birth to ten sons. Thereafter the trunk changed into a dragon. The dragon came out of the water and asked Shayi, "Where are the sons you bore for me?" Seeing the dragon, all the sons were scared and ran away except for the youngest one, who sat with his back against the dragon. And then the dragon licked the boy on his back. In Shayi's own language, "sitting" was pronounced *jiu,* and "back" was pronounced *long.* So the youngest son was named Jiu Long. He had received the dragon father's caresses and was very smart. When Jiu Long grew older, he was elected king by his brothers. These ten brothers married ten sisters who were born in another family nearby. All had their children tattooed with patterns of a dragon on their bodies. This became a convention of their descendants, the Ailaoyi people.

Dragons also appeared as bearers of gods or demigods in many myths. In *Shanhaijing,* these kinds of stories are recorded in several sections. For example, chapter 6 of that book depicts the god Zhurong with an animal's trunk and a human head, and states that he often rode on two dragons. In chapters 7 and 16, two recordings about Qi (the hero Yu's son, the first king of the Xia dynasty) mention that Qi also had two dragons as bearers. Similar depictions can be found in stories of Huang Di, Zhuanxu, Yuqiang, and Rushou, sporadically appearing in *Hanfeizi, Dadai Liji, Liji,* and *Shanhaijing.*

Not all dragons played beneficial roles for human beings. Some dragons were bad and harmful and often brought disasters to people. One famous example is the black dragon killed by the goddess Nüwa. The black dragon caused a deluge, and this flood could not be stopped until the goddess defeated and killed the dragon.

Some renowned stories tell of dragons' rearing. Several such stories are recorded in *Zuozhuan* (*Chronicle of Zuo,* once attributed to Zuo Qiuming, an ancient historian who lived in the last stage of the Spring and Autumn era, but probably compiled in the Warring States period). One is about a dragon raiser. In ancient times there were people who raised and trained dragons. A famous one was Dongfu, descendent of Yangshu'an. He loved dragons and could understand a dragon's will and interests, and for this reason he raised dragons very well. Many dragons went to him to be tamed and fed. With these dragons Dongfu served King Shun, one of the three sage kings. The king therefore bestowed on him Dong and Huanlong ("Dragon Raiser") as his family name. Another story associated with dragon rearing is of Kongjia, the fourteenth king of the Xia dynasty. Because of his obedience to the god of heaven, Kongjia was given two pairs of dragons to ride; each pair included one male and one female. But Kongjia could not take care of them without a dragon raiser. Then a person named Liulei, who had learned the skill of raising dragons from Huanlong, served Kongjia. Kongjia praised him and granted him the surname Yulong ("Dragon Trainer"). One day a female dragon died. Liulei stealthily chopped its meat and cooked it for the king to eat. Kongjia was so pleased with the meat that soon after, he asked Liulei to cook the same meal for him again. This scared Liulei—where and how could he get more dragon meat? He had to escape from the palace.

Many versions of dragon myths orally transmitted in ethnic groups in contemporary China have more complicated plots. A story told by the Miao people, an ethnic group in southwest China, mentions that it was a divine dragon that created human beings. Long ago there were no human beings in the world, but there was a divine dragon that lived in a cave. One day, many monkeys came to the cave to play. The divine dragon blew to those monkeys, and the monkeys all transformed into human beings. As a result the dragon received high respect and worship from Miao people.

Another ethnic group in southwest China, the Bai, say that it was a dragon that gave birth to a couple that later became the ancestors of human beings. In remote antiquity, the earth consisted of five separate parts. The east was occupied by birds. The south was occupied by beasts. The west was occupied by insects, and the north had fishes and shrimp. In the center part lived a female monkey who had three heads and six arms. The kings of birds, beasts, insects, and fishes and shrimp were, respectively, the phoenix, the tiger, the bee, and the giant turtle. They often visited the monkey and had intercourse with her. Long afterward, the monkey became pregnant. After 9,900 years, the monkey produced ninety-nine eggs. However, all the eggs except the biggest one were stolen by the kings of the other four areas. Under the monkey's cautious care, the biggest egg hatched a python. Conforming to his monkey mother's request, the python departed to look for those eggs stolen by the kings. He defeated and devoured those birds, beasts, insects, and fishes and shrimp that tried to hinder him along the way. Therefore his appearance changed completely. He became a strange winged creature that had a bull's head, deer's horns, pig's mouth, hawk's paws, and snake's trunk. He had become a divine dragon that could fly up to the sky and control the wind and rain. The four kings were so scared by the dragon that they returned all the eggs to him. The dragon broke the eggs one by one. Each time he broke an egg, a creature appeared. But all of these creatures ran away from the dragon. The only ones who stayed with the dragon were hatched from the last two eggs; they were a man and a woman. It was they who bore human beings in later time.

Besides these rich myth texts, there are numerous dragon stories that belong to the genre of folktale or legend. These kinds of stories are extremely widespread in China. Their motifs and plots are also diverse. One of the most famous dragon tales is about Ye Gao and the dragons. Ye Gao loved dragons very much. He decorated his whole house with dragon's figures. Because of this display of admiration, a dragon was impressed and came down from heaven to visit Ye Gao. At the glance of a real dragon, Ye Gao was terrified and quickly ran away. This story is often used as a fable of "Yegong Hao Long" (literally meaning "Lord Ye loves dragon") to mock the one who claims to love something but is actually afraid of it.

In a lot of areas, especially in the east, northeast, and central parts of China, among Han people there are plentiful stories about Short-Tailed Old Li. Short-Tailed Old Li is a famous dragon god who is said to have had a short tail. The explanations for why his tail was short are various. One popular version states that his father cut off part of his tail. Short-Tailed Old Li was born into a poor family in Shandong Province as a black dragon. When he was first born and started to suck his mother's breasts, she immediately fainted. Then his father came back from the field. Seeing the strange and ugly newborn baby, the man, already tired of the family burden, became very angry. He hit the baby with a spade and cut off part of the baby Li's tail. The dragon was hurt so severely that he broke the roof of the house and flew away in a cloud of sparks. He never went home again. Many texts state that the place that he flew to was northeast China, where he settled in the Black Dragon River and became the god of that river. He took his mother's family name, Li, so he was called Short-Tailed Old Li. After his mother died, every May 13 of the lunar calendar, the day his mother died, Short-Tailed Old Li flew back to pay respect at his mother's grave. Whenever he came back, it would rain. Therefore people worshiped him as a rain god. They often pray to him for rain.

Texts about the dragon's lineal descendants are also a very important and large part of dragon tales. Differing from the nine varieties of dragon offspring, these descendants all inherited the dragon's nature and power. They are authentic dragon sons or daughters. A renowned story recorded in a document from the Tang dynasty tells of a dragon king's daughter and her ill-fated marriage. A scholar named Liu Yi failed in the examination to become an official. When he was on the journey home, he met a pretty lady who was tending sheep in sadness. She was the daughter of the Dragon King of Dongting Lake and had been married to the son of the Dragon King of the Jing River. But in the years after she got married, her husband treated her badly. Eventually she was banished by her parents-in-law to a desolate place to herd sheep. In obedience to the dragon girl's request and instructions, Liu Yi visited the dragon palace in Dongting Lake and delivered the girl's letter to her family. The dragon girl's uncle, the Dragon King of the Qiantang River, was angry at hearing of his niece's treatment. He flew to the Jing River, defeated the son of the Dragon King of the Jing River, and devoured him. Then the dragon girl was rescued and brought home. The Dragon King of the Qiantang River intended to marry the girl to Liu Yi. Though Liu Yi was fascinated by the girl's beauty and excellence, he refused the Dragon King for ethical reasons. After he went home with countless rare jewels presented to him at the dragon palace, Liu Yi was married twice. But each marriage quickly ended with his wife's death. A month after he got married for the third time, he learned that his third wife was actually the dragon girl. They lived together happily, and eventually both of them became immortals.

As the most powerful divine creature, the dragon's influence is deeply rooted in various facets of Chinese culture and society, not only in oral or literate traditions. The dragon is thought to control rain, and whenever there is a drought people will pray to the dragon for rain. From an ancient era as early as at least the Shang dynasty (1600 BC–1046 BC) to modern times, in China there have been a multitude of rituals of praying for rain. Among many of those rituals, the dragon is often worshiped or given the main role. The ways in which people deal with dragons in the ritual differ greatly in different places and eras. According to *Chunqiu Fanlu (Abundant Dew of the Spring and Autumn Annals)*, a metaphysical book by Dong Zhongshu (former Han, d. 104 BC), as a drought appears, if one makes several statues of dragons with clay and then asks boys or young men to pace and dance among these statues, the rain will come. The number of the statues, their color, and the people who dance in the ritual will be changed according to the season.

Some local records of the areas in southwest China compiled during the Qing dynasty describe that in people's minds a drought can most likely be attributed to the laziness of a dragon. They consequently had specific treatments to motivate the dragon in order to receive rain. One of those was to throw a tiger's bone into the pool where a dragon was thought to live. The dragon would be irritated and would fight with the tiger, and this would cause heavy rain. The reason for this is that the dragon and the tiger are the most fierce and powerful creatures, therefore they cannot bear each other. Whenever they see each other, or even sense a part of the other, they will fight. Another method was to throw dirty things into a pool. Because the dragon could not bear filth, it would create rain to clean its pool.

The praying-for-rain ritual is still very popular in many rural areas in contemporary China, and in the ritual a specific dragon king is usually worshiped as the main god of rain. In parts of northwest China, for example, every village has its own local god that is different in name and the powers it has. These kinds of local gods function as the core being that is worshiped in praying-for-rain rituals, and many of them are dragon kings.

Though the dragon shows up very early in Chinese history and culture, and dragon kings have become popular gods in Chinese belief nowadays, the figures of dragon kings actually did not appear until the Eastern Han dynasty, when Buddhism was imported into China. A deity named Naga was linked with the divine dragon originating in Chinese Buddhism. Because it was thought of as the main god that took charge of rain, a vital resource for agricultural society, the dragon king emerging from Chinese Buddhism received positive feedback from people. Inspired by this, Taoist leaders created their own dragon kings to meet ordinary people's needs and hence attract followers. Therefore, many dragon kings emerged from Chinese Buddhism, Taoism, and folk beliefs. People began to believe that in every sea, river, lake, spring, and even well there must be a dragon king reigning, and numerous temples for dragon kings were built throughout the country. Each dragon king was different in power, rank, and ability, but they all were worshiped as important deities by people in different areas.

The dragon's figure is also visible in other kinds of customs. The most well-known examples are the customs of the dragon dance and the dragon boat race. The dragon dance is an activity held primarily at traditional festivals, such as the Spring Festival, Lantern Festival (on January 15 of the lunar calendar), and many kinds of temple fairs. During these holidays, people will prepare for the dragon dance by constructing a dragon approximately 16 feet long with grass and cloth or with bamboo strips and paper. Conventionally the dragon dance is performed at night, so after shaping a dragon, people will place ornamental candles inside its trunk. These are called dragon lanterns. In the evening several skilled performers will hold the dragon lanterns on handles under its trunk with all of the candles lit, and they will perform the dragon dance in the public square or along main streets. The scale of a dragon dance festival depends on the size of a community or temple. This kind of performance was originally held to bring good weather and good harvests on specific occasions, but nowadays the dragon dance functions as entertainment. At various celebrations, fairs, and new festivals, the dragon dance is performed in a standardized way, and occurs more often in the daytime rather than its traditional evening performance.

The dragon boat race is often held during the Duanwu Festival on May 5 of the lunar calendar in river or lake regions in southern China. Sometimes the race is held among several neighboring villages, and sometimes it is held among teams throughout a county or even an entire province. The scale of the races may be very different according to the region they cover, and the dragon boats, though all carved in the shape of a dragon, also differ in size and quality because of their owners' financial resources. In the race, all participating boats will compete in a race to determine which boat covers the predetermined distance the fastest, while the audience stands along the banks and cheers. This forms the highlight of the Duanwu Festival; accordingly, in many areas in southern China the festival is called the Dragon Boat Festival.

The origin of the dragon boat race, according to a famous legend, is related to Qu Yuan, the first great poet in the Warring States era, who drowned himself in a river on May 5 for the honor of his state and his ambition. When Qu Yuan threw himself into the Miluo River, people rowed boats on the river to rescue him. Though Qu Yuan died, this act brought about the custom of the dragon boat race. However, scholars presume that this custom originated much earlier than the time of Qu Yuan. It was initially a ritual held to avert evil fortune.

During the imperial era from the Han dynasty to the Qing dynasty, the dragon was gradually associated with the symbol of the holy imperial power. Emperors all claimed and tried to testify that they were the sons of heaven as well as the incarnation of a divine dragon. This greatly strengthened the holy image and integrity of royalty in the eyes of ordinary people. Meanwhile, the dragon image that appeared as ornaments on clothes, houses, and many other articles of everyday use was monopolized by emperors. Commoners who dared to use the figure of a dragon to ornament any article of everyday use risked execution. This situation did not change until 1911, when the imperial era ended.

Today more and more ordinary Chinese people identify themselves as descendants of the dragon. And hence the dragon has become a widely accepted symbol of cultural and ethnic identity for contemporary Chinese people.

See also Fuxi; Huang Di; Nüwa; Pangu; Yan Di; Yinglong; Zhulong

References and Further Reading

An, Deming. *Averting Natural Disaster: A Study of Agricultural Rituals from Farming Villages in Tianshui, Gansu Province* (in Chinese). Beijing: Zhongguo Shehui Kexue Chubanshe, 2003, 81–98, 132–144.

Chinese Literature Press, comp. *Dragon Tales: A Collection of Chinese Stories.* Beijing: Chinese Literature Press, 1994.

Dragan, Raymon. "The Dragon in Chinese Myth and Ritual: Rites of Passage and Sympathetic Magic." In *Sages and Filial Sons: Mythology and Archeology in Ancient China,* eds. Julia Ching and R. W. L. Guisso. Hong Kong: Chinese University Press, 1991, 135–162.

Liu, Chenghuai. *Primitive Myth in China* (in Chinese). Shanghai: Shanghai Wenyi Chubanshe, 1988, 21–43.

Liu, Zhixiong, and Yang Jingrong. *The Dragon and Chinese Culture* (in Chinese). Beijing: Renmin Chubanshe, 1994.

Schafer, Edward H. *The Divine Woman: Dragon Ladies and Rain Maidens in T'ang Literature.* New York: Farrar, Straus & Giroux, 1980.

Wen, Yiduo. "Dragon and Phoenix" (in Chinese). In *Myth and Poetry,* by Wen Yiduo. Beijing: Guji Chubanshe, 1956, 69–72.

Xu, Naixiang, and Cui Yanxun. *A Study of the Dragon* (in Chinese). Beijing: Zijincheng Chubanshe, 1987.

Xu, Shunzhan. "A Study of the Descendants of the Dragon" (in Chinese). *Zhongyuan Wenwu* 4 (1994): 1–13.

Yan, Yunxiang. "A Study of the Influence of Indian Naga Tales on the Chinese Dragon King and Dragon Girl Tales" (in Chinese). In *The Origin and Development of Chinese-Indian Literature Relationship,* ed. Yu Longyu. Changsha: Hunan Wenyi Chubanshe, 1987, 373–415.

Yang, Zhengquan. "On Dragon Worship and Dragon Myths among Ethnic Groups in Southwest China" (in Chinese). *Minzu Yishu Yanjiu* 1 (1998): 53–56.

ELIXIR OF IMMORTALITY

Death has been a powerful theme in beliefs, literature, and arts all around the world. Many Chinese myths explain why humans have to die at a certain time. Some also note mythical substances that have the magic power of rejecting death and maintaining life. These mythical substances include special springs, trees, peaches, grasses, drugs of immortality, and numerous other things. For example, *Shanhaijing* mentions the tree of immortality and Chi spring (*chi* means "red"). Guo Pu (276–324 CE), an annotator of *Shanhaijing*, explained that the tree of immortality could bring longevity to the one who took a concoction made from it, and the Chi spring could help one maintain youthfulness. A story recorded in *Bowuzhi* (*A Treatise on Research into Nature*, third to fifth century CE) states that two officers of Fangfeng, a giant god killed by the god Yu, stabbed themselves in the heart with their daggers and died. Yu felt sympathetic about their death, so he pulled out the daggers and revived them with the herb of immortality. The two then became the pioneers of the Pierced-Chest People.

Among these mythical substances, the elixir of immortality is the most famous, because it is often linked with some powerful or well-known deities, such as Xiwangmu (the Queen Mother of the West), Yi, and Chang'e. A popular story appears in *Huainanzi*, noting that Yi got the elixir of immortality from Xiwangmu, but his wife Heng'e stole it from him and consumed it. Then she became immortal and flew to the moon. Yi was very disappointed but could not regain the elixir.

Xiwangmu is the famous possessor of the precious drug. In Han iconography a rabbit often pounds the elixir in a mortar in front of her, and sometimes also in front of her husband, Dongwanggong. Though Chang'e became immortal and flew to the moon, she was transformed into an ugly toad after she reached the moon and had to endlessly pound the elixir there. However, later, the pounding rabbit somehow moved to the moon too and became Chang'e's companion, continuing its work there.

Xiwangmu does not alone own the elixir of immortality; other deities and even shamans also have it. In a text in chapter 11 of *Shanhaijing*, it is written that east of the Kaiming beast, there were several holy shamans named Peng, Di, Yang, Lü, Fan, and Xiang. They each held the elixir of immortality and surrounded the corpse of the god Zhayu in an attempt to revive him.

See also Chang'e; Fangfeng; Xiwangmu; Yi

References and Further Reading

Birrell, Anne. *Chinese Mythology: An Introduction*. Baltimore and London: Johns Hopkins University Press, 1993, 171–176.

Loewe, Michael. *Ways to Paradise: The Chinese Quest for Immortality*. London: George Allen and Unwin, 1979.

Yuan, Ke. *A Survey of Chinese Mythology* (in Chinese). Chengdu: Bashu Shushe, 1993, 240–245.

FANGFENG

Fangfeng was a god and giant killed by Yu for arriving late to the assembly of the gods. Yu, the hero who stopped the world flood, assembled all the gods on

Mount Guiji (located in modern Zhejiang Province), but Fangfeng arrived late. Yu was very annoyed, so he killed Fangfeng. Since Fangfeng was nearly as tall as ten meters (33 feet), the executioner had to build a high dike to reach his head. Another legend also describes Fangfeng as a giant and links him with Confucius. It states that many years after Fangfeng's death, one joint of his skeleton was found but no one except Confucius knew about it. He told Fangfeng's story and thought this bone belonged to him. The bone was so huge that it filled an entire cart. Another Fangfeng myth explains the origin of the Pierced-Chest People. Two officers of Fangfeng were angry about Yu's execution of Fangfeng and wanted to seek revenge for their master. They shot at Yu when he traveled into Fangfeng's land. But then there came a large gale, with thunder and heavy rain, and two dragons ascended to the heavens. The two avengers were so terrified that they stabbed themselves in the heart with their daggers and died. Yu felt sympathetic about their death, so he pulled out the daggers and revived them with the herb of immortality. The two men then became the pioneers of the Pierced-Chest People.

Fangfeng was also a god in folk belief. An account from *Shuyiji* recorded the custom of worshiping Fangfeng in the territory of Wu and Yue (now mainly in the areas of Zhejiang, Jiangsu, and Shanghai) during the Six Dynasties era. Fangfeng's figure in his temple was often portrayed as having a dragon head, one eye, ox ears, and two eyebrows that grew together. When the people of Yue held the sacrifice rite for him, they played a piece of music called "Fangfeng's ancient melody," with bamboo pipes that were three *chi* long (three chi is equal to one meter). These pipes sounded like a howl. During the music, three people danced with their hair draped over their shoulders.

The Fangfeng myth and legend are still told in contemporary China, especially in Zhejiang and Jiangsu provinces. Nearly thirty Fangfeng myths and legends were collected in the late 1980s. Contrary to those unclear and fragmented ancient stories in which Fangfeng is portrayed only as a faulted and lesser god of Yu, with his other attributes and functions ambiguous, these modern narratives show strong affection toward Fangfeng. He is depicted as a great culture hero who worked very hard to control the flood and save people but was wrongly killed by Yu. One story collected in 1987 in Deqing County, Zhejiang Province, explains the origin of the sacrifice rite to Fangfeng and the reason Fangfeng is called "king." After Yu controlled the world flood, he held an assembly on Mount Guiji to celebrate the success. But Fangfeng did not arrive until the assembly was ending. Yu was very upset. He thought Fangfeng was too conceited and defiant, so he decided to execute him as a warning to others. Since Fangfeng was so tall, Yu had to make a platform so that the executioner could behead Fangfeng. When Fangfeng was beheaded, the blood that spilled out was white, not red. This abnormal phenomenon showed that Fangfeng might have been treated wrongly. Yu thus ordered reporters to investigate the true reason for Fangfeng's late arrival at the meeting. They eventually told Yu that when Fangfeng was rushing to Yu's assembly, he encountered a local flood. He stopped to save people from the flood and therefore came to the council very late. Yu felt regret for having wrongly executed Fangfeng. For compensation, he then conferred the honorary title "Fangfeng King" on the dead and ordered a temple built and sacrifices made to him on every August 25. The custom was maintained for 4,000 years, until the initial period of the People's Republic of China.

See also Yu

References and Further Reading

Birrell, Anne. *Chinese Mythology: An Introduction.* Baltimore and London: Johns Hopkins University Press, 1993, 148–152, 245–246.

Yuan, Ke, and Zhou Ming, comps. *A Source Book of Chinese Myth Texts* (in Chinese). Chengdu: Sichuansheng Shehui Kexue Chubanshe. 1985, 258–260.

Zhong, Weijin, ed. *Collected Essays on Fangfeng Study* (in Chinese). Hefei: Anhui Wenyi Chubanshe, 1996.

Zhong, Weijin, and Ouyang Xiyong, comps. *A Source Book of Fangfeng* (in Chinese). Tianjin: Tianjin Guji Chubanshe, 1999.

FENG BO

The wind god Feng Bo helped Chiyou in a battle against Huang Di. In one version he was shot by the archer Yi. *Feng* means "the wind," and *bo* means "the master" (it is also a respectful title for a male elder). Feng Bo also is known as Feng Shi (Wind Master).

There are several gods of the wind in Chinese mythology and beliefs, such as Feng Bo (or Feng Shi), Feilian, Ji Bo (*Ji* refers to the Ji star), Qiongqi, Yuqiang, and Feng Yi (*Yi* means "female elder"). They come from different times or different regional culture traditions, and some of them gradually become confused in later recounts. For example, Feilian was a wind god worshiped by the Chu people in the south during the Eastern Zhou era. It was a divine bird that could make wind. In later accounts, it is described as having a deer's body, a sparrow's head with horns, a serpent's tail, and the markings of a panther. Unlike Feilian, Ji Bo was an ancient wind god worshiped by the central people. Its function was rooted in the early belief that the Ji star managed the wind. Both Feilian and Ji Bo were identified as Feng Bo in at least the Han dynasty. Another wind god, Feng Yi, appeared in texts as late as the Tang dynasty, and he was sometimes also called Feng Bo. Thereafter he was somehow turned into a female goddess in later literature and customs.

Feng Bo appeared as early as the Warring States era. In a text from *Hanfeizi* (written by Han Fei, ca. 280–233 BC), Feng Bo is depicted as a subordinate god of Huang Di. When Huang Di assembled the deities and ghosts on Mount Tai, he was surrounded by many retinues. Elephants and dragons pulled the cart for him, the divine bird Bifang accompanied him, Chiyou led the way, Feng Bo cleaned the road, Yu Shi (the Rain Master) created sprinkles of rain along the way, tigers and wolves ran ahead, and deities and ghosts followed him. However, later Feng Bo rebelled against Huang Di. When Chiyou attacked Huang Di, he asked Feng Bo and Yu Shi to help him, so they released a storm. But Huang Di ordered the drought goddess Ba to descend from heaven, and the rain was stopped. The defeated Chiyou was killed by Huang Di. The text does not mention how Feng Bo and Yu Shi were treated after the battle.

Some other Feng Bo myths link him to the hero Yi. Since Feng Bo was known to have destroyed men's houses, Yi shot him in his knees. In another version, Yi stopped Feng Bo from damaging houses by shooting him at the Qinqiu Marsh. In one version, Yi killed Feng Bo.

Feng Bo's appearance varied greatly among different accounts. In a text of the Yuan dynasty, he was described as having the head of a dog, red hair, the shape of a ghost, the hips of a panther, and red trousers, and he stood on a cloud and carried on his back a sack full of wind. In the Qing dynasty, however, he was often portrayed as an old man with a white beard, and he always carried the wind sack in his hand and directed the wind coming from the sack in any direction he chose.

See also Ba; Chiyou; Huang Di; Yi; Yu Shi

References and Further Reading

Christie, Anthony. *Chinese Mythology.* Rev. ed. New York: Peter Bedrick Books, 1985, 71–72.

Liu, Chenghuai. *Myths in Ancient China* (in Chinese). Shanghai: Shanghai Wenyi Chubanshe, 1988, 126–135.

Ma, Shutian. *Gods of Chinese* (in Chinese). Beijing: Yanshan Chubanshe, 1990, 227–230.

Yuan, Ke, and Zhou Ming, comps. *A Source Book of Chinese Myth Texts* (in Chinese). Chengdu: Sichuansheng Shehui Kexueyuan Chubanshe, 1985, 72, 76.

FLOODS, THE

Flood is a worldwide mythical theme. It is especially popular in Chinese mythology, as Derk Bodde described: "Of all the mythical themes of ancient China, the earliest and by far the most pervasive is that of flood" (Bodde 1961, 398). Chinese flood myths usually tell about how the flood in ancient times imperiled the world, and therefore how the heroes or heroines tried to stop the flood and save the world from the disaster; or how human ancestors tried to re-create human races, and eventually how a new cosmic order is rebuilt and a new civilization appears.

Generally, there are three systems of flood myths in Chinese mythology (Lu 2002, 18). The first one relates to the theme "controlling the flood," and it includes many famous classical myths, such as stories of the god Gonggong causing a flood, the goddess Nüwa patching the sky with colorful stones and accumulating the reed ashes to stop the flood, the god Gun stealing Xirang (the self-growing soil) to dam the flood, and Yu channeling the floodwater into the sea and eventually stopping the flood and making the world fit for cultivation. All these myths can be found in texts of the Zhou dynasty. Among them, the Gun-Yu myth is the most representative one in the sense that it intensively stresses how the flood eventually is controlled by great efforts from two generations. It should be added to Bodde's conclusion that these flood myths belong not only to ancient China but are still told in contemporary China as well.

The second system deals with the brother-sister marriage myth, in which a world flood destroyed all of the human beings except a brother and his sister (father and daughter or aunt and nephew in some versions). The surviving siblings had to marry each other to repopulate the human races, because they could not find other partners. After they got married, they bore normal children or, more often, abnormal babies such as a spherical piece of flesh, a gourd, a melon, or a knife-grinding stone. The "abnormal fetuses" somehow turned into humankind when they were cut into pieces, or when they were opened, humans appeared. This type of myth often serves as an etiological myth about the origin and character of human races or certain ethnic groups. It can be found in writings as late as the Six Dynasties, yet it is hard to correspondingly conclude that this type of myth emerged that late in oral tradition. Today it is still one of the most popular myths in China and is told in more than forty ethnic groups throughout the country (Chen 1996).

The third system is more like a local legend than a myth. It usually links with a local flood that sank a city and destroyed all the people except a single kind one. The typical plot of this story is like this: A good-hearted person (an old lady, a dutiful son, etc.) was told by a god that the city she/he lived in would sink and turn into a lake soon. If she/he found the eyes of a stone lion (sometimes a turtle) turning red, she/he should run away at once. So every day she/he went to see whether the lion's eyes had turned red. A butcher man felt curious when he learned what this person was doing. So the next day he deliberately wiped some blood on the stone lion's eyes as a joke. When the old lady or dutiful son saw the red eyes of the lion, she/he rushed up a mountain. While others were laughing at her/him, the city began to sink, and it soon turned into a lake.

This type of legend also can be found in accounts from the Zhou dynasty, and it is usually used to describe the mythical birth of a great man or to explain the origin of a certain lake. For example, Yiyin, the important politician in the Shang dynasty, was said to be born from a hollow mulberry tree that was transformed from his mother. The mother was the sole survivor of the local flood, but when she turned around to see what had happened to her city—which broke the divine forbiddance—she was turned into a hollow mulberry tree.

However, this legend later became connected to the brother-sister marriage myth, and thus the local flood became a worldwide disaster. In Henan Province in central China, the flood is usually said to be a part of a cosmic disaster, which is often depicted as "the sky collapsed and the earth sank." A myth collected in 1982 in Nanyang County says that in the remote past, there were two sibling students, a brother and his elder sister. There was a temple near their school with an iron lion standing in front of it. The siblings liked to ride the lion for fun. One day, a monk told the siblings that they should feed the iron lion every day with steamed bread. They followed his suggestion. After a period of time, the monk told them that they should pay attention to the lion's eyes, and when the eyes became red, they should get into the lion's stomach. One day, when the sister fed the lion again, she found that the lion's eyes had turned red, so she and her younger brother got into the lion's stomach. Then they saw the sky become dark, and heard the wind blowing fiercely with a loud crash. When it became bright again, they climbed out and found that the sky had collapsed and all the other people were dead. They subsisted on the steamed breads in the lion's stomach and hoped to find a house in which to live. On a mountain, they found an old lady (her status was unclear in the story). They asked her what they should do after the near extinction of all humans. The old lady suggested that they roll one piece of a millstone down the mountain, and if the piece happened to cover another piece of the millstone at the foot of the mountain, they should marry each other. Eventually the two pieces came together, and the siblings got married. Soon they bore five boys and five girls, and these siblings married each other too. Thereafter human beings became plentiful and populated this world.

The flood myth is by no means uniquely Chinese, for it is widely found among other peoples of East and Southeast Asia, Europe, Africa, India Islands, New Guinea, Polynesia, Micronesia, the Americas, and many other places. However, compared to the biblical or other Western flood myths, the Chinese flood myth is distinctive in some regards. The basic difference, as some scholars have suggested, is that in the Chinese version what is emphasized is the conquest of the flood and the origin of civilization rather than the flood that came to punish human sin (Bodde 1961, 402–403; Lu 2002, 18–21). This characteristic is strongly illustrated in the Gun-Yu myth. The essence of this myth is not that one should obey God's will and arrangement or the law of nature. Rather, the spirit is praised for making every effort to conquer the natural disaster, no matter how arduous the task is, in order to save humans. Eventually the demigod Yu stopped the flood and changed the miserable world into a habitable place for humankind. He then became the founder of the first civilized state, Xia. Similarly, the emphasis of the brother-sister marriage myth is not on the flood itself either. The flood only functions as the necessary cause for the sibling incest. The narrative purpose is to explain how humankind was re-created after the cosmic disaster and how a new world order was rebuilt. In some versions, after the repopulation of human beings, the stories also tell how the new descendents get grain seeds or fire, and thereafter start an agricultural civilization. So, as recent research insists, the motifs of "controlling the flood" and "acquisition of the agricultural civilization" contained in the Chinese flood myth make it unique (Lu 2002, 18–19).

See also Gonggong; Gun; Nüwa; Xirang; Yu

References and Further Reading

Birrell, Anne. *Chinese Mythology: An Introduction.* Baltimore and London: Johns Hopkins University Press, 1993.

Bodde, Derk. "Myths of Ancient China." In *Mythologies of the Ancient World,* ed. Samuel Noah Kramer. Chicago: Quadrangle Books, 1961, 398–403.

Chen, Jianxian. "Chinese Flood Myths: Types and Distributions Based on 433 Versions" (in Chinese). *Minjian Wenxue Luntan* 3 (1996): 2–10.

Christie, Anthony. *Chinese Mythology.* Rev. ed. New York: Peter Bedrick Books, 1985, 87–97.

Lu, Yilu. *The Flood Myths: Centered on the South Ethnic Groups and the Aborigines of Taiwan in China* (in Chinese). Taibei: Liren Shuju, 2002.

Walls, Jan, and Yvonne Walls, eds. and trans. *Classical Chinese Myths.* Hong Kong: Joint Publishing Co., 1984, 9–11, 94–109.

FUSANG

Fusang (literally meaning "Leaning Mulberry") is a world-tree in the east where the ten suns stay, bathe, and rise. It is also known as Fumu (Leaning Tree).

The world-tree is a common mythical motif found in many countries and among numerous ethnic groups. It is usually described in various mythologies as a huge divine tree that links earth with heaven and communicates the human and profane condition to the divine and sacred realm. Among its many parallels in Europe, Australia, North America, and other areas, Fusang is one of the most famous Chinese world-trees. According to texts from *Shanhaijing,* Fusang grew in the water of the Tang Valley. The tree was very high; its trunk reached 300 *li* (100 miles) in height, and its leaves were like the leaves of the mustard plant. The ten suns stayed on the tree and bathed in the valley. Nine of them stayed on the lower branches of Fusang while the sun that was going to rise stayed on its top branch. The ten suns rose from the Fusang tree one by one. As soon as one sun came back from crossing the sky, another sun went up. Each sun was carried by a crow. In an account from *Huainanzi*, the sun is said to rise from the Yang Valley (the same as the Tang Valley) and be bathed in the Xian Pool. When the sun swept past Fusang it was called First Dawn. When it climbed up Fusang and was prepared to begin its journey, it was called Daybreak.

In some later versions, Fusang is described as a large tree in the east. Its top reached heaven while its trunk curved down and reached the Three Springs of the earth. However, according to *Shizhouji* (*A Record of Ten Mythic Islets*, said to have been written during the Han dynasty but probably written in the Six Dynasties era), Fusang seemed to be not only a kind of tree but also a mythical place that was located in the middle of the Blue Sea. It was thousands of miles in circumference with a palace for an immortal built on it. Fusang trees grew here. Their leaves were like those of the mulberry, and they also produced the same fruit. The biggest one of them was more than 100,000 feet high and 2,000 *wei* wide (one wei is equal to the diameter of a circle created by a person's arms). Since the trees grew in pairs, every pair of them shared the same root and their trunks leaned toward each other; therefore they received the name "Leaning Mulberry." Though the trees were extremely large, their fruits were rare, because the trees produced fruit only once every 9,000 years. The fruit was red, and it tasted very sweet and savory. When the immortals ate the fruit, their bodies would turn a golden color, and they were able to fly and float in the air.

Other legends state that there were Heaven Chickens on the Fusang tree. The chickens nested in the top of the mythical tree and crowed at midnight each night. Every time they crowed, the crows inside the suns followed them. And then all the chickens in the world would follow and crow loudly.

See also Crow of the Sun; Tang Valley; Xihe

References and Further Reading

Birrell, Anne. *Chinese Mythology: An Introduction.* Baltimore and London: Johns Hopkins University Press, 1993, 38–39, 234.

Yuan, Ke, and Zhou Ming, comps. *A Source Book of Chinese Myth Texts* (in Chinese). Chengdu: Sichuansheng Shehui Kexueyuan Chubanshe, 1985, 211–214.

FUXI

Fuxi is a culture hero, a human ancestor, and one of the most powerful primeval gods in Chinese mythology. He also may be called Paoxi or Baoxi in ancient literature.

In one version of the Fuxi myth, Fuxi was born after his mother trod in a huge footprint in a marshland and then became pregnant. According to some ancient written recordings and iconography, he had a human head with a snake's body, though he gradually became fully human and in later years was a king with great dignity. During the Han dynasty Fuxi often became associated with Nüwa, one of the most powerful and ancient goddesses. Nüwa's achievements include creating human beings by molding yellow earth together and patching the broken sky alone, according to early written sources. Fuxi took the role of Nüwa's brother and husband, and Nüwa was his helper and assistant. They often appeared together in funeral stone bas-reliefs of the Han dynasty, portrayed with human heads or upper bodies and serpents' or dragons' lower bodies, sometimes with their tails intertwined. Fuxi holds a pair of compasses or the sun with a three-footed crow inside it, and Nüwa holds either a carpenter's square or the moon with the divine frog inside. These symbols are interpreted as representing the order that Fuxi and Nüwa created subsequently by establishing the rules of the world and the harmony of the universe between yang and yin, which are important notions in traditional Chinese philosophy, medicine, and other systems. Yang represents the male or positive principle in nature while yin represents the feminine or negative principle.

Fuxi and Nüwa. Funeral stone carving of the Han dynasty, Wuliang Shrine, Jiaxiang County, Shandong Province. Both of them were portrayed with human heads and upper bodies and serpents' lower bodies. Their tails intertwined. Fuxi held a pair of compasses while Nüwa held a carpenter's square. They were surrounded by other winged divine creatures with serpent bodies. (Yang Lihui, Rethinking on the Source Area of the Cult of Nüwa, *Beijing Shifan Daxue Chubanshe, 1999, 71)*

During the Han dynasty, Fuxi was confused with another god, Taihao, who appeared as an independent divinity in pre-Han sources. *Tai* means "great" or "supreme," and *hao* means "expansive and limitless." Therefore, Fuxi not only received the honorary name of Taihao but also took Taihao's function as the god who reigns over the east and controls the season of spring. The wood god, Goumang, became his subordinate.

Most of Fuxi's myths refer to Fuxi inventing cultural items in remote antiquity. He gained the reputation of inventor, and is given credit for many important innovations. From these inventions he achieved status as one of the greatest culture heroes in China. One of his famous inventions, for example, was the Eight Trigrams (*Ba Gua*, the eight possible combinations of three whole or broken lines, used in Chinese divination), which later also became very important in traditional Chinese philosophy and belief. According to *Zhouyi*, "Xi Ci Zhuan" ("Appended Texts" of *The Classic of Change*, written approximately in the Qin and early Han eras), Fuxi carefully watched the images in the sky and on the earth, and he thought about the patterns and colors of birds and beasts as well as the suitability of the land. The images and patterns included not only those of his surroundings but also those of his own body. Then he created the Eight Trigrams in order to communicate the virtue of the divinities and to resemble the character of everything on the earth.

Fuxi also is well-known for inventing hunting and fishing nets by imitating the spider's web. A modern version of the Fuxi myth, collected in Sichuan Province in the 1960s, provides a vivid description of this inventing process. After Fuxi and his sister re-created human beings, there were more and more people in the world. These people survived by hunting wild animals. The more they hunted, the more they ate. If they killed nothing, then they ate nothing. People often suffered from hunger. Fuxi felt very worried about this. He tried to solve this serious problem. One day, he found fish jumping in a river, so he caught several big fish with his hands. He then told his children to catch and eat fish likewise. But the ruler of the water, Dragon King, was very upset and horrified that the humans were eating his fish. He was afraid that this would decrease the population of his subjects. Adopting the suggestion of his prime minister, the tortoise, the Dragon King told Fuxi that he and his children could not catch any fish unless they could do this without using their hands. Fuxi was baffled for several days. One day, when he was lying under a tree and thinking about the problem, he saw a spider weaving its web and catching several insects with it. Fuxi was enlightened by this. He wove a rattan net and put it into the river, then waited on the shore. After a moment, he lifted the net. Lots of fish were jumping inside the net. Fuxi was very pleased because he could catch fish much easier now without using his hands! Soon he taught his children to follow him. The Dragon King was so angry that his eyes protruded from his head from then on. The prime minister tortoise wanted to flatter its king with another idea. But when it crept onto the shoulder of the Dragon King, it was slapped by the king and fell down into an ink plate. That is the reason why the tortoise is black today.

In addition, Fuxi had many other mythical functions. He established the marriage rule. This rule required a young man to give his fiancée two deer skins as an engagement gift. He made some musical instruments, such as the *se* (a twenty-five-stringed plucked instrument, somewhat similar to the zither) and the *xun* (an egg-shaped clay wind instrument with finger holes), and composed the melody of "Jia Bian."

He raised livestock and reined cattle and horses to draw carts and carry heavy goods. He smelted metal and made numerous material objects and tools. He taught people to barbecue food and to pound grain with a mortar and pestle. Fuxi also made cloth and began to rear silkworms. He made coins of copper. He invented written characters for people to record life instead of remembering events by making special knots in cords. He also invented the calendar and laws.

Because he had so many cultural inventions important for human life, he was respected as the first of the Three Divine Sovereigns, along with Nüwa and Shennong, or the Divine Farmer (different names are given in different texts). In a rationalized system of Chinese ancient history, which was primarily formed in the Han dynasty, he was even respected as the first king of the remote past.

In modern Chinese mythology, however, Fuxi is best known as an ancestor of humans. He married his sister and re-created human beings after a great flood. This type of brother-sister marriage myth is widely spread throughout the country, especially in southern and central China. The first couple may only be called "a brother and his sister" rather than by the names Fuxi and Nüwa, or they may take different names in different places and ethnic groups. In some cases they have the title "Fuxi and his sister" or simply "Fuxi and Nüwa." Therefore, Fuxi is known in his first marriage as a human creator to many ethnic groups, including the Han, Miao, Yao, Tujia, Maonan, and Shui.

Fuxi is still worshiped in modern China. Huaiyang County in Henan Province is said to be the capital of King Taihao Fuxi's mythical kingdom and the hometown of Fuxi (Fuxi is said to have been born in Huaiyang). In Huaiyang there is a big temple complex called the Tomb of Taihao, or, more popularly, Renzu Temple (Temple of Human Ancestors). The main god worshiped here is Fuxi. Nüwa is also worshiped here, but her hometown is said to be Xihua, in a nearby county.

Renzu Temple in Huaiyang has a long history. One of the famous legends about its reconstruction refers to Zhu Yuanzhang, the first emperor of the Ming

Pilgrims in front of the Renzu Temple, Huaiyang County, Henan Province, 2005. (Courtesy of Tong Yunli)

dynasty (whose reign lasted from 1368 to 1398). Zhu was chased by his enemies before he ascended the throne of the kingdom, so he hid in Renzu Temple and prayed to Fuxi. He promised Fuxi he would rebuild this rough temple if the ancestor blessed him and protected him from his chasers. Thousands of spiders soon appeared and began to weave webs on the temple door. In minutes the door was covered by cobwebs and looked as if nobody had ever entered the temple. This fooled Zhu's enemies, and they left the temple grounds. Zhu was thus rescued, and he later became the founder of the Ming dynasty. As emperor, Zhu ordered that the temple be reconstructed similar to the structure of his palace. That is why the temple complex looks so grand today.

From February 2 to March 3 in the lunar calendar, the monthlong Renzu Festival is held to celebrate Fuxi's birthday at the Renzu Temple complex. The festival draws thousands of pilgrims daily from nearby villages, counties, and provinces. They come here for many different purposes: to make supplications to the ancestors; to thank the ancestors for fulfilling their supplications; or to pray for children, happiness, health, wealth, or countless other things, such as entrance into college. The pilgrims, especially women, may dance the *danjing-tiao* (a local dance in which women carry a pole on their shoulders), or sing *jingge* (classic songs, a type of folk song) to commemorate and praise the ancestors. As for the contents, many jingge not only tell the myths of their remote creators but also often end with a moral or propagation. The following is the text of a jingge that Yang Lihui recorded in her fieldwork in Huaiyang in 1993:

> Remember the beginning of the world is chaos,
> Without sky, without earth, without Human beings.
> Then, the deity of sky created the sun, the moon, and the stars,
> Then, the deity of earth created the grain and grass.
> Having the sky and earth, the chaos separated,
> Thus appeared Renzu, the brother and sister.
> They climbed to the high mountain Kunlun,
> To throw the millstone and get married.
> They gave birth to hundreds of children,
> That's the origin of Baijiaxing (human beings).
> Therefore, though people in this world look different,
> Yet in fact they belong to the same family.
> How wrong it is struggling for the wealth and fame,
> Because you can't bring them with you when you go into the grave.
> I persuade you to be a good person,
> Because a good person can be blessed by the Renzu on earth.

There is another interesting custom here, that of *ninigou* ("mud dog"), which relates to Fuxi's mythical deeds. Ninigou refers to all toys made of mud, including monkeys, swallows, tortoises, and tigers, and it can also be the clay musical instrument, the *xun*. Why do people make ninigou? The craftsmen explain that this tradition originated with Fuxi, who first made the clay xun and created humans from mud. They want to imitate the mythical activities and thus memorialize their remote ancestors.

See also Dragon; Goumang; Kunlun Mountain; Nüwa

References and Further Reading

Birrell, Anne. *Chinese Mythology: An Introduction.* Baltimore and London: Johns Hopkins University Press, 1993, 44–47.

Christie, Anthony. *Chinese Mythology.* Rev. ed. New York: Peter Bedrick Books, 1985, 87–91.

Wen, Yiduo. "A Study of Fuxi" (in Chinese). In *The Complete Works of Wen Yiduo.* Vol. 1. Beijing: Sanlian Shudian, [1948] 1982, 3–68.

Yang, Lihui. *The Cult of Nüwa: Myths and Beliefs in China* (in Chinese). Beijing: Zhongguo Shehui Kexue Chubanshe, 1997, 94–102, 144–151.

Yuan, Ke. *Myths of Ancient China: An Anthology with Annotations* (in Chinese). Beijing: Renmin Wenxue Chubanshe, [1979] 1996, 42–71.

Zhang, Zhenli, and Cheng Jianjun, comps. *The Collection of Myths Transmitting in Contemporary Central Plain* (in Chinese). Zhengzhou: Zhongguo Minjian Wenyijia Xiehui Henan Fenhui, 1987, 83–126.

GONGGONG

The water god who caused a flood disaster and bumped into Mount Buzhou, giving rise to cosmic disorder, Gonggong is known in some ancient texts as Kanghui. He is often portrayed as having a man's head with red hair, and the body of a serpent.

The Gonggong myth appears in writings of the late Warring States era. One question raised in the poem "Tianwen" asks, "Why did the earth tilt toward the southeast during Kanghui's rage?" This illustrates that the myth about Gonggong damaging Mount Buzhou was current at that time.

In the Han dynasty and thereafter, the Gonggong myth contains much more detail. Gonggong is said to have fought with the god Zhuanxu (or Zhurong, Di Ku, or Shengnong; various names are given in different versions) to be the Supreme Divinity in remote times, but he failed. In his fury he bumped against one of the sky pillars, Mount Buzhou, and damaged it. The cords of the earth also broke during this event. His blunder brought cosmic disruption.

This story is sometimes associated with Nüwa, the great mother of human beings and the one who repaired the cosmos, but with considerable differences. According to *Lunheng* and "Bu *Shiji* Sanhuang Benji" ("Biographies of the Three Divine Sovereigns: A Supplement to the *Historical Records*," written during the Tang dynasty), the Gonggong story is followed by that of Nüwa. The recording in "Bu *Shiji* Sanhuang Benji" combined various myth versions and tried to form a coherent ancient history. Gonggong was described as a rebellious nobleman. He became powerful by using shrewdness and punishment. He ruled with tyranny instead of benevolence. Toward the end of Nüwa's reign, Gonggong fought with Zhurong, the God of Fire, but he failed. He was so angry that he struck his head against Mount Buzhou and caused this sky pillar to collapse, snapping the cords of the earth. To repair this damage, Nüwa melted stones of five different colors to mend the sky. She cut the legs off a huge tortoise and set them up to support the four corners of the sky. Then she collected ashes of reeds to stop the flood. Through her effort, Nüwa cleared up the chaos and put the world in order again. However, in texts from *Liezi* and *Bowuzhi* (*A Treatise on Research into Nature*, written during the Jin dynasty), the chronological order of these two stories is reversed. That is, Nüwa repaired a defect in the cosmos first, and later Gonggong fought with the god Zhurong and upset the normal established order. Gonggong's damage often served as an etiological myth of the current Chinese topography. Since then, heaven tilts toward the northwest, and that is why the sun, moon, and stars move in that direction. Earth sinks toward the southeast, and that is why the rivers of China flow toward the ocean in the east. The loose connection between these two stories suggests that they might have been independent of each other in early stages of the myths and were loosely combined in later development.

Gonggong is not only the destroyer of the sky pillar and cords of the earth but also plays a chief role in a disastrous flood. A text from *Guoyu* (*Discourses of the States,* from the Spring and Autumn era), for example, states that in ancient times Gonggong abandoned the right way. He wanted to damage the world by damming the rivers, reducing the high land, and blocking up the low land. But the heavens did not give him good fortune, and ordinary people refused to help him. Disasters and disorders spread everywhere. Therefore Gonggong was ruined at last. In another version, from *Huainanzi* (chapter 8), the Gonggong story is linked with that of the mythical sovereigns Shun and Yu. In Shun's time, Gonggong created a flood that swept near the place of Kongsang. At that time, the mountains Longmeng (meaning "Dragon Gate") and Lüliang did not open up and hence blocked the channels. So the flood spread everywhere, and rivers throughout the land joined together. People had to climb the mountains and trees to escape from the vast deluge. Then Shun ordered Yu to dredge the rivers and lakes, open up the waterways, and channel the flood to the east sea. As a result, the flood ran out and the world became dry, and people became settled again.

After his failure, Gonggong came to a sticky end. One version of the myth states that he was killed by the god Zhuanxu because he created the flood disaster. Other versions state that he was killed by Di Ku or Yao because of his tyrannical and conceited domination. A popular story says that he was banished by Yu when Yu brought an end to the flood. But other variants state that Gonggong was exiled to the place of Youzhou by Shun or, in another version, by Yao because Yao wanted to give the throne to Shun but Gonggong opposed this.

See also Buzhou, Mount; Cords of the Earth; Houtu; Nüwa; Pillars of the Sky; Shennong; Shun; Yu; Zhuanxu; Zhurong

References and Further Reading

Birrell, Anne. *Chinese Mythology: An Introduction.* Baltimore and London: Johns Hopkins University Press, 1993, 69–72, 97–98, 146.

Bodde, Derk. "Myths of Ancient China." In *Mythologies of the Ancient World,* ed. Samuel Noah Kramer. Chicago: Quadrangle Books, 1961, 386–389, 398–399.

Yuan, Ke, and Zhou Ming, comps. *A Source Book of Chinese Myth Texts* (in Chinese). Chengdu: Sichuansheng Shehui Kexueyuan Chubanshe, 1985, 141–144.

GOUMANG

The wood god and the inventor of the *luo* (a net for catching birds), Goumang is the descendant of Shaohao, the god who reigns over the western region, but he somehow assists Fuxi (also called Taihao) to reign over the eastern region and the spring season. However, in some versions, "Goumang" is a title for the officer of wood, instead of being a special deity.

Goumang often appears with a bird's body and a human face that is square-shaped, and he wears white and rides upon two dragons. He is said to be the offspring of the god Shaohao, and his name is Zhong (different from the god Zhong who separated the heaven from the earth). He assists Fuxi, who takes wood as the emblem of his reign, to rule the eastern region and the season of spring. Both Goumang and Fuxi hold compasses in their hands. When Goumang died, he became the God of Wood.

A legend about Goumang from *Mozi* (written mainly by the philosopher Mo Di, ca. 468–376 BC) suggests that Goumang may also function as the God of Life. The legend states that Zhengmugong, the Duke Mu of the Zheng state, was a man of virtue. One time when he was in the temple during the day, there came a god with a bird's body and a square face, wearing white. The duke was horrified and wanted to run away. Then the god said, "Do not be afraid. The Supreme Divinity ordered me to add nineteen years to your life as an award for your virtue. We hope you will make your state prosperous, with descendants flourishing. Do not lose your state." The duke kowtowed to the god and asked who he was. The god answered: "I am Goumang." In some versions the duke is said to be Qinmugong (the Duke Mu of the Qin state).

As noted previously, the name "Goumang" seems sometimes only a title for the official of wood (Muzheng) instead of a certain deity. A text from *Zuozhuan* shows that "Goumang" is the title for the Muzheng (Official of Wood), and this title was assumed by one of Shaohao's uncles named Zhong (different from the deity Zhong who separated heaven from the earth with another deity, Li).

See also Fuxi; Shaohao

References and Further Reading

Liu, Chenghuai. *Myths in Ancient China* (in Chinese). Shanghai: Shanghai Wenyi Chubanshe, 1988, 192–195.

Ma, Changyi. *The Classic of Mountains and Seas: Ancient Illustrations with Annotations* (in Chinese). Jinan: Shandong Huabao Chubanshe, 2001, 493–494.

Yuan, Ke, and Zhou Ming, comps. *A Source Book of Chinese Myth Texts* (in Chinese). Chengdu: Sichuansheng Shehui Kexueyuan Chubanshe, 1985, 19–20.

GUN

Gun is a popular culture hero in Chinese mythology. He stole Xirang, the self-growing soil, from the Supreme Divinity in order to stop the flood, but failed in his mission and was killed by the God of Fire, Zhurong, at Mount Yushan. His corpse turned into a yellow bear and dove into the pool of Yuyuan. His son Yu was miraculously born from the belly of his corpse and continued to fight the flood until he succeeded.

Gun is said to be a descendant of Huang Di. Though there are slim accounts describing his image, the written character for his name (鯀, which includes the radical 鱼, which means "fish") reveals that his figure might have originally been a fish. His myth is mainly recorded in the two written classics of Chinese mythology, *Shanhaijing* and "Tianwen." According to a text from *Shanhaijing* (chapter 18) and the annotations of it by Guo Pu (276–324 CE) and Yuan Ke (1916–2001), there was a flood in ancient times. It was so fierce that it gushed up into the sky. Gun wanted to stop the flood, so he stole Xirang from the Supreme Divinity without waiting for his permission. Xirang was a kind of mythical soil that was able to grow ceaselessly by itself. If it was excavated, it would grow more. Gun used it as a barricade against the overflowing water. The Supreme Divinity was angry, so he ordered the fire god Zhurong to kill Gun at the outskirts of Yushan (which literally means "Feather Mountain"). Gun's corpse was not tampered with for three years. Then, when his belly was opened with a sword, his son Yu emerged. The Supreme Divinity then commanded Yu to spread Xirang to control the floodwater and stabilize the world.

Comparatively, the Gun myth is more detailed in "Tianwen." Though in this text the myth is described in question form and hence it inevitably appears fragmented and sometimes vague, it gives many details of the Gun myth. The following is a translation of this text.

If Gun was not able to control the flood,
Why did the others recommend him?
They all said: "Don't worry!
Why not let him try and then see whether he can restrain it?"
When the sparrow hawk and turtle joined together (and offered strategies),
Why did Gun accept their suggestions?
He obeyed everybody's advice to stop the flood,
Why did the Supreme Divinity kill him?

His corpse was abandoned at Yushan,
Why did it not rot for three years?
When his belly was opened up, his son Yu emerged,
How could this miraculously happen? . . .
He was imprisoned at Yushan and was not allowed to go west,
How did he surmount those lofty and precipitous peaks?
He metamorphosed to a yellow bear after his death,
How could those magicians revive him?
He told people to plant black millet,
And to grow cattail and reed.
He had done so much for people,
But why was he rejected, and thus considered a notoriety forever?

From this text, we may infer that when Gun tried to control the flood, he adopted the suggestions of the sparrow hawk and turtle. It could have been they who suggested that Gun steal Xirang from the Supreme Divinity. After Gun was executed and gave birth to Yu from the belly of his corpse, he turned into a yellow bear. Then he managed to climb over the high mountains to the west and ask the powerful shamans to bring him back to life. In other versions he is said to have turned into a yellow dragon, a yellow turtle with three legs, or a black fish. Then he dove into the Yuyuan (which literally means "Feather Pool").

A legend recorded in the Jin dynasty states that after his failure to control the flood, Gun committed suicide by sinking into the Yuyuan. He then turned into a black fish, which often raised its feeler, shook its scales, and lay crosswise in the waves. People who saw it said it was the spirit of the river. Fishermen built Gun's temple on Mount Yushan and offered sacrifices to him throughout the year. Another version written in the Six Dynasties era states that after Gun was executed by Yao at Yushan, he metamorphosed into a yellow bear and dove into the Yuquan (Yu Spring). Thus, when the Guiji people (in modern Zhejiang Province) make offerings at Yu Temple, they do not give bears as sacrifices.

Other myths about Gun can be found in early sources such as *Shujing* (*Book of History*, ca. tenth century BC) and *Lüshi Chunqiu* (*Annals of Master Lü*, third century BC), but these sources have a tendency to historicize or interpret each story. In the *Shujing* Gun was depicted as opinionated and destructive. This source states that in ancient times, the flood brought great damage to the world. The water reached the sky, and people suffered from it. So Di, the Supreme Divinity, asked the gods of the Four Mountains to suggest someone who might be able to stop the flood. The four gods recommended Gun. But the Supreme Divinity was hesitant to use him because he thought Gun was a conceited man who would only damage the human species. Since the four gods urged Di to let Gun try, the Supreme Divinity finally sent Gun to stop the flood. But nine years later, Gun still had not succeeded. Another story from *Lüshi Chunqiu* describes Gun as a nobleman who competed against Yao for power. The sage king Yao wanted to give his throne to Shun. Gun felt that this was unfair because he thought he himself should be one of the Three Dukes. So he rebelled against Yao and Shun. It is said that when he was angry, he was even more ferocious than a wild animal. In the wilderness, Gun led a group of beasts. If the beasts' horns were put together, they could form a big wall. And if Gun raised his tail, it looked like a flag. In this way he evaded the strengths of Yao and Shun, and Gun wandered in the wilderness worrying about Shun getting the throne. He was later executed at Yushan, his belly cut open with a sword produced in Wu.

Besides being a fallen hero who failed at damming up the flood, Gun is said to be the culture hero who first tamed cattle and invented the plow (*lei* and *si*) and introduced city walls. One interpretation states that he built the inner wall of the city to protect the ruler and the outer wall to guard the common people.

The Gun story told in contemporary China usually appears as a mixture of related myths and other mythical themes and motifs; its plot often is complicated. Gun often is set in an orderly pantheon that formed late. Furthermore, despite his failure and tragic death, Gun often is described in popular literature and folk belief as a respectful hero who tried to save the world and its people. One legend collected in the 1980s in central Sichuan Province explains the origin of the Yellow Dragon Temple located near the headwaters of the Min River. Gun was the grandson of Tian Di (the Emperor of Heaven). One day, he went to Lingxiao Palace (*lingxiao* literally means "reach to the clouds") to worship his grandfather. When he passed by the south gate of the palace in the heavens, he found there was a gap in the Milky Way and the water was flowing down onto the earth. The world of humans was covered by a flood, and people fled to the top of the mountains. Gun remembered that his grandfather dug here and brought home some black mud called Xirang. This created a flaw in the river of heaven and caused water to overflow into the human world. He knew that only Xirang could stop the flood. So, when Gun saw his grandfather, he asked him to put Xirang back where it belonged or scatter it directly onto the earth to stop the water. But Tian Di did not agree with him. Gun asked again and again, and Tian Di became impatient and drove him out of the palace. Gun then decided to steal Xirang and save the humans, but he did not know where to find the special mud in his grandfather's palace. His friends, the divine swallow and turtle, told him that Xirang was in a jade cupboard in Lingxiao Palace. Furthermore, they had a good idea of how to go about getting the magic mud. The next day, Tian Di went to the Grand Cold Palace on the moon to watch Chang'e dance. Gun and his two partners tricked the heavenly guards that protected the mud and made them drunk. Then they opened the cupboard and caught Xirang. Xirang was so heavy that it overloaded the turtle's shell and created several cracks. Gun and his partners flew to the earth and scattered the mud onto the overflowing waters. The mud quickly began to grow, and soon there appeared mountains and dams. People happily came down from the mountaintops and began to rebuild houses, till the land, and sow seeds.

Tian Di was very angry when he learned of Gun's theft. He ordered Gun, the swallow, the turtle, and the palace guards all to be executed. After Gun was killed at Yushan by the cruel god Zhurong, his corpse did not rot, and his eyes remained open and his heart kept beating. Zhurong then was ordered to open Gun's chest. When he did so, a yellow dragon emerged from Gun's chest and flew toward Canglongshan (Mount Hiding Dragon) above the Min River.

Later, Gun's son Yu grew up and continued to battle the flood. One day, when he investigated the flooding at the Min River, he was caught by a sudden storm and his boat was thrown back and forth by huge waves and became caught in a whirlpool. At this critical moment, the yellow dragon appeared, dove into the river, and carried the boat out of the whirlpool. The places the dragon passed were each channeled, and the floodwater was confined. From then on, the Min River had a stable channel.

Years later, a Yellow Dragon Temple was built near the headwaters of the Min River for commemorating the meritorious yellow dragon. Every June 16, people of many nationalities, including Tibetan, Han, and Qiang, come here to worship the yellow dragon and pray to him for happiness.

See also Chang'e; Shun; Xirang; Yao; Yu; Zhurong

References and Further Reading

Birrell, Anne. *Chinese Mythology: An Introduction.* Baltimore and London: Johns Hopkins University Press, 1993, 79–83, 121–123.

Bodde, Derk. "Myths of Ancient China." In *Mythologies of the Ancient World*, ed. Samuel Noah Kramer. Chicago: Quadrangle Books, 1961, 399–403.

Christie, Anthony. *Chinese Mythology.* Rev. ed. New York: Peter Bedrick Books, 1985, 91–92.

Hou, Guang, and He Xianglu, comps. *Selected Myths from Sichuan Province* (in Chinese). Chengdu: Sichuan Minzu Chubanshe, 1992, 325–327.

Liu, Chenghuai. *Myths in Ancient China* (in Chinese). Shanghai: Shanghai Wenyi Chubanshe, 1988, 361–377.

Walls, Jan, and Yvonne Walls, eds. and trans. *Classical Chinese Myths.* Hong Kong: Joint Publishing Co., 1984, 94–97.

Yuan, Ke, and Zhou Ming, comps. *A Source Book of Chinese Myth Texts* (in Chinese). Chengdu: Sichuansheng Shehui Kexueyuan Chubanshe, 1985, 239–243.

HE BO

He Bo is the god of the Yellow River who helped Yu stop the flood by providing him a map of the rivers' locations. In some versions he was shot by the hero Yi because he drowned men.

See also Yi; Yu

HOUJI

Houji is an important culture hero who brought varieties of grain to people and taught them cultivating and harvesting; he was widely known as the God of Agriculture. He was miraculously born by Jiang Yuan, the first consort of the god Di Ku, and later became the ancestor of the Zhou people (the Zhou dynasty dates from the eleventh century BC to 256 BC). In many historicizing biographical materials he was set in the time of the sage kings Yao and Shun. In his name, *hou* means "sovereign" or "lord" and *ji* means "millet." Therefore, Houji can be translated as "Lord Millet" or "Sovereign Millet" in English. He was also called Qi ("the Abandoned"; this name is different from another Qi, the ancestor of the Shang people born by Jiandi).

The Houji story appears very early in the first Chinese poetry collection, *Shijing* (*The Classic of Poetry*, also translated as *Book of Odes*, compiled in or before 500 BC). The poem "Shengmin" ("Giving Birth to Our People") highly praised Houji, the ancestor and founder of the Zhou, and minutely described the process of his miraculous birth, his supernatural ability to plant, his great benefits to people by bringing them grains and teaching them cultivating, and the sacrifice rite he invented and offered to God to pray for the harvest:

> The first birth of [our] people,
> Was from Jiang Yuan.
> How did she give birth to a person?
> She had offered a sacrifice to the Supreme Divinity,
> To ward off the misfortune of childlessness.
> By chance she stepped into a huge toe-print made by the Supreme Divinity,
>   and her body was stirred.
> She then began to live in a separate room undisturbed.
> Jiang Yuan became pregnant, and she behaved even more devoutly and
>   solemnly.
> She gave birth to [a son],
> Who was Houji.
> When her pregnancy had come to full-term,
> Her first-born son was delivered as easy as the birth of a lamb.

His afterbirth didn't burst,
And there was no injury to him.
It was a result of the Supreme Divinity showing his mythical power.
The Supreme Divinity was satisfied and calm,
Accepting and enjoying her offering and sacrifice,
And she easily brought forth her son.
[Scared by his abnormal conception,] Jiang Yuan abandoned her son on a narrow lane,
But the sheep and oxen protected him and fed him.
Jiang Yuan then tried to place him in a forest,
But gave up for there happened to be many wood-cutters there.
She then threw him away on the cold ice,
And a bird sheltered and supported him with its wings.
When the bird flew away,
Houji began to wail.
His cry was so long and loud,
That his voice filled all his surroundings.
[He then was taken back home.]
When he just learned to crawl,
He looked intelligent and knowledgeable,
And was able to feed himself.
When he started to plant large beans,
The beans grew vigorously.
The paddy of millet he planted was abundant;
His hemp and wheat grew strong and thick,
His melons and gourds came in great yields.
The husbandry of Houji,
Developed the technique of helping [the crop's growth].
He cleared away the thick weeds,
And sowed the ground with fine seeds of grain.
The seedlings of crops were ready to burst as soon as they emerged,
And they grew up quickly,
With strong stems and plentiful ears.
Their grains were full,
And Houji had a bumper harvest.
He thus dwelt in Tai as the appointed lord.
The Supreme Divinity bestowed to him fine grains:
The black millet, and the double-kernelled;
The red, and the white.
The black and the double-kernelled millet were planted extensively,
Which made a tremendous harvest.
The red and white millet were planted extensively,

And there was need for many people to carry it on their shoulders and backs at
   the harvest.

Being home, he offered sacrifices to the Supreme Divinity.

And how as to the sacrifices?

Some hull the grain, some take it from the mortar;

Some tread it, some winnow it.

It is rattled as it is washed in the dishes,

And the steam emanates as it is distilled.

We consulted seriously about the rites.

We burn southernwood with the fat;

We sacrifice a ram to the Spirit of the path,

Offering roast and broiled flesh,

We pray for a more wonderful coming year.

The offerings are loaded in the wood stands,

And fill the earthenware stands.

As soon as the fragrance ascends,

The Supreme Divinity will receive all the offerings with pleasure;

They are so fragrant and in their peak season.

Houji created the sacrifice rites,

By which to pray for absolution and fortune.

This has lasted through the present day.

Similar stories can be found in later writings. For example, in the chapter
"The Basic Annals of Zhou" in *Shiji*, the exemplary historical book written in
the early ages of the Western Han dynasty, the Houji story was narrated, clearly
based on the poem above, but with some historicization. Houji became the subordinate of Yao and Shun. It said that Houji of the Zhou named Qi. His mother,
Jiang Yuan, is the daughter of the Youtai clan. Jiang Yuan is the first consort of
Di Ku. When she went out into a field one day, she saw a huge footprint. She
was very curious and pleased and so she stepped in it. As soon as she did this,
there was a movement in her body as if she had become pregnant. She bore a son
in due time. However, since Jiang Yuan's motherhood of this child was miraculous, she considered the baby to be something inauspicious, so she threw it
away in a narrow alley. When the oxen and sheep passed the alley, they all detoured to avoid stepping on the baby. Jiang Yuan next attempted to throw it into
a forest, but she happened to meet many people in the forest. Jiang Yuan threw it
again on the ice, but the birds covered and warmed it with their wings. Jiang
Yuan thought Houji must be a god, so she brought the child home and raised it.
Because she wanted to abandon it in the beginning, she named it Qi ("the Abandoned"). When he was a child, he was very ambitious. He liked to plant hemp
and cereals as a game, and they grew very well. When he grew up, he liked to

sow and cultivate. He conducted research and found the lands fit for grain, and there he sowed grain seeds. People all followed him. When Yao learned of his extraordinary specialty, he chose him to be the Master of Farming. Thus the whole world received benefits from Houji. Later Shun told him to sow grain in order to save people from hunger. At the place called Tai, Shun honored him and gave him the name Houji.

Like many deities in Chinese mythology and belief, Houji also died and was buried. Even after his death, he was still associated with cereals and plants. According to *Shanhaijing* (chapter 18), Houji was buried in the wilderness of Duguang, where the Black River went through. Here grew good-tasting beans, rice, sticky millet, and unsticky millet. There were hundreds of grains that self-seeded here and grew naturally whether it was winter or summer. Here the male phoenix sang while the female phoenix danced freely. The tree of Lingshou (*ling* means "good" or "animated," and *shou* means "long life") bore fruits and flowers, and grasses and trees flourished. Here hundreds of beasts lived together, and grasses would not wither in winter and summer.

Houji enjoys a high status in the traditional pantheon in China, where agriculture plays a key role in people's lives and in the national economy. He is worshiped not only as the god of agriculture but also as the founding ancestor of farming. For instance, in Zouping County, Shandong Province, Houji was said to be the first to teach farmers how to cultivate and harvest crops. He was offered sacrifices in the temple every July 15 of the lunar calendar. Farmers would hang some bad grain outside their gates on this date, by which they hoped that Houji would teach them more about how to make the cereals grow better (Shanman et al. 1988, 44). In Shanxi Province, especially its southern counties like Jishan, Wenxi, Wanrong, and Yuncheng, there are many relics linked to the Houji story, such as the Mountain of King Ji, temples of King Ji or of Ji and Yi (in which both Houji and Boyi are worshiped), Jiang Yuan's Mausoleum, and Ice-pool Village. Houji is believed to have been born there, abandoned there (in the Ice-pool Village, for instance), and to have taught people cultivating there. Among the stones on the Mountain of King Ji are some bright jadelike ones. Their shapes are like types of cereals. Some look like the millets, some like corn, some like sesame, some like the seeds of pumpkins or watermelons, and so on. These stones are called "Stones of Cereals." Local people said they are transformed from the seeds left by Houji and Jiang Yuan after they taught sowing. They often serve to testify to Houji's close relationship with this area and his great contributions to humans.

Houji's descendants continue to make contributions in agriculture, too. In the same chapter of *Shanhaijing*, Houji's grandson, Shujun, is said to be the inventor who started to till by using cattle.

See also Di Ku; Jiang Yuan; Shujun; Shun; Yao

References and Further Reading

Birrell, Anne. *Chinese Mythology: An Introduction.* Baltimore and London: Johns Hopkins University Press, 1993, 54–55, 116–117.

"Jishan County: Where Houji Taught People Cultivating" (in Chinese). http://www.daynews.com.cn/mag6/20030424/ca27605.htm.

Li, Zixiang. "Reflections on Houji's Teaching Cultivating When Visiting the Mount of Ji" (in Chinese). In *Critiques of Ancient History* (in Chinese), Vol. 2, ed. Gu Jiegang. Shanghai: Shanghai Guji Chubanshe, 1982, 96–98.

"Remembering Houji's Benefits of Teaching Cultivating on the Mount of King Ji" (in Chinese). http://www.sxta.com.cn/lvwh/lvwh26.htm.

Shanman, Li Wanpeng, Jiang Wenhua, Ye Tao, and Wang Dianji. *Customs in Shandong Province* (in Chinese). Jinan: Shandong Youyi Chubanshe, 1988, 44.

Yuan, Ke. *Myths of Ancient China: An Anthology with Annotations* (in Chinese). Beijing: Renmin Wenxue Chubanshe, [1979] 1996, 208–214.

Yuan, Ke, and Zhou Ming, comps. *A Source Book of Chinese Myth Texts* (in Chinese). Chengdu: Sichuansheng Shehui Kexueyuan Chubanshe, 1985, 147–151.

HOUTU

Houtu is a shadowy figure in Chinese mythology whose gender is ambiguous. He functions as the Deity of Earth. In some versions he is said to be the descendant of Yan Di, son of Gonggong, grandfather of Kuafu, and the assistant god of Huang Di. Both Houtu and Huang Di hold cords and reign over the central part of the world. Houtu also is sometimes described as the ruler of the netherworld. However, Houtu's gender is gradually described as female in later writings and beliefs. In his name, *tu* means "earth" or "soil," and *hou* means "divine sovereign," which can equally be used to address males and females.

The name Houtu appears early in Zhou writings such as *Guoyu* (*Discourses of the States*), *Zuozhuan* (*Chronicle of Zuo*), *Chuci,* and the early Han accounts such as *Liji* (*Record of Ritual*) and *Huainanzi.* However, in these writings "Houtu" has several meanings and the gender it refers to is ambiguous. Sometimes "Houtu" is used as a respectful title for the earth. This usage is similar to the custom of addressing heaven as Huangtian ("Grand Heaven"). Since the earth produces plants, fruits, and grains on which humans live, it is often regarded as a mother figure. Accordingly, Houtu is frequently interpreted as a female (Ma 1990, 37–39; Birrell 1993, 161–162). But sometimes "Houtu" also refers to a certain male god named Houtu. A text from *Guoyu,* for instance, states that Gonggong possessed the world, and he had a son named Houtu. Houtu was able to level and reclaim the ground of the world, so he was worshiped as the God of

Earth. In Wang Yi's annotations to *Chuci*, Houtu also functioned as the ruler of the netherworld, Youdu (which literally means "Dark Capital"). Houtu had a terrible assistant named Tubo ("The Master of the Earth") to guard the gate of Youdu. In addition to these two meanings of the word, "Houtu" sometimes may be used as a title for a kind of mythical official who takes charge of affairs on earth. According to a text from *Zuozhuan*, the title for the Tuzheng (Official of Earth) was "Houtu," namely "She" (the deity of the earth), and this title was assumed by Gonggong's son, named Goulong. In another version from *Huainanzi*, Yu became She after he died of exhaustion in his work controlling the great flood. Gao You wrote that Yu was worshiped as Houtu after his death.

In spite of these variants, Houtu regularly appeared as a female earth deity in later developments, at least after the Sui dynasty. She often is respectfully addressed as Madame Houtu or Goddess Houtu in folk religion and popular literature. Many temples are dedicated to her. In Wanrong County, Shanxi Province, for example, there is a Houtu temple. According to local documents, this temple was first built in the early Han dynasty thanks to the distinguished Emperor Wu. Thereafter, from the Han through the Song dynasties, there were more than ten emperors who went there to offer sacrifices to Houtu. In this place Houtu is popularly called "Houtu the Sacred Mother," and she is portrayed as a graceful and poised queen wearing a coronet, silk cape, and skirt with embroidered phoenixes on it (in Chinese tradition, the phoenix is often used as a symbol of the queen or empress). She is said to have been born on March 18 of the lunar calendar, so a temple fair commemorates her on this day each year. On April 19, 2003 (lunar March 18), the local government sponsored a large Houtu Temple Fair (the official title that year was "The First Houtu

The statue of "Houtu the Sacred Mother" in Houtu Temple, Wanrong County, Shanxi Province, 2003. (Courtesy of Li Hongwu)

Tourism Culture Festival") in order to exploit Houtu as a "Culture Resource" to propagate the rich local culture, attract more travelers and traders, and therefore develop the local economy. Houtu functions as more than a Deity of Earth in the local belief system. Like most mythical gods in Chinese folk belief, Houtu is an almighty goddess in the pantheon. People offer her sacrifices and pray to her for harvest, rain, children, health, wealth, safety when boating in the Yellow River, and the tide when a boat is stranded. In local legends, Houtu often is depicted as a kind, wise, and powerful goddess. One story says she helped Yu solve his problem in channeling the flood to the sea. When Yu channeled the Yellow River, he wrongly opened it toward the west. Because the rocks and stones in the west were extremely hard, his work progressed very slowly. As he worked, Yu felt worried because the flood season would soon come. When Houtu the Sacred Mother heard this news, she drew a map of the Yellow River and thought over possible solutions. Then she had an idea. She ordered one of her divine birds to tell Yu that he should open the channel eastward. Yu took her suggestion and finally succeeded in directing the floodwater toward the east sea. The place where he wrongly dredged later received the name "River Wrongly Opened." At another time, Houtu visited Yu and was sympathetic about his bad living conditions. She used her great power and in minutes made a huge cave for Yu and his helpers to live in. To thank Houtu, Yu suggested naming this cave "the Sacred Mother's Cave." But Houtu was modest; she thought Yu brought more benefits to the world, so she insisted the cave be named "King Yu's Cave." Furthermore, Houtu learned that Yu was unable to supply enough food for his workers, so she and her daughter cooked a large pot of rice gruel every day for the hardworking laborers. No matter how much the laborers took, the pot of gruel was never emptied. The place where Houtu and her daughter cooked was later called "Rice Gruel Temple." In another story, Houtu is described as a heroine who drove off a harmful ogre. A turtle ogre that lived in the Fen River in Shanxi Province often took humans as its food. To eliminate the evil creature, Houtu the Sacred Mother transformed into a man who chopped firewood on the riverbank. The ogre soon found him and rose up from the bottom of the river to eat the man. Houtu then showed her true self and reprimanded the ogre for its evil behavior. The ogre knew that it would be punished by the Sacred Mother, so it fled. But it ran into another deity named Juling and was kicked by him into the Yellow River. Houtu arrived soon after and affixed it in the center of the river. The huge turtle shell then turned into a large island, which is now known as "Chicken-heart-shaped Beach."

See also Gonggong; Huang Di; Kuafu; Yan Di; Youdu; Yu

References and Further Reading

Birrell, Anne. *Chinese Mythology: An Introduction.* Baltimore and London: Johns Hopkins University Press, 1993, 161–162.

Ma, Shutian. *Gods of Chinese* (in Chinese). Beijing: Yanshan Chubanshe, 1990, 37–39.

Xue, Wenliang, and Wang Xiaohua, comps. "A Source Book of Houtu Culture" (in Chinese). Wangrong: Local Chronicles Office, 2003.

Yuan, Ke, and Zhou Ming, comps. *A Source Book of Chinese Myth Texts* (in Chinese). Chengdu: Sichuansheng Shehui Kexueyuan Chubanshe, 1985, 49–50.

HUANG DI

Huang Di, or the Yellow Emperor, is one of the most renowned legendary figures in Chinese mythology and culture. He is the son of Shaodian, the half brother of Yan Di, and the forebear of some ethnic groups and many notable deities. He is also the most important of the Five August Emperors (names differ in different texts). He defeated Yan Di, Chiyou, and other deities and became the most powerful ruler of the central part of ancient China in mythical history. In later tradition he is highly respected as a common ancestor of all Chinese people. Additionally, he is depicted as a great culture hero by inventing almost all of the necessary cultural items in ancient times. In some descriptions he functions as the Thunder God. In his name, *huang* means "yellow," and *di* means "emperor"; therefore he may be called the Yellow Emperor in some English translations. He is also named Xuanyuan.

Huang Di's name was already quite popular in written texts during the Warring States era. From then on, he became more and more prominent in Chinese myths, legends, beliefs, and political lives, and hence diverse versions of stories are told about him.

According to a text from *Shizi* (written in the Warring States era, but now preserved only in later collections), Huang Di is portrayed as a human being with four faces. Another version describes his miraculous birth. His mother, Fubao, saw a great bolt of lightning one night circling one of the stars in the Great Bear. (In traditional Chinese belief, astronomical phenomena are often connected with special and momentous events of the world. The eclipse, the brightness or dimness of the stars, the falling of meteors, and the unusual interaction between stars and planets are taken as the signs of the birth or death of a great man, or the prosperity or decline of a dynasty.) It was so bright that it lit up the area nearby. Then Fubao became pregnant, and after twenty-five months she gave birth to Huang Di. A text from *Dadai Liji* (*The Elder Dai's Records of Ritual,* ca. first century BC) describes that when Huang Di was just born, he was smart; when he was a baby, he could talk; when he was a child, he was quick; when he grew up, he was honest and clever; when he was an elder, he was wise. In some writings, Huang Di was 300 years old when he died.

In writing of the Warring States era and the Han dynasty, Huang Di often appears as the ruler of the central part of the world. A text from *Huainanzi* (chapter 3) sets Huang Di and the other four divine emperors in an orderly pantheon distributed in five directions (east, south, west, north, and center) and five elements (wood, fire, metal, water, and earth; in traditional Chinese philosophy, the whole world is made of these five elements). It says that the east belongs to wood. Its god is Taihao. His subordinate is Goumang. Both of them hold the compasses and control the season of spring. The south belongs to fire. Its god is Yan Di. His subordinate is Zhuming. Both of them hold the beams of steelyards and control the season of summer. The center belongs to earth. Its god is Huang Di. His subordinate is Houtu. Both of them hold the ropes and control the four directions. The west belongs to metal. Its god is Shaohao. His subordinate is Rushou. Both of them hold the carpenter's squares and control the season of autumn. The north belongs to water. Its god is Zhuanxu. His subordinate is Xuanming. Both of them hold the sliding weights of steelyards and control the season of winter.

Huang Di. Funeral stone carving of the Eastern Han dynasty, Wuliang Shrine, Jiaxiang County, Shandong Province. The inscription reads, "Huang Di made numerous creations and transformations. He invented weapons, wells, and the field system. He invented clothes and the house." (Feng Yunpeng and Feng Yunyuan, Re-search on Stone Carving, 1821)

Being the most powerful ruler of the center and the other four directions, Huang Di enjoys high status and distinction. A text from *Hanfeizi* (written by Han Fei, ca. 280–233 BC) indicates that when Huang Di assembled the deities and ghosts on Mount Tai, he was surrounded by many entourages. Elephants and dragons pulled the cart for him, the divine bird Bifang accompanied him, Chiyou led the way, Feng Bo cleaned the road, Yu Shi created sprinkles of rain along the way, tigers and wolves ran ahead, and deities and ghosts followed him.

Some Chinese mythologists argue that there must have been several wars between Huang Di and the other four divine emperors, and only after Huang Di defeated all of them could he become the most powerful (Yuan 1996, 105). According to a text written in the Three Kingdoms era (which now can only be seen in later collections), at the beginning of Huang Di's era he cared about cultivating his temperament and loved his people. He did not like war at all. But the other four emperors boasted about their own directions and colors. (The east belongs to wood, so its color is therefore green; the south belongs to fire, so its color is red; the west belongs to metal, with the color white; and the north, water, has the color black. The center belongs to earth, with the color yellow; therefore Huang Di is called Yellow Emperor.) They conspired to attack Huang Di. Huang Di's soldiers were so concentrated on preparing for the fight that they did not remove their armor. Huang Di sighed and said, "If the ruler on high is in danger, his people will suffer from instability; if the ruler loses his kingdom, his subordinates will have to serve another country. Now I am a ruler on high, but the four emperors attack me and put my army on constant alert. How can I bear this situation?" So he went to the fortified walls and commanded the army himself. In the end, he defeated the four emperors.

Though Huang Di is often depicted in later tradition as a peaceable and benevolent ruler, he fought with various mythological deities. Thus, he is sometimes interpreted as "a warrior-god" (Birrell 1993, 130). The most well-known wars perhaps are the ones between Huang Di and Yan Di, and between Huang Di and Chiyou.

Yan Di is the half brother of Huang Di, the god of the south. In a text from *Xinshu* (*New Documents,* written by a Han dynasty writer, Jia Yi, 201–168 BC), Yan Di is said to have controlled half of the world while Huang Di controlled the other half. Huang Di ruled his kingdom based on benevolence and love, but Yan Di did not follow these principles. Thus they fought at the open plain of Zhuolu (which now belongs to modern Hebei Province). The battle was so fierce and brutal that the victims' blood flowed like a stream that could float the pestles. At last Huang Di killed Yan Di and took his land. The world then became peaceful. In another version, from *Liezi,* when Huang Di fought against Yan Di in the countryside of Banquan, he ordered black bears, grizzly bears, wolves, panthers, cougars, and tigers to be his vanguards, while the eagles, fighting pheasants, falcons, and phoenixes were his banners. Another Huang Di myth states that the battle between the two brothers lasted for a long time. Huang Di fought against his brother many times before finally winning the war.

The battle between Huang Di and Chiyou seems much fiercer and larger in scale. Chiyou is the descendant of Yan Di. In some accounts he is said to have eighty brothers (seventy-one brothers in another version), each with an animal body, bronze head, and iron forehead, speaking a human language. They used sand and stone as their food. Other versions state that Chiyou had a human body, horned head, ox hooves, four eyes, six hands, and ears and temples like swords and spears. He seems to be a former subordinate of Huang Di (see the text above from *Hanfeizi*), but later he somehow became a rebel. According to a text from *Shanhaijing* (chapter 17), Chiyou made weapons and attacked Huang Di, so Huang Di commanded Yinglong to launch an attack against Chiyou in the wilderness of the central plain. Yinglong began by storing all of the water. Chiyou asked Feng Bo and Yu Shi to release a cloudburst. Then Huang Di asked the drought goddess Ba to descend from heaven, and the rain was stopped. Eventually Huang Di killed Chiyou.

There are many stories describing the course and circumstances of the war. One story states that Chiyou was able to soar into the sky and surmount the dangerous and difficult obstructions. But Huang Di made a drum from the hide of Kui, a one-legged mythical creature, and beat it many times. The sound it made was so great that it prevented Chiyou from flying away, and he was caught and killed by Huang Di. Another version states that Chiyou led many ferocious mythical animals to attack Huang Di on the Zhuolu plain. In response, Huang Di ordered his subjects to blow horns sounding like dragons to threaten them. Another version asserts that Chiyou could stir up clouds and mist. When he fought with Huang Di, he made heavy fog for three days. Huang Di's army was caught in it and could not determine their direction. Huang Di then invented the compass cart and guided his army out of the fog. Thus, Huang Di defeated Chiyou and killed him. Some versions maintain that after Huang Di fought against Chiyou many times and still could not win, he retreated with his army to Mount Tai. There was a thick fog lasting for three days. In the fog, Huang Di saw a lady with a woman's head and a serpent's body. He kowtowed, bowed twice, flattened himself against the ground, and did not dare to stand up. The lady said, "I am Xuan Nü [literally means 'Dark Lady,' a Taoist goddess in later tradition]. What do you want to ask me?" Huang Di answered, "I hope I can get myriad attacks, myriad wins." So the goddess taught him the art of war, and he defeated Chiyou in the end.

In some accounts Huang Di is said to "have fought fifty-five times and then the whole world obeyed him." Some Chinese historians believe that Huang Di is a legendary clan leader in primitive China, the same as Yan Di. During the process of their clans' growth and expansion, Huang Di and Yan Di commanded many battles against other clans. They ultimately became the most powerful clan leaders in the central plain. Since their clans formed the basic part of the Huaxia ethnic group, which later made up the main body of Han Chinese, Huang Di and Yan Di were thus worshiped as the ancient ancestors of the Han Chinese and, furthermore, of the whole Chinese nation. Today Han Chinese still identify themselves as "the descendants of Huang Di and Yan Di."

Besides these stories about Huang Di's wars, another big cluster of Huang Di myths refers to his many cultural inventions. In these myths he is depicted as the fountainhead of Chinese culture and civilization. He drilled the wood for fire, and then cooked fresh meat. By following his lead, his people did not suffer stomach diseases from then on. He hollowed a tree trunk to make a boat and cut branches to make oars. Therefore people could go to distant places by water. He tamed cattle and horses to draw carts so that people could use them to carry heavy goods. Inspired by the erigeron that could endlessly rotate in the wind, he made the wood cart. And that is why he was also called Xuanyuan (*xuan* refers to a high-fronted, curtained carriage used in ancient times, and *yuan* refers to the shafts of a cart). He cut trees and used them to build a variety of houses to protect people from wind and rain. He invented hats, crowns, and clothes. He cut wood to make pestles, and dug earth to make mortar. He made a caldron to steam rice. He made coins. He found the way of measuring weight, and invented the clepsydra as a device for measuring time. He started the football game. After he met the goddess Xiwangmu, he made twelve mirrors, and used one in each month. So it was also Huang Di who invented the mirror. He invented coffins for the dead. After he killed Chiyou, he buried him, and that originated the custom of burial. Various myths and legends continue to attribute many inventions and discoveries to him, such as music, writing, Chinese medicine, the art of war, the interpretation of dreams, and astronomy. In other myth versions he is said to have made the rules for wedding ceremonies, distributed lands and built the country, and started rituals and markets. All in all, as an ancient writer noted, "All of the techniques and crafts are started from Xuanyuan" (*Shiwu Jiyuan, The Origin of Items*, written in the Song dynasty, chapter 7).

Among his numerous inventions, the compass cart is famed. A legend collected in the 1980s in Xinzheng County, Henan Province (said to be Huang Di's hometown), explained how Huang Di invented the compass cart. Huang Di was a chieftain in the central plain, and Yan Di was a chieftain in the east. Admiring the better life in the central plain, Yan Di commanded his clan to attack Huang Di's. Though Yan Di failed in the battle, the winner, Huang Di, wanted to ally with him. They became sworn brothers, and their clans were united into one large country. Meanwhile, in the southeast, there was another clan, and its leader was Chiyou. Chiyou also coveted the prosperity of the central plain, so he ordered his people to invade the central plain. Huang Di then commanded his army to fight Chiyou. It was the middle of autumn, and there often was heavy fog. Having difficulty discerning the direction, Huang Di's army was defeated several times. Therefore, Huang Di spent much time in discovering a means for telling the directions. At length he found that a kind of magnetite could help. He then made a carved wooden man with a magnetite hand installed on it. No matter where he was, the magnetite hand always pointed to the south. Therefore, Huang Di named it Fang ("Direction"). Later Huang Di built a cart and fixed the carved man on it, so it could easily be moved around. Huang Di called the whole system Xuanyuan Fang. Sometime later the name was changed to "compass cart."

In addition to these inventions directly made by Huang Di himself, many cultural items were made by his officials, sometimes under his instructions. For example, according to texts from *Shiben*, he asked Xihe to make a system for observing the sun, Changxi to make a system for observing the moon, Yuqu to create methods to observe the stars, Linglun to make music, Danao to compile the Heavenly Stems and the Earthly Branches (the Ten Heavenly Stems and Twelve Earthly Branches are used in combination to designate years, months, days, and hours), Lishou to formulate arithmetic, Rongcheng to create the calendar, and Juyong and Cangjie to create writing. In other texts, his officers also invented the mortar and pestle, boats, bows and arrows, crowns, cloth, shoes, drums, mirrors, domesticated cattle, and other things. Even one of his four wives, Leizu, is a famous culture heroine. She started sericulture, the cultivation of silkworms and production of silk, and therefore she was worshiped as "the Sericulture Goddess" after she died (one myth version holds that she died while on an inspection tour with Huang Di, so Huang Di honored her as the Road Goddess).

Huang Di has a grand family. Another wife of his, Momu, is also well-known. Though she seems not to have made any special discoveries or creations, she still wins much respect. She was unsightly in appearance, but of great virtues, so Huang Di married her and let her supervise his other concubines. Today some Chinese women without good looks still call themselves "Momu," implying that they have virtue inside.

Huang Di has many distinguished descendants, such as Gun and Yu, the great heroes who controlled the flood; Zhuanxu, the mythical emperor; Zhong and Li, the heroes separating heaven from earth; Shujun, the Cultivation God; and Yuqiang, the Sea God. Huang Di also is said to have originated some ancient ethnic groups, such as Huantou, Miaomin, and Quanrong.

Huang Di has some relationship with Taoism. During the Warring States era, he was adopted into the Taoist philosophy and respected as a great ancient saint who advocated silence and inaction and encouraged the worship of nature. Later he became a god in the Taoist pantheon. Likewise, there are stories that depict Huang Di as an immortal. Some popular legends describe how Huang Di "ascended to heaven" at the end of his secular life. According to the historicized descriptions of Huang Di's life history in *Shiji*, Huang Di gathered copper at Mount Shoushan. He used it to make a big *ding* (a tripod caldron). When the ding had been made, a dragon with a long beard descended from heaven to meet him. Huang Di rode on it, and more than seventy of his officials and concubines followed him. Since there were too many lower subordinates to ride on the dragon, they grabbed on to the dragon's beard and were dragged along underneath. They were so heavy that they pulled the beard out before the dragon could ascend to heaven. Huang Di's bow also fell. With Huang Di ascending to heaven, people on the ground held his bow and the dragon's beard and cried. From then on, the place was called Ding Hu (*hu* means "beard"), and the bow was called Wuhao (meaning "cry"). Some other sources suggest that Huang Di chose his death date himself. When the day came, he said goodbye to his officials. After he died, he was buried at Mount Qiao (now in Huangling County, Shaanxi Province, in northwest China). But the mountain soon collapsed, and his coffin was found empty except for his sword and shoes.

Today Huang Di's myths and legends are still told in China. In Xinzheng County, for example, nearly twenty Huang Di myths and legends were collected from local oral tradition in the 1980s and were published in 1990. They tell various stories about Huang Di's divine birth and marriage, his wars with Yan Di and Chiyou, his wonderful reign over the mythical kingdom, and his ascension to heaven. One legend explains why the local crab has ten legs rather than the normal eight: Huang Di's officials found a huge stone cave for their industrious emperor to spend his summer. It was very cool inside, and there was a pond in front of it. Huang Di was satisfied with living in the cave except that there were groups of mosquitoes, fleas, scorpions, and mice disturbing him. He said unconsciously to his subordinates, "If only these disturbances could be exterminated." The crab living in the pond heard this and it cleared these pests away. When Huang Di found that it was the crab in the pond that had helped him, he rewarded it with two more legs. Thereafter, only the crab in the local pond has ten legs.

As the prominent hero and common ancestor of Han Chinese people, Huang Di receives great respect in Chinese history. During the Late Imperial era, he was respected as one of the common ancient ancestors of everyone in the Chinese nation (Zhonghua Minzu) in the process of constructing a modern nation. He no longer belonged only to the Han. All of the non-Han ethnic groups, whether Mongolian or Qiang, were also the offspring of Huang Di. Now the collective memory of "the descendants of Huang Di and Yan Di" is widely held by Chinese all over the world. Huang Di has become a cultural symbol that is often used to reinforce the unified identity of Chinese people and to solidify group attachments among the fifty-six ethnic groups in China.

On April 5, the Tomb-sweeping Day of 2003, a large sacrificial ritual offering to Huang Di was held at the Xuanyuan Temple in Huangling County, Shaanxi Province. Among the people who attended the ceremony were many

New statues of Huang Di and Yan Di, Xinzheng County, Henan Province, 2004. (Courtesy of Dai Gaizhen)

important officials of the Communist Party and representatives of overseas Chinese from Hong Kong, Taiwan, Macao (Aomen), Canada, Australia, and Southeast Asia. They came together to worship "the Common Ancestor of the Chinese People" and "the Founder of Human Civilization."

See also Ba; Cangjie; Chiyou; Feng Bo; Goumang; Gun; Houtu; Kui; Li; Leizu; Linglun; Shaohao; Shujun; Yan Di; Yinglong; Yu; Yu Shi; Yuqiang; Zhong; Zhuanxu

References and Further Reading

Birrell, Anne. *Chinese Mythology: An Introduction.* Baltimore and London: Johns Hopkins University Press, 1993, 130–137.

Bonnefoy, Yves, comp. *Asian Mythologies.* Translated under the direction of Wendy Doniger. Chicago and London: University of Chicago Press, 1993, 246–247. Originally published as *Dictionnaire des mythologies et des religions des sociétés traditionnelles et du monde antique.* Paris: Flammarion, 1981.

Christie, Anthony. *Chinese Mythology.* Rev. ed. New York: Peter Bedrick Books, 1985, 96.

Editorial Committee for the Folk Literature Collection in Xinzheng County, ed. *Legends from Xuanyuan's Hometown* (in Chinese). Zhengzhou: Zhongyuan Nongmin Chubanshe, 1990.

Liu, Chenghuai. *Myths in Ancient China* (in Chinese). Shanghai: Shanghai Wenyi Chubanshe, 1988, 673–732.

Tian, Jizhou. *The History of Ethnic Groups before the Qin Dynasty* (in Chinese). Chengdu: Sichuan Minzu Chubanshe, 1988.

Walls, Jan, and Yvonne Walls, eds. and trans. *Classical Chinese Myths.* Hong Kong: Joint Publishing Co., 1984, 40–52.

Xu, Xusheng. *The Legendary Period in Ancient Chinese History* (in Chinese). New ed. Beijing: Shangwu Yinshuguan, 1985.

Yuan, Ke. *Myths of Ancient China: An Anthology with Annotations* (in Chinese). Beijing: Renmin Wenxue Chubanshe, [1979] 1996, 101–143.

Yuan, Ke, and Zhou Ming, comps. *A Source Book of Chinese Myth Texts* (in Chinese). Chengdu: Sichuansheng Shehui Kexueyuan Chubanshe, 1985, 64–118.

HUNDUN

Hundun is an obscure mythical figure in Chinese mythology. The word *hundun* is used in Chinese language as both a noun and an adjective that literally refers to the primeval chaos as well as a person who is ignorant or muddleheaded. Mythical stories about Hundun may personify these two aspects of his name.

Ancient recordings about Hundun are often quite different from or even contradictory to each other, which perhaps suggests that they come from different narrative traditions. Therefore, it is almost impossible to find a consistent character and function of Hundun.

Perhaps the most often cited Hundun myth appears in *Zhuangzi*. It portrays Hundun as the god of the central region who has not a single aperture. Shu (literally meaning "fast") was the god of the south sea while Hu ("swift") was the god of the north sea. They often met each other at the central region reigned by Hundun. Hundun treated them very well, so Shu and Hu hoped to pay a debt of gratitude to him. They presumed that everyone had seven apertures in his head (two eyes, two ears, two nostrils, and one mouth) with which to see, hear, eat, and breathe, but Hundun had none; therefore, if they could make seven apertures in Hundun's head, they could repay him for his kindness. They tried to chisel openings in Hundun's body. They chiseled one hole each day. However, after seven days of their work, Hundun died.

Like many other myths or legends appearing in this classic, the Hundun story has clearly been reshaped by Zhuang Zhou to illustrate his Taoist philosophy. The two meddling gods Shu and Hu are used to symbolize the artificial order (time and direction), whereas Hundun symbolizes the primeval chaos that is a natural, unspecified, unified whole. In the story the artificial order destroyed the natural and harmonic whole. Zhuang thus expresses his idea that one should respect nature and not insist on doing something that is not natural; politicians should let things take their own course and should not construct uninformed interventionist policies.

However, contrary to his depiction as a kind and innocent god of the central region in *Zhuangzi*, Hundun is at times described as a bad and ferocious deity in other writings. In an account from *Zuozhuan*, Hundun was said to be Dihongshi's unintelligent son (according to some commentators, Dihongshi is in fact Huang Di, the ruler of the central part of the world), one of the "Four Evil Ones" (Si Xiong), who was later exiled by the sage king Shun. He concealed justice and did not take righteous actions. He liked to treat people cruelly and do harm to them secretly. He made close friends with those evil beings who acted and spoke against justice and virtue. Because he was so muddled and incompetent, he was called Hundun.

Some scholars believe that a minor deity, Dijiang, who appeared in *Shanhaijing* is in fact Hundun (Yuan 1993, 66; Birrell 1993, 98–100). According to a text from *Shanhaijing*, Dijiang lived in a western mountain called Tianshan ("Sky Mountain"). His shape was like a yellow bag, and his color was as red as the cinnabar flame. He had six feet and four wings but no head and face. He knew how to sing and dance. Though Dijiang and Hundun have similar appearances of featureless heads, it remains difficult to conclude that Dijiang can be identified as Hundun himself, because they share few functions and behaviors.

Another account relating to Hundun appears in a later book, *Shenyijing* (*The Classic of Spirits and Strange Things*, once said to have been written by a Han writer, Dongfang Shuo, 154–93 BC, but probably compiled later by an anonymous author). It clearly combines the two contradictory narrative traditions about Hundun in *Zuozhuan* and *Shanhaijing*. It states that there was an animal on the west side of Kunlun Mountain. It looked like a dog with long hair and four feet, or like a brown bear without claws. It had two eyes but could not see. It had two ears but could not hear. It had a stomach yet was without the five internal organs. It had intestines, but they were so straight that food would go immediately through his body. When the creature found someone of virtue, it would run and butt him; but when it found someone of evil, it would lean on him. When doing nothing, it often bit its own tail, turning around and around, looking up at the sky and laughing. It is also called Hundun.

See also Huang Di; Kunlun Mountain; Shun

References and Further Reading

Birrell, Anne. *Chinese Mythology: An Introduction.* Baltimore and London: Johns Hopkins University Press, 1993, 98–100.

Christie, Anthony. *Chinese Mythology.* Rev. ed. New York: Peter Bedrick Books, 1985, 51–52.

Girardot, Norman J. *Myth and Meaning in Early Taoism: The Theme of Chaos (Hun-tun).* Berkley and Los Angeles: University of California Press, 1983.

Yuan, Ke. *The Classic of Mountains and Seas: A Collation and Annotation* (in Chinese). Chengdu: Bashu Shushe, 1993, 66.

Yuan, Ke, and Zhou Ming, comps. *A Source Book of Chinese Myth Texts* (in Chinese). Chengdu: Sichuansheng Shehui Kexueyuan Chubanshe, 1985, 2–3.

JIANDI

Jiandi is the ancestress of the Shang people and the second wife of Di Ku. She ingested a swallow's egg and miraculously gave birth to Qi, the founder of the Shang people.

Most gods or goddesses and heroes or heroines in Chinese mythology have miraculous birth stories. Huang Di, for example, was conceived after his mother saw a great bolt of lightning circling one of the stars in the Great Bear, Houji was conceived after his mother stepped into a huge footprint, Yu was born from the belly of his father's corpse, and there are numerous other stories of miraculous births. The mythical births show the deities' sacred origins, testify to their unusual abilities, and promise their significant achievements.

Myths about Jiandi's miraculous conception and the birth of Qi can be found in some ancient classics. Poems in *Shijing* (*Eulogy of Shang*, for example) mention that the founder of the Shang people comes from a swallow. The famous Zhou poet Qu Yuan clearly names Jiandi in his well-known poem "Tianwen." He asks, "Jiandi stayed on the terrace, why did Di Ku go there and seduce her? The swallow sent two eggs to her, why did she devour them?" Wang Yi, the Han commentator of this poem, explains these questions with the story that when Jiandi was serving Di Ku on the terrace, a swallow passing by dropped its egg. Jiandi was pleased and devoured it. Then she gave birth to Qi.

In another version that appears in *Shiji*, Jiandi is said to be a daughter of the Yousong clan and the second concubine of Di Ku. One day when she went out to take a bath with Di Ku, she saw a swallow dropping an egg. She picked it up and swallowed it. Then she inexplicably became pregnant, and later gave birth to Qi.

In addition to Jiandi's main mythological function as the ancestress of the Shang people, a text in *Lüshi Chunqiu* illustrates another role Jiandi played as a culture heroine: In the Yousong clan there were two beautiful girls (according to some accounts, one was Jiandi and the other was named Jianci). They lived in a terrace nine stories high. Each meal they ate had to be accompanied by drum music. One day the Supreme Divinity (Di) sent a swallow to visit them. The swallow sweetly sang, repeating "Yiyi." The two girls loved it so much that they tried to catch the swallow. Finally they covered it with a jade basket. When they lifted up the basket after a while, the swallow flew away immediately toward the north, leaving two eggs behind. The girls were so disappointed that they composed a song, singing "Swallow, swallow, you flew away," which is credited with being the origin of northern music. This story does not mention Jiandi's extraordinary conception. But Gao You, the Han commentator of *Lüshi Chunqiu,* wrote that the Supreme Divinity was in fact the God of Heaven; it was he who ordered the swallow to lay two eggs for the girls of the Yousong clan to swallow so that one would give birth to Qi.

A Han dynasty book, *Lienüzhuan* (*Biographies of Exemplary Women,* written by Liu Xiang, 79–8 BC), rationalized and demythologized the Jiandi myth and set Jiandi as an exemplary mother of female virtues who could educate women to obey Confucian ethical rules. The story of Jiandi is set in the time of the sage king Yao. She was the elder sister of the Yousong clan. One day Jiandi and her sisters went out to take a bath in a river of Xuanqiu when they saw a swallow passing by and dropping a colorful egg. They all competed with each other to catch it, and Jiandi won. Protecting it from being seized by her sisters, she put the egg into her mouth, but swallowed it by accident. Then she became pregnant and later gave birth to Qi. Jiandi was good at managing the ways of the world, and she was quite knowledgeable and benevolent. When Qi grew up, she taught him the rules of truth and order, and eventually helped him to succeed. Thus she was respected by honorable men as a model mother who had the virtues of benevolence, reason, and subservience.

Jiandi has some correlation with the ancient custom of worshiping Gaomei, the Supreme Matchmaker. Gaomei was originally and probably a divine stone that was believed to have the magic power of bestowing children to people. Later it became anthropomorphized in some places as a great mother or ancestress like Nüwa, Jiandi, or Jiang Yuan, and its main function became matching people and bestowing children. According to recordings from *Shijing* and *Liji* (*Record of Ritual,* the early Han accounts), as well as some of their Han commentators' annotations, Jiandi reinforced the custom of worshiping Gaomei. They said that every spring when swallows flew back from the south, people would go to the countryside to offer sacrifices to Gaomei and pray for children. The emperor would also lead all of his consorts there, and they usually offered a pig, a sheep, and a bull as the sacrifices. By displaying bows and arrows in front of the statue of Gaomei, they hoped that they could bear intelligent sons. Once when Jiandi went to worship Gaomei with her husband, Di Ku, she caught a falling swallow egg and ate it. Afterwards she became pregnant and gave birth to the founder Qi. Her mythical experience was interpreted as the effectiveness of Gaomei's sacred power, so the emperors later built a temple to worship Gaomei.

However, according to a text cited by *Taiping Yulan* (*An Imperial Reading of Texts Compiled in the Taiping Era* [977–984 CE], compiled by Li Fang, 925–996 CE, chapter 529), the Gaomei custom originated from the Jiandi story. It states that in 296 CE, the divine Gaomei stone that rested on the sacrificial altar was broken into two pieces. The emperor and many officials wondered why a stone was put on the altar and whether they should salvage it. Then a knowledgeable consultant explained that at the time of Di Ku, Jiandi swallowed an egg and then gave birth to a great son. Thereafter, ordinary people put an egg-shaped stone on the altar to pray for children. The old broken stone thus was buried, and a new one was installed.

There are some Chinese scholars who argue that the role of Gaomei was actually assumed by the ancestress Jiandi in ancient times. For example, Jiandi was in fact the Gaomei worshiped by the Shang people, and Nüwa and Jiang Yuan were the Gaomei worshiped by the Xia and Zhou people (Wen 1982). Thus, rather than believing in a Gaomei stone, people searched for Gaomei magic power from these special goddesses.

> **See also** Di Ku; Houji; Huang Di; Jiang Yuan; Nüwa; Qi; Yu
> **References and Further Reading**
> Birrell, Anne. *Chinese Mythology: An Introduction.* Baltimore and London: Johns Hopkins University Press, 1993, 113–118.
> Bonnefoy, Yves, comp. *Asian Mythologies.* Translated under the direction of Wendy Doniger. Chicago and London: University of Chicago Press, 1993, 242. Originally published as *Dictionnaire des mythologies et des religions des sociétés traditionnelles et du monde antique.* Paris: Flammarion, 1981.
> Liu, Chenghuai. *Myths in Ancient China* (in Chinese). Shanghai: Shanghai Wenyi Chubanshe, 1988, 510–520.
> Wen, Yiduo. "Analyses on the Legends of Gaotang Goddess" (in Chinese). In *The Complete Works of Wen Yiduo.* Vol. 1. Beijing: Sanlian Shudian, [1948] 1982, 81–116.

JIANG YUAN

Ancestress of the Zhou people, the first consort of Di Ku, and the mother of Houji, Jiang Yuan stepped into a huge footprint in a field and miraculously gave birth to Houji, the God of Agriculture and the founder of the Zhou people.

The Jiang Yuan myth appears very early in the first Chinese poetry collection, *Shijing.* The poem "Shengmin" ("Giving Birth to Our People") highly praised her and her son Houji. It describes in detail her miraculous conception and bearing of Houji:

The first birth of [our] people,

Was from Jiang Yuan.

How did she give birth to a person?

She had offered a sacrifice to the Supreme Divinity,

To ward off the misfortune of childlessness.

By chance she stepped into a huge toe-print made by the Supreme Divinity, and her body was stirred.

She then began to live in a separate room undisturbed.

Jiang Yuan became pregnant, and she behaved even more devoutly and solemnly.

She gave birth to [a son],

Who was Houji.

When her pregnancy had come to full-term,

Her first-born son was delivered as easy as the birth of a lamb.

His afterbirth didn't burst,

And there was no injury to him.

It was a result of the Supreme Divinity showing his mythical power.

The Supreme Divinity was satisfied and calm,

Accepting and enjoying her offering and sacrifice,

And she easily brought forth her son.

[Scared by his abnormal conception,] Jiang Yuan abandoned her son on a narrow lane,

But the sheep and oxen protected him and fed him.

Jiang Yuan then tried to place him in a forest,

But gave up for there happened to be many wood-cutters there.

She then threw him away on the cold ice,

And a bird sheltered and supported him with its wings.

When the bird flew away,

Houji began to wail.

His cry was so long and loud,

That his voice filled all his surroundings.

. . .

Another version of the Jiang Yuan myth is given in the exemplary historical book *Shiji* ("The Basic Annals of Zhou" chapter), in which Jiang Yuan is said to be the daughter of the Youtai clan and the first consort of Di Ku. One day when she went into a field, she saw a huge footprint. She was very curious and pleased and so she trod in it. As soon as she did this, there was a movement in her body as if she had become pregnant. She bore a son in due time. However, since Jiang Yuan was miraculously pregnant, she considered the baby to be something inauspicious, so she abandoned it in a narrow alley. When the oxen and sheep passed the alley, they all detoured to avoid stepping on the baby. Jiang Yuan attempted to throw it into a forest, but she happened to meet many people in the forest. Jiang Yuan threw it away again on the ice, but the birds covered and warmed it with their wings. Jiang Yuan thought Houji must be a god, so she brought the child home and raised it. Because she wanted to abandon it in the beginning, she named it Qi ("the Abandoned"), who later became the founder of the Zhou people and the god of agriculture.

Though Jiang Yuan was the receiver of a miraculous conception and wanted to abandon her baby in the beginning, she is portrayed as an ideal woman and an exemplary mother in some historicized writings. A story recorded in *Lienüzhuan*, for instance, presents Jiang Yuan as a model mother who has the female virtues praised by Confucians, such as chastity and constancy. Being set in the time of the emperor Yao, in the story she is said to be the daughter of the Marquis Tai. When she stepped in the huge footprint and became pregnant, she felt very strange and disgusted about the coming baby. She divined and offered sacrifices to the gods in order to abort the fetus. However, her son was born anyway. No matter where she threw him, he received protection and survived. She realized the baby must be something unusual, so she brought it back home. She was a pure and quiet woman with concentrated attention, and she was good at cultivating. So when Houji grew up, she taught him to sow and cultivate. Because of the education she gave him, Houji became a famed minister of agriculture in administration of Yao and Shun. Therefore she was respected by men of honor as a virtuous mother who was pure, chaste, and successful in civilizing her son.

Jiang Yuan is also worshiped in folk belief as a goddess. An article written by a scholar named Cui Yingke in the 1920s introduced the rituals and legends about Jiang Yuan in his hometown in Wenxi County, Shanxi Province. There was a Jiang Yuan mausoleum in this area, popularly called "Goddess Jiang's Temple." On every lunar March 1, a temple fair would be held there to offer sacrifices to Jiang Yuan. Local operas would be performed for her for three days. During the fair, people often polished coins on the stone tablet in front of the mausoleum, by which they believed that the coins would become powerful and thus could keep their holders (especially children) healthy and safe. Stories orally transmitted in that area clearly show that the Jiang Yuan myth may have become localized and demythologized in later times. In the stories, Jiang Yuan is usually portrayed as a miserable farm girl who suffered a lot from her miraculous conception and finally became respected because of her notable son. One legend says that when Goddess Jiang was still a young girl, one snowy day in winter she went to the threshing ground to fetch some firewood. The snow was so heavy that she could hardly walk. Then she found two lines of huge footprints along the road where she should go, and she stepped in them. Because the footprints were made by a god, she got pregnant by stepping in them. When she was ready to give birth and was going to be brought to bed in her home, her mother made her ride a mule and go to the field to give birth since she felt shamed by her daughter's pregnancy. When the baby was ready to appear, the mule also happened to be ready to give birth. Worried that this might disturb her own childbirth, Goddess Jiang used a gold needle to block the mule's birth canal. From then on the mule could no longer bear offspring. When the baby came out, she threw it into a pool. It was in June, but the pool water suddenly iced up. While the baby lay on the ice, birds flew over to cover and warm him. Since that time, the pool would ice up every June; the village where the pool was located was named "Ice-pool Village." Meanwhile, Jiang's sister-in-law sent a pot of dough drop soup to the field, but the pot was broken halfway there, and the soup flowed down a local hillside, so it later was called "the Hillside of Dough Drop Soup." Believing that Jiang's miraculous conception would bring misfortune to the village, some of her neighbors chased after her and tried to beat her. Goddess Jiang ran away. When they had almost caught her, there suddenly came a gale that blew for three days. When the gale stopped, the people found that Goddess Jiang had disappeared and that a mausoleum appeared in her place. They called the building "Jiang Yuan's Mausoleum."

Another legend states that Goddess Jiang's son loved to cultivate everywhere and was respected as "Ji the Highness." He often asked his mother about his father, to which Goddess Jiang replied, "You have no father." He felt very upset. When the local operas were sung for the goddess in her temple during the fair, the statue of Ji the Highness would always be carried down the Mountain of King Ji to visit his mother. When they met each other, the statue of the son would always be arranged to turn his back to his mother, which was said to be because he still felt upset about being born without a father.

See also Di Ku; Houji

References and Further Reading

Birrell, Anne. *Chinese Mythology: An Introduction.* Baltimore and London: Johns Hopkins University Press, 1993, 116–118.

Cui, Yingke. "Legends and Biographical Sketch of Jiang Yuan and Supposition on Her Mausoleum" (in Chinese). In *Critiques of Ancient History.* Vol. 2, ed. Gu Jiegang. Shanghai: Shanghai Guji Chubanshe, 1982, 99–104.

Yuan, Ke, and Zhou Ming, comps. *A Source Book of Chinese Myth Texts* (in Chinese). Chengdu: Sichuansheng Shehui Kexueyuan Chubanshe, 1985, 147–149.

JIANMU

See Sky Ladder

JINGWEI

Jingwei is a mythical bird that metamorphosed from Yan Di's daughter and indomitably tried to fill up the sea with pebbles.

Yan Di, the Flame Emperor, had a young daughter named Nü Wa (different from the great mother and cosmic repairer Nüwa; *nü* means "female," *wa* means "child"). Nü Wa was playing in the eastern sea but was fatally drowned and never returned. She turned into a bird called Jingwei. Jingwei lived on Fajiu Mountain, located in the north. It looked like a crow but had a colorful head, white beak, and red claws. Its name is derived from the sound of its call, which sounds like "jingwei." It always carried a pebble or a twig in its mouth and dropped it into the eastern sea, where Nü Wa lost her young life. Jingwei tried unyieldingly to fill up the vast sea with its tiny efforts, never stopping.

In one version Jingwei was said to have mated with a sea swallow. Their female children looked much like Jingwei, and the male children looked much

Jingwei. Originally drawn in the 17th century by Hu Wenhuan. (Ma Changyi, The Classic of Mountains and Seas: Ancient Illustrations with Annotations, *Shandong Huabao Chubanshe, 2001, 253)*

like the sea swallow. Because Jingwei was drowned in the eastern sea in its pre-existence, it swore not to drink the water of the eastern sea. Thus it was also called Oath Bird. And since it had not yet received revenge for its grudge and resentment, Jingwei was also called Grudge Bird. Jingwei persistently tried to fill up the sea in spite of the great difficulty and impossibility, so it was also called Resolve Bird. Since Jingwei was formerly the emperor's daughter, it was sometimes called Emperor's Daughter Bird.

The myth of Jingwei is well-known to most Han Chinese people. Many feel sympathetic to Jingwei's misfortune and admire the bird for its bravery, toughness, and unyieldingness. This myth continues to appear in many poems, novels, and dramas, combining the diverse themes of pathos, courage, and the refusal to accept defeat. "Jingwei Tries to Fill the Sea" has become an idiom that encourages people to learn from Jingwei's spirit and to work bravely and persistently, no matter how hard the task seems.

See also Yan Di

References and Further Reading

Birrell, Anne. *Chinese Mythology: An Introduction.* Baltimore and London: Johns Hopkins University Press, 1993, 214–215.

Walls, Jan, and Yvonne Walls, eds. and trans. *Classical Chinese Myths.* Hong Kong: Joint Publishing Co., 1984, 29–30.

Yuan, Ke. *Myths of Ancient China: An Anthology with Annotations* (in Chinese). Beijing: Renmin Wenxue Chubanshe, [1979] 1996, 89–91.

KUAFU

Kuafu is the grandson of Houtu and the mythical hero who chased the sun to compete with it in a race but died of thirst in the end. His stick then transformed into a forest of peach trees.

"Chasing the sun" is a striking motif in Chinese mythology, especially in Han Chinese myths. Besides the Kuafu myth, there is another type of myth containing this motif. Being well-known by the common name of "Erlang Carried Mountains and Chased the Sun," the myth usually tells how a hero named Erlang (literally meaning "the second son") carried mountains on a shoulder pole and chased the superfluous suns; eventually he caught them and pressed them down under the mountains. The story is often used to explain the character of the sun's circulation (why it rises every morning and rests during the night, for instance) and the origins of some local mountains or hot springs.

Comparatively, the myth "Kuafu Chased the Sun" is much more popular, and it boasts a rather long recorded history. The earliest and most comprehensive recordings of his myth can be found in *Shanhaijing,* a major repository of ancient Chinese mythic narratives. A text from that book (chapter 17) states that there was a mountain called Chengdu Zaitian in the great wilderness. A god named Kuafu lived in it. There were two yellow snakes circling his ears and another two yellow snakes in his hands. He was the grandson of Houtu. Kuafu overvalued his own strength, so he wanted to chase the sun's shadow and catch the sun at Yugu (Yu Valley). He felt very thirsty halfway there, so he decided to drink from the river. Since the river water was not enough for him, he then decided to go to the great marsh. But he died of thirst on his way. Another text from the same book (chapter 8) states that Kuafu competed with the sun in a race. He entered into the aureole of the sun. Being very thirsty, he went to drink in the Yellow River and the Wei River, but they were not enough for him. Then he decided to go northward to the great marsh. He died of thirst before he arrived there. His walking stick transformed into a forest of peach trees. Another version appearing in *Liezi* adds that after Kuafu died of thirst in his race with the sun, he abandoned his walking stick. Nourished by the fat from his corpse, the stick turned into a peach tree forest, which extended for thousands of miles.

Some other myth versions portray Kuafu as a divine animal who looked like a big monkey with spotted arms and a panther's tail. He was good at casting and often threw stones at people. Others say that Kuafu died of execution instead of thirst. He was killed by Yinglong, the executioner who also killed Chiyou. Scholars have interpreted that the reason for his execution was that both Chiyou and Kuafu were the descendants of Yan Di (Kuafu's grandfather, Houtu, was said to be the descendant of Yan Di too), so they both fought against Huang Di to seek revenge for the defeated Yan Di. They failed in the battle and were executed by Huang Di's subordinate, Yinglong (Yuan 1996, 144–150).

Among these many myth versions, "Kuafu Chased the Sun" is the most influential one. It sometimes even serves as an etiological myth to explain many local landforms. According to some ancient documents, for instance, there were three mountains in the east of Chenzhou Prefecture (now part of Hunan Province), standing like three legs of a tripod caldron thousands of feet high. They were said to be the legs of the caldron used by Kuafu when he competed with the sun in a race and cooked there along the way. In Anding County (now in Gansu Province), there was a knoll named "Mound of Shaking Shoes," which was said to be formed by the sand and earth shaken out of Kuafu's shoes. When Kuafu was chasing the sun, he took off his shoes and shook them there to pour out the sand and earth bothering him. In Taizhou Prefecture (now part of Zhejiang Province), there was a huge footprint on Mount Fufu, which was said to be made by Kuafu while he was chasing the sun.

A modern fieldwork report from Lingbao County in Henan Province shows that the myth of "Kuafu Chased the Sun" is still told in contemporary China, and Kuafu is worshiped as a supreme god in the local pantheon (Zhang Zhenli and Cheng 1987, 270–283). Several traces of the Kuafu myth were found in Ling-bao County, such as "Mount Kuafu," "Kuafu Valley," and "Kuafu Barrack" (it is said that there were barracks there in ancient times). A Qing stone tablet (1837 CE) in Kuafu Valley was found during the fieldwork, and the epigraph inscribed on it explained why the mountain was named Mount Kuafu: Kuafu was a man who lived at the shore of the east sea. He was good at walking and running very fast. He was familiar with the sunrise, but wondered how it set, so he took a stick and chased the sun. When he ran to this mountain, he was so thirsty that he died there. Therefore, the mountain was called "Mount Kuafu."

A modern Kuafu myth collected in the village of Kuafu Barrack states that Kuafu died of anger rather than thirst. Kuafu wondered how the sun set, so he decided to chase the sun to have a look. When he ran to this mount, he felt very thirsty. He drank some water and took a nap. When he awoke, he saw that the sun was just about to set. Realizing that he could not catch up with the sun, he was extremely angry and at last died of anger. Because he was buried there, the valley got the name "Kuafu Valley," and the mountain was called "Mount Kuafu." Other versions say that after Kuafu died, his stick turned into a forest of peach trees. To commemorate him, later generations planted more peach trees there. A rule was established that these peach trees must not be chopped down. For Kuafu's sake, the peach trees in that area flourished, and the forest extended for hundreds of miles.

Kuafu was worshiped as the god of Mount Kuafu. Until the 1960s, in every lunar October (some versions say February), villagers in Kuafu Valley would offer sacrifices and perform local operas for him. The fair usually lasted for three to five days. The villagers were proud that they were the descendants of Kuafu, and they believed he would protect them.

"Kuafu Chased the Sun" has long been used as an idiom. Though it may occasionally be used to criticize those people who overrate their own ability and act blindly against reality, it is often used as a positive metaphor for man's courage, toughness, persistence, and unyieldingness. Tao Yuanming (365–427 CE), a renowned Jin poet, highly praised Kuafu in one of his poems:

Kuafu cherished a great ambition,
He then competed with the sun in a race.
At the same time they reached Yü Valley, where the sun set down,
It seemed neither of them won.
Because Kuafu possessed such divine power,
How could the water in the rivers be enough for him to drink, even if they
    were drunk up?

His remains metamorphosed into the forest of peach trees,
And his merit was achieved after his death.

The Kuafu myth appears in many other Chinese poems, novels, operas, and cartoon films. Kuafu is usually depicted as a tragic but great hero who bravely challenges the difficult and impossible, and he intrepidly acts in order to realize his dream and ambition.

See also Chiyou; Houtu; Yan Di; Yinglong

References and Further Reading

Birrell, Anne. *Chinese Mythology: An Introduction.* Baltimore and London: Johns Hopkins University Press, 1993, 215–216.

Cheng, Jianjun. *Myths Transmitted in Contemporary Henan Province* (in Chinese). Zhengzhou: Haiyan Chubanshe, 1997, 156–163.

Walls, Jan, and Yvonne Walls, eds. and trans. *Classical Chinese Myths.* Hong Kong: Joint Publishing Co., 1984, 31–33.

Wang, Xiaolian. *The Chinese Mythological World: A Study on the Creation Myths and Relevant Beliefs in Ethnic Groups of China* (in Chinese). Taibei: Shibao Chuban Gongsi, 1987, 707–762.

Yuan, Ke. *Myths of Ancient China: An Anthology with Annotations* (in Chinese). Beijing: Renmin Wenxue Chubanshe, [1979] 1996, 144–150.

Zhang, Zhenli, and Cheng Jianjun, comps. *The Collection of Myths Transmitted in the Contemporary Central Plain* (in Chinese). Zhengzhou: Zhongguo Minjian Wenyijia Xiehui Henan Fenhui, 1987, 270–283.

KUI

Kui is the one-legged mythical monster killed by Huang Di. Its hide was used to make a drum for defeating Chiyou.

Descriptions about Kui in ancient writings vary greatly. Among them, the most well-known Kui myth appears in *Shanhaijing.* In that book (chapter 14), Kui was said to be a divine beast who lived on Mount Liubo (*liubo* literally means "flowing wave") in the east sea. It looked like an ox but was gray, hornless, and one-legged. Whenever it came out or dived into the sea, a storm would follow. Its light was like the sunlight and moonlight, and its sound was like the thunder. Later it was caught by Huang Di, who made a drum by using its hide as the cover. When struck with the bone of the Thunder God, the drum made a great sound that could be heard over five hundred miles away. Huang Di used the drum to show his power to the whole world. In some versions, this drum made by Kui's skin played an important role in the battle between Huang Di and Chiyou.

Chiyou was the offspring of Yan Di. He was the god of war and the inventor of military weapons. He had eighty brothers (seventy-one brothers in another version), each of them with an animal body, bronze head, and iron forehead, who spoke human language. Chiyou was said to be able to soar into the sky and surmount the dangerous and difficult obstructions. When he rebelled against Huang Di, Huang Di had a difficult time defeating him. But eventually Huang Di caught Kui and made a drum from its hide. He thus beat it many times during war. The sound it made was so great that it prevented Chiyou from flying away and escaping him during their great battle. So Chiyou was caught in the end and was beheaded by Huang Di.

Other versions depict Kui as a one-legged horned dragon. Its scales shone like the sun and moon. If it happened to be seen, it would bring a drought to the place where it was seen. Sometimes Kui was said to look like a monkey with a man's face, and had the ability to talk. Kui was also described as a drum-shaped animal with one leg. It was the spirit of the mountain. If one called its name, then it could help one to catch the tiger and panther.

In written texts in which scholars have rationalized to explain history, Kui is said to be a humanized master of music under the administrations of the sage kings Yao and Shun. According to a text from *Shangshu* (*Ancient History*, which may also be called *Shujing*, *The Classic of History*, traditionally said to have been compiled by Confucius, 551–479 BC, but later mixed with some other texts), Shun appointed Kui to be his official of music and to educate his descendants. Kui answered that if he beat and stroked a stone, all animals would follow his melody and dance. Another recording from *Lüshi Chunqiu* (*Annals of Master Lü*, third century BC) clearly illustrated Kui's role as a culture hero who invented music. Being the master of music of Yao, Kui (originally written as "Zhi," but many commentators thought he was in fact Kui) invented song by imitating the sound he heard in the mountain forest and gully. He made a drum by stretching a beast's hide over an earthen jar. He beat and stroked stone, trying to imitate the sound made by the Supreme Divinity's jade chime stone. The melody he invented was so pleasant and tuneful that all the animals began to dance along with it.

Another popular story related with Kui is that its one-legged character was cunningly interpreted by Confucius as a lesson in life that "one is enough." Confucius used the term *zu* as a pun to create a fabled lesson from the Kui myth. In the Chinese language, *zu* can be used as both a noun meaning "foot" and an adjective meaning "enough." So, *yi zu* can mean either "one leg" or "one is enough" (in which *yi* means "one"). When Confucius was asked whether Kui was really one-legged (*yi zu*), he replied that Kui was indeed *yi zu*: one is enough. Confucius described Kui as an accomplished and talented official who contributed much to society. He explained that Kui was the master of music for the sage king Shun, and he adjusted the tune and harmonized the music. Since music was highly revered during this time as contributing to the education and governance of society, Kui's work helped to bring order to the world, and people became convinced that Kui was indeed a model official. Therefore, Confucius explained, if an emperor had an excellent official like Kui, one was enough. In this way, Confucius skillfully dissolved this myth and rationalized the Kui story. He turned Kui, the one-legged mythical monster, into a virtuous and talented historical official.

> **See also** Chiyou; Huang Di; Shun; Yao
> **References and Further Reading**
> Birrell, Anne. *Chinese Mythology: An Introduction.* Baltimore and London: Johns Hopkins University Press, 1993, 134–135.
> Ma, Changyi. *The Classic of Mountains and Seas: Ancient Illustrations with Annotations* (in Chinese). Jinan: Shandong Huabao Chubanshe, 2001, 553–555.
> Yuan, Ke, and Zhou Ming, comps. *A Source Book of Chinese Myth Texts* (in Chinese). Chengdu: Sichuansheng Shehui Kexueyuan Chubanshe, 1985, 95–97.

KUNLUN MOUNTAIN

One of the most remarkable mythical mountains in Chinese mythology, Kunlun Mountain is the earthly residence of the Supreme Divinity, a paradise of deities and immortals, one of the pillars of the sky that prevents heaven from collapsing, and a sky ladder that links the earth to heaven.

Descriptions about the mystery, grandeur, or magnificence of Kunlun Mountain in ancient writings are indeed abundant. The renowned Zhou dynasty poet Qu Yuan sketchily depicted it in his inquisitive poem "Tianwen." Among those various descriptions, one of the earliest and most comprehensive depictions comes from *Shanhaijing*. In a text from that volume (chapter 11), Kunlun was said to be a huge mountain located in the northwest. It was the earthly residence of the Supreme Divinity and the dwelling of other gods. It was 800 *li* (400 kilometers, or 248 miles) square and 80,000 feet high. On the summit were nine wells, nine gates, and magic grain. The balustrades of the wells were made of jade. The gates were all guarded by the divine beast Kaiming ("Enlightened"), which looked like a big tiger with nine heads and human faces. The magic grain, named *Muhe* (literally meaning "Tree Grain"), was forty feet tall and five spans wide. To the west of Kunlun Mountain were phoenixes that wore snakes on their bodies and stepped on snakes. To the north of the mountain were the Pearl Tree, the Jade Tree, the Tree of Immortality, Tree Grain, the Sweet Spring, and Shirou (meaning "Seeing Flesh"). Shirou was a substance shaped like a cow's liver with two eyes. It could never be completely consumed. Every time it was eaten, it would regenerate. To the east of Kunlun Mountain were six shamans who surrounded Yayu's corpse and rescued him with the elixir of immortality. Yayu was a deity with a human face and snake body who was killed by the deities Erfu and Wei; the six shamans were ordered to revive him. To the south of the mountain were a six-headed bird, a hornless dragon, snakes, panthers, and others. Kunlun was a place where the deities dwelled. It was so rocky and steep that only the benevolent and talented hero Yi could ascend the mountain.

Another text from *Shanhaijing* (chapter 2) also sets Kunlun Mountain in the west as the earthly capital city of the Supreme Divinity, which is rich in odd animals and plants. It was ruled by the deity Luwu, who had a man's face, tiger's body and paws, and nine tails. He was also the ruler of the nine parts of heaven and the seasons of the Supreme Divinity's garden.

A magic beast named Tulou lived on Kunlun Mountain. It looked like a sheep with four horns, and it ate human beings. There was a bird named Qinyuan, shaped like a bee but as big as a mandarin duck. If it stung other birds and beasts, they would die; and if it stung trees, the trees would wither. Another magic bird, Chunniao, resembled a phoenix and took charge of the Supreme Divinity's clothes and utensils. The Shatang Tree was waterproof; one who consumed its wood would float in water instead of sinking. Also found on the mountain, the Pincao Grass could make one who consumed it forget his troubles and always be happy. Kunlun Mountain was said to be the source of four rivers: the Yellow River, Red River (Chishui), Yang River, and Black River (Heishui).

In various pictures drawn in *Yubenji* (written in the Warring States era, cited by *Shiji*), *Huainanzi, Shiyiji,* and other writings, Kunlun appears as a pillar of the sky (in one version a pillar of the earth) located at the center of the world. This was the paradise of the deities and immortals, the place where the sun and the moon hid in turn while the other one glared out of the blue sky, and a huge divine mountain that contained numerous marvelous and wonderful items. Among them were the Sweet Spring and Emerald Lake (Yaochi); colorful clouds and waters; Tree Grain; the Pearl Tree, the Jade Tree, and the Tree of Immortality; Cinnabar River (Dan Shui), whose water prevented its drinker from death; and Weak River (Ruoshui), whose water was so weak that it could not even float a feather. Some versions state that Kunlun Mountain was composed of three tiers. The lowest one was called Fantong, the middle one was Xuanpu (literally meaning "the Suspending Garden"), and the highest one was Zengcheng (literally meaning "the Increased City"), which was also named the "Palace of Heaven" and was the residence of the Supreme Divinity (Tai Di). Others say that even Zengcheng was nine stories tall. According to a text from *Huainanzi* (chapter 4), however, the first tier of Kunlun Mountain was Liangfeng (Cool Wind Mountain). Anyone who climbed it would receive immortality. The second tier was called

Xuanpu. Persons who climbed this tier would acquire spiritual power and could control the wind and rain. And if one climbed further, one would arrive at heaven, the residence of the Supreme Divinity, and thereafter one would become a spirit. Here Kunlun Mountain functioned not only as a pillar of the sky but also as a sky ladder that connected the earth with heaven. In some later traditions, Kunlun was rebuilt into a Taoist paradise for immortals. An account appearing in *Shiyiji* depicts Kunlun as a mountain that was even higher than the sun and moon. It had nine tiers that were separated from each other by 5,000 kilometers (3,100 miles). The clouds surrounded them and the wind blew from the four directions. Immortals often went there to play by riding on dragons and cranes.

Though Kunlun is quite famous, it became much better known because of its association with an important goddess in Chinese mythology, Xiwangmu, or the Queen Mother of the West. Some sources suggest that Kunlun Mountain is also the residence of the goddess (other versions say that she presides over the Jade Mountain, which is very close to Kunlun). A text from *Shanhaijing* (chapter 16) states that Kunlun Mountain was located south of the west sea, on the shore of the Liusha (meaning "Flowing Sand"), behind the Red River, and in front of the Black River. A spirit dwelled in the mountain. It was human-headed with a tiger's body and white spotted tail. The Weak River circled the bottom of the mountain, and a flaming mountain surrounded it. A deity named Xiwangmu inhabited a cave there. She (or he; the text makes this unclear) wore a Sheng crown and had tiger's teeth and a panther's tail. Other versions say that Kunlun Mountain was surrounded by the Weak River and that only deities and immortals could arrive there by riding on dragons. Three green divine birds flew in and out, fetching food for Xiwangmu. Xiwangmu is popularly known as the keeper of the elixir of immortality and the magic peaches; both of them have the power to keep one's vitality and prevent death. In the Yi myth, the hero Yi is said to have received the elixir of immortality from Xiwangmu. Since the text in *Shanhaijing* (chapter 11, mentioned above) says that only the benevolent and talented hero Yi could ascend the mountain, it might be deduced that Yi scrambled up Kunlun Mountain and asked Xiwangmu for the precious elixir. But, unfortunately, the elixir of immortality was eventually stolen by Yi's wife Chang'e, and Chang'e then flew to the moon and became the spirit of the moon.

Kunlun is a divine space where some important mythological events happened. Besides the Yi and Xiwangmu myths, a Tang dynasty account from *Duyizhi* (*A Treatise on Strange Beings and Things*, by Tang dynasty writer Li Rong, ca. 846–874 CE) states that the great mother Nüwa married her brother on this mountain and they became the first ancestors of the world. At the very beginning of the world, there were no other people except for Nüwa and her elder brother. They lived on the mythical Kunlun Mountain. They wanted to become husband and wife so that they might have children and populate the earth, but felt shamed by this because of their blood relationship. They prayed to heaven from the top of the mountain: "If Thou wouldst send us two forth as man and wife, then make this smoke gather. If not, then make the smoke disperse." The smoke gathered immediately, so they married. However, Nüwa still felt very shy and ashamed so she weaved grass into a fan to cover her face. That is why brides often hold fans during their wedding ceremonies.

Kunlun still plays a significant role in later traditions, including legends, tales, novels, and operas. In the popular legend of Lady White Snake, for instance, Kunlun appeared as a paradise where the grass of immortality and numerous other precious plants grow. It was presided over by an immortal named Nanji Xianweng (meaning the "Immortal Grandfather of South Pole"). A white crane guarded those treasured plants. The legend states that the special creature, the White Snake, had magic power and transformed into a beautiful lady and married a man named Xu Xian. A green snake changed into her maidservant. When Xu Xian was horrified to death when he unexpectedly saw the original figure of his wife, Lady White Snake flew to Kunlun Mountain and tried to steal the grass of immortality to revive her husband. Her true love moved the Immortal Grandfather, so she was granted her wish. Upon returning home, she boiled the grass and poured the juice into her husband's mouth. After a little while, Xu Xian awakened.

A distinguished Chinese historian, Gu Jiegang, argues that the classical Chinese myth system can be divided into two branches: one is the Kunlun myth system, the other one is the Penglai myth system (Gu 1979). Based on Gu's analysis, another mythologist, Wang Xiaolian, maintains that there are two systems of Chinese mythical paradises. One is the East Paradise, which is made up of those immortals; alchemists; Penglai, the paradise floating on or under the sea; and Guixu ("Returning Mountain") located under the sea and containing five divine mountains. The other is the West Paradise, which is made up of deities; shamans; Kunlun, the earthly residence of the Supreme Divinity; and the head stream of the Yellow River. The two traditions of the paradises are transmitted separately, and they gradually became confused during the late Warring States era (Wang 1987, 529–563).

See also Fusang; Tang Valley; Xihe; Yi

References and Further Reading

Birrell, Anne. *Chinese Mythology: An Introduction.* Baltimore and London: Johns Hopkins University Press, 1993, 38, 234, 255.

Bonnefoy, Yves, comp. *Asian Mythologies.* Translated under the direction of Wendy Doniger. Chicago and London: University of Chicago Press, 1993, 246–247. Originally published as *Dictionnaire des mythologies et des religions des sociétés traditionnelles et du monde antique.* Paris: Flammarion, 1981.

Christie, Anthony. *Chinese Mythology*. Rev. ed. New York: Peter Bedrick Books, 1985, 96.

Gu, Jiegang. "The Combination of the Two Myth Systems of Kunlun and Penglai in *Zhuangzi* and *Chuci*." *Zhonghua Wenshi Luncong* 2 (1979): 31–57.

Walls, Jan, and Yvonne Walls, eds. and trans. *Classical Chinese Myths*. Hong Kong: Joint Publishing Co., 1984, 31–33.

Wang, Xiaolian. *The Chinese Mythological World: A Study on the Creation Myths and Relevant Beliefs in Ethnic Groups of China* (in Chinese). Taibei: Shibao Chuban Gongsi, 1987, 529–563.

Yuan, Ke, and Zhou Ming, comps. *A Source Book of Chinese Myth Texts* (in Chinese). Chengdu: Sichuansheng Shehui Kexueyuan Chubanshe, 1985, 64–118.

LEIZU

The first wife of Huang Di, the grandmother of Zhuanxu. She started sericulture, the cultivation of silkworms and production of silk, and was worshiped as the Sericulture Goddess after she died.

As the famed cradle of sericulture in the world, China boasts various myths and legends about the origin of silkworms and silk production. One myth is about Cancong, the founder of the ancient Shu kingdom (now in modern Sichuan Province, southwestern China), and his contribution in teaching the techniques of sericulture to humans in local mythology. Another well-known legend about the silkworm's origin is the "Horse-headed Lady" story, which explains that the silkworm (its head looks like a horse's head) is transformed from a girl wrapped in a horsehide: A father went away with the army while his daughter and horse stayed at home. After a period of time the daughter missed her father very much. One day she joked with the horse that if it brought her father back home, she would marry it. The horse then ran away, located the army, and brought her father back. Upon learning what had happened, the father was shocked, and he killed the horse to prevent it from marrying his daughter. Its hide was exposed to the sun in the yard. When the daughter played in the yard one day, the horsehide suddenly flew over, wrapped her up, and flew away. The father searched for his daughter in the horsehide for several days, and then found she had changed into a silkworm on a mulberry tree. Later the daughter was worshiped as the goddess of sericulture, and people offered sacrifices to her to pray for a good silk harvest. Her figure was a young woman cloaking a horsehide. She was popularly known as the Horse-headed Lady.

Among the variety of sericulture myths and legends, the Leizu myth is a popular one. According to a text from *Shiji* (chapter 1), the exemplary historical

The Leizu temple at Xinzheng County, Henan Province, 2004. (Courtesy of Dai Gaizhen)

book written in the first century BC, Huang Di married a girl from the Xiling clan. Her name was Leizu. As the first wife of Huang Di, she gave birth to two sons, and one of them later fathered Zhuanxu, one of the Five August Emperors in the mythical history of China. In many other ancient writings, Leizu was commonly said to have started sericulture, so she was worshiped as Xiancan, the ancestress of sericulture. One myth version holds that she died on an inspection tour with Huang Di, so Huang Di honored her as the Road Goddess.

The Leizu story continues to be told in contemporary China. For example, a myth collected in the 1980s in Xinzheng County, Henan Province (said to be Huang Di's home), portrays Leizu as a guilty maidservant of Xiwangmu, the Queen Mother of the West. Without getting the goddess's permission, she ate some fruits of a mulberry tree that originally belonged to heaven. She thus was able to vomit silk. In addition, she fed some colorful moths the mulberry leaves, and they changed into the silkworms and were able to produce silk, too. Her actions broke the rule of heaven, so she was punished and ousted from heaven to the earth, where she became an ordinary farm girl. But she brought some silkworms and mulberry tree seeds with her. After she met Huang Di and married him, she taught people of his clan all the techniques of raising the silkworm, reeling the silk, and weaving the silk. Because of her contribution, people began to wear clothes. For this reason, she was worshiped as the ancestress of sericulture.

Another myth collected in the same period in Dujiangyan City, Sichuan Province, gives more details about Leizu's inventions. This myth states that at the time of Xuanyuan (another name of Huang Di), Leizu, who was Xuanyuan's wife, took charge of food and clothing in the clan. When Xuanyuan led men to hunt wild animals outside, Leizu led women at home in peeling off the animals' hides for clothes and boiling their flesh for food. The animal-skin clothes were uncomfortable for wearing because they were hard, rough, and not ventilated. One day Leizu went out with Xuanyuan to hunt wild pigs. She found herself coming to a place where she had never been. There were lots of mulberry trees, and the silkworms were eating the tree leaves. She found some cocoons there and investigated them. The silk threads that came out of those cocoons were so light, soft, and tough! Leizu was excited when she realized that she could make cloth from the silk. She then picked many cocoons and took them back home. She ordered women to reel the silk from the cocoons. Because the silk thread from each cocoon was very long and there were many women reeling at the same time, the silk threads were often tangled with each other. Leizu had no idea of how to solve this problem.

Later, when she saw Xuanyuan turning a waterwheel, she had an idea. She had a small wooden spinning wheel made with a handle fixed on it. When she turned the handle and reeled the silk, the threads orderly rolled onto the wheel. From then on, the silk threads were never tangled.

Then Leizu began to weave. At first, she tried to imitate the spider's weaving but failed, because the silk was not as sticky as the spider's thread. One day when she went out to fish, she saw a big fish swimming back and forth freely between the reeds. She then thought that she could weave by using a shuttle shaped like a fish to weave back and forth between the silk threads. Her method proved effective. She quickly wove a piece of fabric and formerly named it "silk." She then taught all the women of her clan the skill of weaving. Quickly she faced another puzzle. Since many people now were in the mulberry field gathering the cocoons, the cocoons became rare. To solve this problem, Leizu brought some silkworms home and let them lay eggs there. She fed them mulberry leaves that she picked up from the field and brought back. Because it was so inconvenient to get more leaves, the silkworms soon died of hunger. Leizu then asked Xuanyuan to dig up some of the wild mulberry trees and plant them nearer to her home. A year later, mulberry trees were growing everywhere. Leizu then began to show people how to plant the mulberry tree, how to raise the silkworm, and how to reel and weave the silk. In the end, all the women in the world learned these techniques.

Because of her great contribution to human life, Leizu won considerable respect. She is popularly worshiped by sericulturists as the Sericulture Goddess. In Yuan'an County, Hubei Province, there is a Leizu temple (also named the Temple of the Sericulture Goddess). Since Leizu is said to have been born on March 15 in this county, a temple fair is held on every lunar March 15. During the fair, people play operas in front of the temple and pray for Leizu's blessing and protection of their silk productions. In Yanting County, Sichuan Province, there is a Leizu mausoleum. Leizu is said to have been born there in Leizu Village. On March 31, 2003, a large sacrificial ceremony was held in Mianyang City (to which Yanting County belongs) to commemorate Leizu. Hosted by the local government, the ceremony's purpose was "commemorating Leizu, the Mother of Huaxia [Han Chinese], and developing our Chinese virtues." More than 10,000 people from Sichuan and Shaanxi provinces attended the ceremony.

See also Cancong; Huang Di; Xiwangmu

References and Further Reading

Editorial Committee for the Folk Literature Collection in Xinzheng County, ed. *Legends from Xuanyuan's Hometown* (in Chinese). Zhengzhou: Zhongyuan Nongmin Chubanshe, 1990.

Gu, Xijia. *Research into Sericulture in Southeast China* (in Chinese). Beijing: Zhongguo Minjian Wenyi Chubanshe, 1991.

Hou, Guang, and He Xianglu, comps. *Selected Myths from Sichuan Province* (in Chinese). Chengdu: Sichuan Minzu Chubanshe, 1992, 221–230.

Yuan, Ke, and Zhou Ming, comps. *A Source Book of Chinese Myth Texts* (in Chinese). Chengdu: Sichuansheng Shehui Kexueyuan Chubanshe, 1985, 64–118.

LI

The Governor of Fire and the offspring of Zhuanxu, Li cut off the connection between the sky and the earth with another deity, Zhong.

The motif of separating heaven from the earth is worldwide. In China, many myths tell how at the very beginning, the sky and the earth were tightly linked with each other or that there was only a narrow crack between them. Then, by some means, they were separated from each other and remain apart through today. Widely spread in ethnic groups such as the Han, Miao, Yao, Yi, Naxi, Buyi, Dulong, and Paiwan (in Taiwan), these myths are quite varied in the reasons for the separation and the means by which this separation occurred. Some state that the earth was separated from the heavens to punish human sins or to eradicate inconveniences in human life (for instance, humans could not walk upright because there was too little space, and they could not lift the pestle to pound rice freely). Others state that the separation was caused by a deity's action, such as lifting the sky up and pressing the earth down, setting up a pillar or pillars between them, cutting off their contact with an axe, or using a broom to sweep the sky up high and the earth down low. In some myths the separation was caused by animals. For example, ants bite the sky tower and make it collapse, the ox and wolf cause the separation, or a crab is to blame. One popular myth version asserts that the sky was lifted up by a woman pounding rice using mortar and pestle. She disliked the close connection between the sky and earth and the inconvenience caused by this (it was hard for her to lift the pestle and pound the rice), so she poked the sky with her pestle. The sky felt so much pain that it rose very high to where it is today. Another well-known myth version holds that the separation was caused by a mistake made by a dung beetle. At the very beginning of the world, the Supreme Divinity in the sky asked a dung beetle to send a message to human beings on the earth that they should have one meal every three days. But the dung beetle wrongly told people that they should have three meals a day. People ate much food from then on, and thus they excreted more. The world was soon full of dirty excrement. The Supreme Divinity was shocked when he smelled a foul odor emanating from the earth. Therefore he decided to raise the sky far away from the earth. He punished the dung beetle by making it clean up the excrement on the earth forever.

Among these various myths, a prominent one in ancient Chinese writings is the myth that Zhong and Li broke off the connection between the sky and the earth. The earliest record of this myth can be found in the most ancient Chinese history book, *Shangshu*. A text from this book states that Chiyou started a revolt and brought disaster to the common people. Influenced by him, people on the earth gradually were corrupted. They began to cheat, steal, and rob. However, the Miao people did not obey Chiyou, so he designated five brutal punishments to deal with them. Then, little by little, the Miao people also became corrupt. They began to cheat each other within their own group, mistreat people from other groups, disobey their faith, and violate the oath between them and the Supreme Divinity. Many innocent people brought complaints against them to the Supreme Divinity. The Supreme Divinity thus ordered two of his subordinates, the deities Zhong and Li, to cut off the link between the sky and the earth. From then on, the Miao people could never ascend to the sky again, but at the same time, the deities could never descend to the earth.

The same story also appeared in another notable ancient historical book, *Guoyu*, but here the story was much historicized and demythologized. A king of the Chu state asked one of his officials, "According to *Shangshu*, Zhong and Li broke off the way between the sky and the earth. Why? If not so, could people then ascend to the sky?" The official rationally interpreted that this was not the case. He interpreted that in remote antiquity, human beings did not intermingle with the gods. There were five special officials to take charge of sacrificial affairs.

They clearly directed people to offer sacrifices to gods, and directed the gods in sending their blessings back to people. But at the end of Shaohao's time, human beings began to intermingle with the gods. People lost their awe for the gods, and they offered sacrifices erratically. The gods did not consistently bestow their blessings on humans, either. Famine and calamity occurred frequently. To solve this problem, Zhuanxu ordered Zhong, the Governor of the South, to administer heaven, which belonged to the gods; meanwhile Li, the Governor of Fire, was charged to control the earth, which belonged to humans. Since then, the gods and human beings do not intermingle with each other. And that was interpreted as the real meaning of "cutting off the connection between the sky and the earth."

Another Li myth version recorded in *Shanhaijing* (chapter 16) asserts that Li was one of the grandsons of Zhuanxu. It says that in the great wilderness, there was a "Sun and Moon Mountain," which was the hinge of heaven. Its main peak was Mount Wuju Tianmen (*Tianmen* means "the gate of heaven"), where the sun and the moon set. There was a deity named Xu on it. He had a human face, no arms, and two feet crossing his neck. Zhuanxu fathered Laotong, and Laotong fathered Zhong and Li. The Supreme Divinity ordered Zhong to lift up the sky, and told Li to press down the earth. After Li went down to the earth, he fathered Ye (according to some analysts, Ye is in fact Xu), who stayed at the west pole of the earth and directed the movements of the sun, the moon, and the stars.

See also Chiyou; Sky Ladder; Zhong; Zhuanxu

References and Further Reading

Birrell, Anne. *Chinese Mythology: An Introduction.* Baltimore and London: Johns Hopkins University Press, 1993, 91–95.

Bodde, Derk. "Myths of Ancient China." In *Mythologies of the Ancient World*, ed. Samuel Noah Kramer. Chicago: Quadrangle Books, 1961, 389–394.

Christie, Anthony. *Chinese Mythology.* Rev. ed. New York: Peter Bedrick Books, 1985, 58–60.

Maspero, Henri. *Myths in Shujing* (in Chinese). Trans. Feng Yuanjun. Beiping: Shangwu Yinshuguan, 1939, 49–93. Originally published as "Légends Mythologiques Dans le Chou Jing [Shu Jing]." *Journal Asiatique* 204 (1924): 1–100.

Walls, Jan, and Yvonne Walls, eds. and trans. *Classical Chinese Myths.* Hong Kong: Joint Publishing Co., 1984, 18–20.

LINGLUN

Linglun is the culture hero who invented music and many musical instruments. In written texts that have been heavily historicized, he was said to be the Governor of Music of Huang Di.

There are numerous myths explaining how music and musical instruments were invented in the remote past. Among them, Linglun and his inventions are the most famous. In ancient writings such as *Shiben (The Origin of Hereditary Families,* ca. third century BC), *Lüshi Chunqiu (Annals of Master Lü,* third century BC), and *Fengsu Tongyi (Popular Customs and Traditions,* second century CE), Linglun was often said to be the Governor of Music under Huang Di, ordered by Huang Di to establish music. So he went to the west of Daxia Marsh, and to the north of Ruanyu Mountain, and located a kind of bamboo from the Xiexi Valley. He made a pipe from it, and its sound made the base of ancient Chinese musical modes. He then made twelve bamboo pipes and blew them by imitating the phoenix's singing. And that made up the twelve *lü* (a series of standard bamboo pitch pipes used in ancient music). In this way, he invented the five notes of the ancient Chinese five-tone scale (*gong, shang, jiao, zhi,* and *yu,* equivalent to 1, 2, 3, 5, and 6 in the numbered musical notation, or *do, re, mi, so,* and *la* in the Western solfeggio), and the eight sounds made by eight musical instruments—the *xun* (an egg-shaped, holed, clay wind instrument), *sheng* (a pipe wind instrument made of gourd), drum, bamboo pipe, strings, *qing* (ancient percussion instrument made from jade or stone), bell, and *zhu* (ancient percussion instrument made from wood).

Because of his great contribution to music, Linglun is respected in later tradition as the God of Music and the divine ancestor of actors. To this day, musicians and actors are generally called Linglun or Lingren (*ren* means "human").

See also Huang Di

References and Further Reading

Liu, Chenghuai. *Myths in Ancient China* (in Chinese). Shanghai: Shanghai Wenyi Chubanshe, 1988, 588–610.

Yuan, Ke, and Zhou Ming, comps. *A Source Book of Chinese Myth Texts* (in Chinese). Chengdu: Sichuansheng Shehui Kexueyuan Chubanshe, 1985, 80–81.

NÜWA

Nüwa is the Great Mother of humans, a culture heroine, and one of the most important and powerful primeval goddesses in Chinese mythology. She repaired the broken sky and created human beings by molding them from yellow earth. In other versions she married her brother and propagated humans.

Nüwa's name appears as early as the late Warring States era in two ancient pieces of Chinese literature, *Shanhaijing* and "Tianwen" in *Chuci.* In the former record, Nüwa's gut turned into ten spirits, and each took different routes and settled into the wilderness. Her mythic action was even more vague and enigmatic in the latter recording, in which there was a question raised about her creation: "Who shaped the body of Nüwa?" This was interpreted by many scholars as "Nüwa has created humans, but who created her?" These written interpretations of the story that Nüwa's insides turned into spirits imply that Nüwa was the creator of humans.

Nüwa's mythical role and achievements are clearer in records from the Han dynasty. According to *Huainanzi*, Nüwa repaired the broken sky. The four poles supporting the sky collapsed at some point in remote antiquity. The record in *Huainanzi* does not explain why this disaster occurred. In other texts, this cosmic disorder was said to be caused by a war between the gods Gonggong and Zhuanxu. Gonggong lost in the war, and he was so angry that he butted into Mount Buzhou (literally meaning "Not Full"), one of the four pillars supporting the sky. This version of the myth explaining how the sky fell states that only

Nüwa creates humans. A folk paper-cutting made by Miao ethnic people. (From Yang Lihui, Rethinking on the Source Area of the Cult of Nüwa, *Beijing Shifan Daxue Chubanshe, 1999, 23)*

one pillar fell, not all four pillars, as stated in *Huainanzi*. Because this story conflicts with the description in *Huainanzi*, some scholars are suspicious of their logical connection and argue that they may be two separate myths.

The collapse of the sky caused great cosmic chaos. Fires raged fiercely and could not be extinguished. Water overran everywhere and did not ebb away. The violent birds and fierce beasts seized and devoured people. At this crucial moment, Nüwa melted stones of five different colors to patch the sky, and cut the legs off a huge tortoise and set them up to support the four extremities of the sky. Then she defeated the ferocious Black Dragon to save the people, and collected ashes of reeds to stop the flood. Her arduous work cleared up the chaos and put the world in order again. In some versions collected in the twentieth century, Nüwa not only mended the broken sky but also repaired the broken earth that was damaged in the same disaster. Her mythical actions serve as an etiology to explain why people today can see colorful clouds in the sky, and why the western land of China is high while the east is low: Nüwa used colorful stones to patch the sky, and she used the longer legs of the tortoise to support the west, and the shorter legs to support the east.

Another ancient writing, *Fengsu Tongyi* (*Popular Customs and Traditions*, second century CE), records another well-known myth relating to Nüwa. Nüwa created human beings by molding them from yellow earth with her hands, since the sky and the earth had been created but no humans yet existed. The work drained her strength and took a lot of time, so she took a cord and pulled it through the mud, then she lifted the cord and shook it. All of the sludge that fell down from the cord became men and women. Thus, rich and noble people were those made by Nüwa's hands, while poor and lowly people were those made by Nüwa dragging a cord through the mud.

A different explanation of the origin of humans, which appears comprehensively in *Duyizhi* (*A Treatise on Strange Beings and Things*, by Tang dynasty writer Li Rong, ca. 846–874 CE), involves Nüwa's brother-sister marriage. At the very beginning of the world, there were no other people except for Nüwa and her older brother. They lived on the mythical mountain Kunlun. They wanted to become husband and wife so that they might have children and populate the earth, but they felt shamed by this because of their blood relationship. They prayed to heaven from the top of the mountain: "If Thou wouldst send us two forth as man and wife, then make this smoke gather. If not, then make the smoke disperse." The smoke gathered immediately, so they got married. However, Nüwa still felt very shy and ashamed, so she weaved grass into a fan to cover her face (which explains why brides often hold fans during their wedding ceremonies).

Today, Nüwa's myths are still orally spread in modern China. Compared to those myths mentioned above that come from classical texts, most of her modern myths are the same type while differing in their details and explanations. For example, myths relating to Nüwa's brother-sister marriage today are widely spread with many versions in different ethnic groups, such as the Miao, Yao, Tujia, and Shui. In these versions Nüwa and her brother, often Fuxi, divined to decide whether they should marry to re-create human beings, usually after a great flood. They both agreed if certain things happened, they should get married. First, they rolled two pieces of a millstone down different sides of a mountain, and if the two pieces were recovered, they should marry. Then, they each lit a fire from different places. If the two lines of smoke joined each other instead of dispersing, they should marry. Other trials included one person taking a thread while the other took a needle, and if the needle could be threaded from a long distance, they should marry. If the broken shell of a tortoise could be restored, they should marry. The sister ran around a mountain and her brother ran after her. If he caught her, they should marry. Of course, these things all happened perfectly, so the two were married. A popular ending of this type of myth often serves to explain the origin of the Chinese *Baijiaxing* (literally "100 family names," meaning the main surnames of Chinese). After their marriage, Nüwa gave birth to a spherical piece of flesh. The couple felt so strange about this that they cut the flesh into small pieces and scattered these pieces in the woods. When the pieces touched different species of trees, they turned into human beings. Those people who touched the Li tree (plum tree) took Li as their surname, those people who touched the Tao tree (peach tree) took Tao as their surname, and so on. In central China, including Henan and Hebei provinces, this myth type often ends with an explanation of the origin of disabled people. After Nüwa and Fuxi were married, they created men and women by molding them in clay. Then they dried the wet models in the sun. While they were drying, it began to rain. So they hurriedly swept the models with a broom into a dustpan and carried them into the cave. During this process, some models lost their legs or arms and some were hurt in the eyes and ears. That is why there are both healthy people and disabled people today in this world.

Whereas these contemporary myths are similar to those in ancient recordings, there are other new types of Nüwa myths that are not found in classical literature. In one version collected in Sichuan Province in the 1980s, Nüwa was said to help Shennong, the Divine Farmer, to solve a difficulty of his. The Divine Farmer sowed grain at the beginning of his many seeding works, but it grew into chaff. He did not know what to do. Nüwa squeezed out some of her milk into the empty shell at noon. The chaff began to grow grain from then on, and it always flowers at noon. In another myth collected in the same province, Nüwa later became a member of a systematic pantheon of gods and saved her children for the second time. The supreme god Yu Di (the Jade Emperor) ordered the God of Plague to extinguish humans on the fifth day of the fifth lunar month. As the creator of humankind, Great Mother Nüwa wanted to stop him from doing this. Accepting the Bodhisattva Guanyin's suggestion, Nüwa told every family in the world to hang some mugwort wormwoods outside their doors. When the God of Plagues went down from heaven to the earth, he saw wild grass everywhere. He thought there were no people living there, so he went back without killing anyone. From then on, people hang mugwort wormwoods outside their doors on May 5 according to the lunar calendar, which forms the main custom in the Duanwu Festival.

Besides these divine deeds, Nüwa also was the first go-between, or Supreme Matchmaker. She encouraged males and females to marry each other in order to have children. Because of marriage between men and women there was no more need for Nüwa to create humans from mud. Nüwa also invented some musical instruments, such as the *shenghuang* (a reed-pipe wind instrument) and *xiao* (a vertical bamboo flute), to entertain the children she created.

Nüwa was depicted in early Chinese literature as having a lady's head and a serpent's body. In most grave paintings of the Han dynasty, she often appeared with her brother, Fuxi. Both had human heads and serpent bodies, with their tails often weaving together. She gradually became an elegant and graceful goddess in later developments.

Corresponding with her noble status in mythology, Nüwa also takes a high position in Chinese beliefs. She was respected in some ancient literature as one of the Three Divine Sovereigns. The other two sovereigns usually are Fuxi and Shennong (different names are given in different texts). In the dynasties of Song, Ming, and Qing, she was offered sacrifices by the feudal governments.

Today, Nüwa is still an important goddess in some regions. In Shexian County, Hebei Province, there is a large temple called Wa Huang Gong (The Palace of Empress Nüwa). Nüwa is said to have patched the broken sky and created humans here in this county. Every year from February 15 to March 18 in the lunar calendar, people gather here to worship Nüwa, their "great-grandmother." Most of the pilgrims come from local counties of Hebei Province; some may even come from Henan and Shanxi provinces. March 15 is said to be Nüwa's birthday. From the late afternoon of March 14 until the early morning of March 15, the pilgrims sit in the yard and inside the palace, which is locally called *zuoye* (sitting during the night). Some sing sacred songs for Nüwa. Some dance for her. By accompanying their great-grandmother during her birthday, they believe they will get Nüwa's blessing and all they hope for children, health, safety, and happiness.

In Huaiyang County, Henan Province, there is a temple complex called the Tomb of Tai Hao, popularly called Renzu Temple (Temple of Human Ancestors).

A team of women performing the folk dance danjingtiao *during the temple fair of the Renzu Temple complex, 2005. (Courtesy of Tong Yunli)*

From lunar February 2 to March 3, the monthlong Renzu Festival at the Renzu Temple complex is held to celebrate Fuxi's birthday. Although Fuxi is the main god worshiped during the festival, Nüwa is also worshiped. Some female pilgrims make embroidered shoes and bring them to Nüwa. They call the shoes Nüwa's Shoes. They sacrifice the shoes to Nüwa by displaying them in Renzu Temple or burning them with incense, paper money, or paper buildings (intended as ancestors' dwellings). Women often dance *danjingtiao* (wherein a pole is carried over one's shoulder) for their ancestors. This local folk dance is sometimes called *danhualan* ("carrying flower baskets on shoulder"). It is usually danced by women and passed on matrilineally.

There is a local legend explaining the origin of this dance and the reason why only women can dance it. After Nüwa repaired the broken sky, she mistakenly reincarnated (transmigrated) into a black dog. Her daughter missed her very much, but she did not know where her mother was. So she made two flower baskets and put them on her shoulder, and then she traveled and danced in many places to look for her mother. At last, she found her mother Nüwa and rescued her. Therefore, women imitate Nüwa's daughter and dance the danjingtiao to worship and give sacrifice to Nüwa. The one who dances well is considered to have true filial piety and thus can receive more blessings from Nüwa.

See also Buzhou, Mount; Fuxi; Gonggong; Kunlun Mountain; Pillars of the Sky; Shennong; Zhuanxu

References and Further Reading

Birrell, Anne. *Chinese Mythology: An Introduction.* Baltimore and London: Johns Hopkins University Press, 1993, 33–35, 69–72.

Bodde, Derk. "Myths of Ancient China." In *Mythologies of the Ancient World,* ed. Samuel Noah Kramer. Chicago: Quadrangle Books, 1961, 386–389.

Christie, Anthony. *Chinese Mythology.* Rev. ed. New York: Peter Bedrick Books, 1985, 87–91.

Walls, Jan, and Yvonne Walls, eds. and trans. *Classical Chinese Myths.* Hong Kong: Joint Publishing Co., 1984, 6–11.

Yang, Lihui. *The Cult of Nüwa: Myths and Beliefs in China* (in Chinese). Beijing: Zhongguo Shehui Kexue Chubanshe, 1997.

Yang, Lihui. *Rethinking on the Source Area of the Cult of Nüwa* (in Chinese). Beijing: Beijing Shifan Daxue Chubanshe, 1999.

Yuan, Ke. *Myths of Ancient China: An Anthology with Annotations* (in Chinese). Beijing: Renmin Wenxue Chubanshe, [1979] 1996, 16–49.

PANGU

In Chinese mythology, Pangu (*pan* means "coil up," and *gu* means "antiquity") is the creator of the world, the first divine human who was miraculously born within the cosmos egg. It is he who separates heaven and earth, and when he dies, his body transforms into the universe.

Though Pangu created the world, his myth did not appear in ancient Chinese literature until as late as the Three Kingdoms era. According to *Sanwu Liji* (*Historical Records of the Three Sovereign Divinities and the Five Gods,* third century CE), Pangu was born in chaos and grew up while shaping the heaven and the earth. At the very beginning, heaven and earth were in chaotic formlessness like a chicken's egg. Within this chaos Pangu was born. After 18,000 years, the egg somehow opened and unfolded. The limpid and light part of it rose and then became heaven, while the turbid and heavy part of it sank down and became the earth. Pangu lived inside heaven and earth. One day he transformed many times and became more divine than heaven and more sacred than earth. Each day heaven rose ten feet higher, the earth grew ten feet thicker, and Pangu grew ten feet taller. This situation lasted for another 18,000 years. By then heaven was extremely high, the earth was extremely deep, and Pangu was extremely tall. Then there appeared the Three Sovereigns, who were the earliest divine lords in Chinese mythical history.

In other variants orally transmitted in contemporary China, Pangu created heaven and earth by stretching himself and shattering the egg's shell into pieces while he was confined in the egg-shaped chaos. The egg white is light, so it became heaven, and the yolk is heavy, so it became earth. Some versions even relate that Pangu cut the connection between heaven and the earth with an adze and chisel. In order to keep heaven and earth from merging again after he separated them, Pangu himself served as a huge pillar by standing between them.

Another great deed of Pangu is that his body transformed into the universe after his death. This was first recorded in *Wuyun Linianji* (*A Chronicle of the Five Circles of Time*, third century CE), a book compiled during the Three Kingdoms era. When Pangu was dying, his body began to transform: his breath became the winds and

Pangu, the creator of the world and the first divine human who was miraculously born within the cosmos egg. (From Wang Qi and Wang Erbin, comps., Sancaituhui, Jinchang Baohanlou Kanben, *1609. Preserved in the Library of Literature Institute, Chinese Academy of Social Sciences)*

clouds, his voice became the thunder, his left eye became the sun, his right eye became the moon, his four limbs and trunk became the four extremes of the earth and the Five Mountains, his blood became the rivers, his veins became the earth's arteries, his flesh became fields and soil, his hair and beard became the stars, his skin and body hair became plants, his teeth and bones became various metals and rocks, his semen and marrow became pearls and jade, his sweat became the rain and the dew, and the various insects on his body reacted to the wind and turned into human beings.

The Pangu myth is widespread. Besides being known to Han people, his myth is also well-known to the Miao, Yao, Lisu, Gelao, Bai, Buyi, Zhuang, and many other ethnic groups. Today people continue to tell the Pangu myth, and its details vary. In some versions Pangu's two main deeds are combined and systematized, and the stories are much more elaborate than those recorded in ancient literature. Moreover, many myths tell about other divine actions of Pangu. One popular version associates Pangu with the brother-sister marriage myth type. Pangu and his sister survived a great flood that destroyed all other people, so they married each other in order to re create human beings. They subsequently bore a lot of children and then were worshiped as parents of human beings.

A myth told by people in Henan Province in central China describes Pangu as the protector of humankind and the manager of the world. This myth states that the world was still in dimness after Pangu created humans. Pangu was worried about it and had been thinking of a solution for a long time. One day he was attracted to a gleam of light from the east. Along the light beam he found two beautiful sisters. One had fair skin, and the other appeared to glow. The fair one was the elder; her name was Moon, and her sister's name was Sun. Their clothes were made of brilliant golden and silver silk, which lit the whole place where they stayed. Pangu invited them to light the world by standing on the top of a high mountain. The two sisters agreed. Then Pangu suggested to them that they each appear in turn by daytime and nighttime. Sun was afraid of the darkness and did not go out during the night. She also was ashamed to show herself in front of people during the daytime, so her elder sister, Moon, gave her a handful of golden needles. She told Sun that with the needles she could prick the eyes of those who dared to stare at her. From then on, the two sisters gave light to the world day and night.

In another myth spread throughout Gansu Province in northwestern China, Pangu is associated with the mythical cause of earthquakes. In order to separate heaven and earth, Pangu asked a god to lift heaven and tried to find another spirit to hold up the earth. Since the earth was very heavy, Pangu molded an ox with clay and his own saliva. He blew on the clay ox and it came alive. Then this divine ox was made to carry the earth. Additionally, Pangu molded a clay rooster as a supervisor to keep the ox from falling asleep so as to keep the earth from sinking. After thousands of years of supporting the earth on its back, the ox felt so tired that it wished to take a nap. But the rooster insisted on fulfilling Pangu's instruction and did not allow it. The ox was so annoyed that it shook its head and body three times. As a result, the earth on the back of the ox shook as well. That is the origin of earthquakes.

Pangu's appearance is first depicted in *Wuyun Linianji*. He is described as having a dragon's head and a serpent's trunk. In some versions collected today, Pangu is described as a giant with a cat's head, a serpent's trunk, and a tiger's paw. In these myths his extraordinary figure corresponds to his super power. However, in portraits and temple statues, Pangu usually appears as a manlike giant with a horn. A myth told by people in Henan Province gives an explanation for the horn on Pangu's head. In Pangu's time, all people were horned. They used the horn as a weapon in hunting. Moreover, the horn had the very important function of providing a signal at one's time of death. When a person was dying, his horn would get soft and loose. Usually people worked very hard at hunting, but a person who felt his horn become soft and loose would cease working to wait for death. During a later period, there were so many people whose horns got soft and loose that few people were working. This annoyed the God of Heaven. He sent divine troops and took back the horn of humankind. From then on, ordinary people had no horns, and they became much more industrious than ever before. However, the divine Pangu kept his own horn and mythical powers.

As creator of the universe, Pangu receives a high status in Chinese beliefs. Several temples were built for him in Henan, Guangdong, Jiangxi, and Zhejiang provinces, and in the Guangxi Zhuang Autonomous Region. Many of them were founded before Tang or Song times. In these regions, Pangu continues to be worshiped by people today. For instance, in the Tongbai Mountains region of Henan Province, there is a large Pangu temple on the top of Mount Pangu, which is said to be the former residence of Pangu. During special occasions and ordinary ones, people of this vicinity often go to the temple to worship Pangu, the great god. Every March 3 of the lunar calendar there is a huge temple fair. Pilgrims from rural areas in Henan, Shanxi, Shaanxi, Hebei, Hubei, Anhui, and Shandong

The Pangu temple on Mount Pangu in the Tongbai Mountains region of Henan Province, 2004. (Courtesy of Liu Junqi)

provinces gather here to pay religious homage and offer sacrifices to the god Pangu. These activities actually will last seven or eight days, from March 1 to March 7 or 8. It is said that the number of pilgrims may amount to nearly 100,000. During the fair, besides visiting the temple, people will perform dramas for Pangu for several days and nights. Many people believe that every time dramas are performed, it will rain. They explain that this is because Pangu wants to wash off the garbage many people leave at the fair. This explanation can be conjoined with another of Pangu's mythical powers that people of this vicinity believe in, that Pangu has a special power to create rain three times each year. According to popular Chinese belief, it is only the supreme god, the Jade Emperor, who has the right to send rain. Those gods who create rain without the Jade Emperor's permission will receive a severe penalty. However, some gods who take charge in affairs that are vital to human beings, or who have made great contributions to gods or humankind, will be given special permission by the Supreme God to create rain several times a year. By praying to these gods in times of drought, people may receive rain. Pangu himself belongs to this special group of gods for his great deeds. That is why drought seldom occurs in the Tongbai Mountains region where Pangu is worshiped. Similar beliefs can also be seen in Yudu County, Jiangxi Province. It is said that Yudu used to suffer from heavy droughts each year. However, since a Pangu temple was built, this area has always received favorable weather.

Based on the fact that the Pangu myth was not recorded in literature until as late as the Three Kingdoms era, some Chinese scholars believe that the Pangu myth migrated from non-Han Chinese culture. One of the hypotheses links the Pangu myth to the Panhu myth, the ancestral myth of the Miao, Yao, She, and Li ethnic groups in southern China. Panhu was a dog of Di Ku, a mythical Chinese sovereign. When Di Ku got into trouble during an invasion, it was Panhu that brought the enemy general's head to Di Ku and thus helped him to win the war. As a reward that had been previously promised by its imperial master, Panhu received the emperor's daughter as his wife. The dog then carried the princess to mountains in southern China, where they created children who became the ancestors of the Miao, Yao, She, and Li ethnic groups. However, except for the phonetic similarity between "Pangu" and "Panhu," the two types of myths are actually quite different in theme. Another important assumption supposes that the Pangu myth originated in India. In the *Rig Veda* and *Aitareya Upanishad*, as well as several other texts of the Sutra, stories similar to Pangu's two great deeds are recorded. Nevertheless, many Chinese scholars insist that the Pangu myth is of Han Chinese origin. A deity recorded in two texts in *Shanhaijing* is thought to be the prototype of the Pangu figure. This deity is called Zhulong ("Torch Dragon") or Zhuyin ("Torch Shadow"). He was a god with a human face and a serpent's trunk, and his body was a thousand miles in length. When his eyes opened there was daylight, and when they closed it became night; his hard breath made winter and his hot exhalation made summer. His appearance and abilities are almost the same as Pangu's. Hence, it is argued that Pangu possibly evolved from this god. *Shanhaijing* was compiled much earlier than the time when the Panhu myth was first recorded, and also earlier than the time when Indian tradition had an impact on Chinese culture. Some scholars have suggested that instead of looking for the non-Han Chinese origin of the Pangu myth, the myth actually could be traced to its pure Han Chinese root. Moreover, modern Chinese mythologists also have found that the two fundamental themes contained in the Pangu myth, the theme of the universe starting from an egg-shaped chaos and the theme of a dying deity's body transforming into the universe, correspond with cardinal concepts in ancient Chinese mythology and cosmology. These ideas, such as the notion that the universe started from chaos and that there are correspondences between humans and the universe, can be found as early as the Zhou dynasty. This is thought to provide additional support for Pangu's Han Chinese origin.

See also Di Ku; Nüwa; Zhulong

References and Further Reading

Birrell, Anne. *Chinese Mythology: An Introduction.* Baltimore and London: Johns Hopkins University Press, 1993, 26–33, 118–120, 190–191.

Bodde, Derk. "Myths of Ancient China." In *Mythologies of the Ancient World,* ed. Samuel Noah Kramer. Chicago: Quadrangle Books, 1961, 382–386.

Lü, Simian. "A Study of Pangu" (in Chinese). In *Critiques of Ancient History.* Vol. 7, book 2, eds. Lü Simian and Tong Shuye. Shanghai: Kaiming Shuju, 1941, 14–20.

Ma, Huixin, ed. *The Deity of Pangu* (in Chinese). Shanghai: Shanghai Wenyi Chubanshe, 1993.

Walls, Jan, and Yvonne Walls, eds. and trans. *Classical Chinese Myths.* Hong Kong: Joint Publishing Co., 1984, 1–3.

Yuan, Ke. *Myths of Ancient China: An Anthology with Annotations* (in Chinese). Beijing: Renmin Wenxue Chubanshe, [1979] 1996, 69–76.

PILLARS OF THE SKY

The pillars of the sky are huge pillars that support the sky, keeping it from collapsing or swinging into the earth. They are sometimes used to separate the sky from the earth.

The motif of "supporting the sky" is worldwide. In China, the motif of sky pillars is also widely spread in many myths. It can be found in Han, Naxi, Yi, Miao, Yao, Bai, Luoba, and other ethnic groups. The number of the sky pillars may be different in various stories. It may be four, five, eight, or sometimes twelve. The main functions of the sky pillars are to support the sky so that it doesn't fall down, to keep it from swinging out of place, and to separate the heaven from the earth. The pillars may be huge mountains, trees, stone pillars, turtle feet, tiger bones, a deity's body or human's body, a deity's corpse, or pillars made of gold and silver, jade, pearl, iron, and the like.

Corresponding with pillars of the sky, there are also pillars of the earth, which function to protect the earth from collapsing or swinging. They sometimes appear together with the sky pillars in some myths.

One of the earliest recordings about the sky pillars appears in "Tianwen," the written treasure of Chinese mythology. In it, the distinguished poet Qu Yuan expressed his doubt about the sky pillar myth: "Where are the eight sky pillars? Why is there a gap in the southeast?" "Why did the earth tilt toward the southeast during the rage of Kanghui [another name for Gonggong]?" This illustrates that myths about eight sky pillars, and one of them being ruined by the deity Gonggong, were current in the late Warring States era.

During the Han dynasty and thereafter, myths about sky pillars were very detailed. One known myth states that in remote antiquity, the four poles of the sky collapsed, and this caused great cosmic chaos. Fires raged fiercely and could not be put out. Rivers overran their banks and did not decline. Violent birds and fierce beasts seized and devoured people. At this moment, the goddess Nüwa melted stones of five different colors to patch the sky, and she cut the legs off a huge tortoise and set them up to support the four extremities of the sky. Then she defeated the ferocious Black Dragon to save the people and collected the ashes of reeds to stop the flood. Her arduous work cleared up the chaos and put the world in order again.

Another popular myth holds that one of the sky pillars was Mount Buzhou, but it was damaged by the water god Gonggong in his contest with another deity, Zhuanxu (or Zhurong, Di Ku, or Shengnong; various names are given in different versions), to be the Supreme Sovereign.

These two myths are sometimes associated with each other, but with considerable differences. According to *Lunheng* (*Critical Essays*, written by Wang Chong, ca. 27–100 CE) and "Bu *Shiji* Sanhuang Benji" ("Biographies of the Three Divine Sovereigns: A Supplement to the *Historical Records*," Tang dynasty), the Gonggong story is followed by that of Nüwa. The recording in "Bu *Shiji* Sanhuang Benji" combined various myth versions and tried to form a coherent ancient history, thus: toward the end of Nüwa's reign, Gonggong fought with Zhurong, the God of Fire, but failed. He was so angry that he struck his head against Mount Buzhou and caused this sky pillar to collapse, which snapped the cords holding up the earth. To repair this damage, Nüwa melted stones of five different colors to mend the sky, and cut the legs off a huge tortoise and set them up to support the four corners of the sky (somehow she reestablished four sky columns instead of one). Then she collected ashes of reeds to stop the flood. Through her effort, Nüwa cleared up the chaos and put the world in order again. However, in texts from *Liezi* (which was said to have been written in the Warring States era but probably was gathered from some original texts and rewritten in the Jin dynasty, 265–420 CE) and *Bowuzhi* (*A Treatise on Research into Nature*, Jin dynasty), the chronological order of these two stories is reversed. That is, Nüwa repaired the broken sky first and supported it with four sky columns, then later Gonggong ruined one of the columns and destroyed the normal established order. Gonggong's damage often served as an etiological myth about the current Chinese topography. Since then, the sky tilts toward the northwest, and that is why the sun, moon, and stars move in that direction. Earth sinks toward the southeast, and that is why the rivers of China flow toward the ocean in the east. The loose connection between these two stories suggests that they might have been independent of each other in early stages of the myths and were loosely combined later.

The sky pillars myths are quite rich among other ethnic groups. A myth collected in the 1990s from the Yi people in Xinping County, Yunnan Province, says that at the very beginning, the sky had not been separated from the earth, and the gods lived together with humans. Because the living space was limited, the gods and humans worked together and made four gold pillars. They used the pillars to sever the sky from the earth, and then the gods lived on high in heaven, and humans lived below on earth. And this formed the basic order of the universe.

A famed Miao creation epic, "Ancient Songs of Miao People" ("Miaozu Guge"), vividly describes in detail the reason for setting up the twelve pillars of sky and earth, the process of making and fixing them, the divine persons who made them, and the places where they are set. This epic is usually sung by two or more singers (one asks questions, and the others answer) on the occasions of traditional festivals and special ceremonies such as weddings or funerals. One version of the epic, which was collected from Guizhou Province and was translated from the Miao language into Chinese and published in the 1990s, goes,

In remote antiquity, what kind of pillar supported the sky?
What kind of pillar supported the earth
So that the sky and the earth would not collapse?
In remote antiquity, the sky was supported by the Wubei Tree,
And the earth was supported by the Wormwood Tree,
So that the sky became round,

And it would not collapse. . . .
A man named Jinsong'ang,
He was very clever.
He had nine arms and nine hands,
Nine legs and nine knees.
He could ascend up to heaven,
And he could descend down to the earth.
He ascended up to the sky and jostled it,
He jostled the outside and inside of the sky,
He jostled the east and the west of the sky,
He looked carefully at the sky,
And he looked carefully at the earth,
The sky was still unstable;
The earth was still unstable. . . .

Fufang was smart,
Fufang had great strength,
He pulled out the Wubei Tree,
He pulled out the Wormwood Tree.
He used the silver pillars to support the sky,
And the gold pillars to support the earth.
The sky then became stable,
The earth then became stable. . . .
The steelyard was smart,
It was the go-between.
It borrowed silver from Grandfather Bao,
It borrowed ten thousand *ba* [one ba equals the amount held in one palm] of
    silver,
To make a silver pillar,
A silver pillar to support the sky.
It borrowed millions of *liang* [one liang equals 0.05 kilogram] of gold,
To make a gold pillar,
A gold pillar to support the sky. . . .
There were Grandpa Bao and Grandpa Xiong,
There were Grandpa Qi and Grandpa Dang,
The four grandpas,
The four to make the pillars. . . .
The first hit they hammered like a bird flying,
The second hit they hammered like the snow flying in the air,
The hammer hit swiftly like a whirlwind.
The third hit caused the level ground to sink,
The level ground sank into a deep hollow. . . .

They used up the ten thousand ba of silver,
They had been working for twelve days and nights,
And they made twelve pillars. . . .
Fufang was smart,
Fufang set up the pillars.
The pillars supported the sky straightly,
The pillars supported the earth straightly. . . .
The first pillar was set up at Taigong,
The second pillar was set up at Fangxi,
The third pillar was set up at Wengyang,
The fourth pillar was set up at Deyen,
The fifth pillar was set up at Xennin,
The sixth pillar was set up at Paijiu,
The seventh pillar was set up at Paile,
The eighth pillar was set up at the sea.
Then there were four pillars left,
They were all cut off two meters,
Then one was used to support the east,
The second one was used to support the west,
The third one was used to support the left,
And the fourth one was used to support the right.
When the twelve pillars were all set up,
The sky became round,
The earth became stable. . . .

Another version of this epic mentions the change of the sky columns. After the twelve pillars were erected, a drought arrived on the earth. Because the pillars were all the same height, the rain could not fall down. To solve the problem, the four grandfathers cut about one meter (about 3.3 feet) off the gold pillars in the east; meanwhile, they extended the pillars in the west by one half of a meter. In this way, the sky tilted toward the east and the rain began to fall onto the earth, and the land was not dry anymore.

See also Buzhou, Mount; Cords of the Earth; Gonggong; Kunlun Mountain; Nüwa; Zhuanxu; Zhurong

References and Further Reading

Birrell, Anne. *Chinese Mythology: An Introduction.* Baltimore and London: Johns Hopkins University Press, 1993, 69–72.

Christie, Anthony. *Chinese Mythology.* Rev. ed. New York: Peter Bedrick Books, 1985, 57–68.

Liu, Chenghuai. *Myths in Ancient China* (in Chinese). Shanghai: Shanghai Wenyi Chubanshe, 1988, 779–780.

Yan, Bao, comp. and trans. *Ancient Songs of Miao People* (with Miao pronunciation and translation in Chinese). Guiyang: Guizhou Minzu Chubanshe, 1993, 299–321.

QI

The founder of the Shang people and the son of Di Ku, Qi was miraculously born by Jiandi after she ingested a swallow's egg and became pregnant.

The most well-known Qi myth is perhaps his birth story. Like most heroes and gods in Chinese mythology, Qi's birth was miraculous. According to a text in *Shiji*, Qi's mother was Jiandi, who was a daughter of the Yousong clan and the second concubine of Di Ku. One day Jiandi went out to take a bath with Di Ku and another person and she saw a swallow dropping an egg. She picked it up and swallowed it. Then she inexplicably became pregnant and later gave birth to Qi. When Qi grew up, he helped Yu restrain the great flood. As a reward, he was bestowed the fief of Shang by the sage king Shun. Later he and his state became very powerful and prosperous.

Another version recorded in *Shiyiji* (chapter 2) is more mystical. It says that at the beginning of the Shang dynasty, a divine woman named Jiandi traveled in the field. She found a black bird dropping its only egg. There were two colorful words written on it, "eight hundred." Jiandi picked it up, covered it with a red silk belt, and protected it under a jade basket. During that night, she dreamed that a mother goddess told her, "You possess this egg, and thus you will give birth to a great son. He will inherit the emblem of Metal" (according to the theory of five elements, the Shang dynasty belongs to metal, *jin*). Jiandi then held the egg to her bosom. After one year, she became pregnant. After fourteen more months, she gave birth to Qi, the founder of the Shang dynasty. As the goddess predicted, the Shang dynasty lasted for 800 years (in fact, historically, the Shang dynasty lasted for approximately 600 years).

Other versions say that Qi was so distinctive and extraordinary, like Yu and Houji, that when he was born, he came out from his mother's back, or breast, instead of her belly.

See also Di Ku; Houji; Jiandi; Shun; Yu

References and Further Reading

Birrell, Anne. *Chinese Mythology: An Introduction.* Baltimore and London: Johns Hopkins University Press, 1993, 113–118.

Bonnefoy, Yves, comp. *Asian Mythologies.* Translated under the direction of Wendy Doniger. Chicago and London: University of Chicago Press, 1993, 242. Originally published as *Dictionnaire des mythologies et des religions des sociétés traditionnelles et du monde antique.* Paris: Flammarion, 1981.

Liu, Chenghuai. *Myths in Ancient China* (in Chinese). Shanghai: Shanghai Wenyi Chubanshe, 1988, 510–520.

SHAOHAO

One of the most notable supreme gods in Chinese mythology, Shaohao founded his capital in the east, but later was known as the god who reigns over the west and controls the season of autumn. He is also known as Jintianshi (literally meaning "Metal Sky"), Zhi, Zhuxuan, and Baidi ("White God"; according to the theory of five elements and five colors, the west belongs to metal, and its color is white).

Like most gods in Chinese mythology, Shaohao experienced a miraculous birth, which functions as testimony to his extraordinary and supernatural qualities. One version of his birth story states that during the time of Huang Di, a big star shining like a rainbow fell down to the Hua Islet. A divine lady named Nüjie caught it in her dream. Then she got pregnant and later gave birth to Shaohao (Zhuxuan). Another version maintains that he was the son of *Jin Xing* (the planet Venus) and a beautiful divine lady named Huang'e. Appearing in the Jin dynasty book *Shiyiji (Researches into Lost Records)*, the story states that Shaohao's mother, Huang'e (literally meaning a beautiful divine woman), lived in a jade palace and wove at night. Sometimes, during the day, she traveled far away by a raft to the boundless reach of Qiongsang, which, in that story, was located on the shore of the west sea. There was a mulberry tree on the shore. It was 8,000 feet in height, and it produced fruit every 10,000 years. If one ate its fruit, one was able to live even longer than heaven. At that time, there was a handsome child-god named "the Son of White God" (here Shaohao became the grandson of White God instead of being the White God himself) who actually was the spirit of Jin Xing (the planet Venus) descended at Qiongsang. He feasted and played with Huang'e. They floated on the sea; meanwhile they played fantastic music and sang songs in response to each other. To discern the wind direction, they set up a mast in the front of their raft, tied thatched grass to the mast as a flag, and carved a jade cuckoo bird on the top of the mast, because the cuckoo bird knew the four seasons. What they did originated the custom of *xiangfeng* (whereby people carve a wooden or copper bird and then put it on the top of their roofs or masts to discern the wind direction). Later Huang'e gave birth to Shaohao. He was also named Qiongsangshi or Jintianshi (*shi* here is a respectful title for gods and nobles). Since five colorful phoenixes came to his yard when he was born, he was also called Fengniaoshi (meaning "Phoenix Bird").

Though the text from *Shiyiji* asserts that Shaohao was born in the west, some ancient writings show that he perhaps originated in the east. An account recorded in *Shizi* (which was said to have been written during the Warring States era but now is known only in later quotations) holds that Shaohao founded his state at Qiongsang. The five colors of the sun's light shone and enlightened that place. Some Chinese scholars deduced that Qiongsang should be a place close to Qufu, which now belongs to modern Shandong Province, in eastern China (Yuan 1996, 170; Rao 1996, 67). Shaohao Mausoleum was built in Qufu city (according to local legend, during the Song dynasty) and remains there today, just east of Qufu city. Another text in *Shanhaijing* (chapter 14) not only links Shaohao with the east but connects him to Zhuanxu, one of the supreme gods in ancient times. Beyond the east sea was a huge valley. That was the state of Shaohao, where Shaohao nursed Zhuanxu. Some musical instruments once played by young Zhuanxu and later abandoned could be found there.

As for Shaohao's state, perhaps the most notable and striking character of it is that he named all of his officials by using the names of birds. A text recorded in *Zuozhuan* (*Chronicle of Zuo*, Duke Zhao, 17th Year) described that when Shaohao founded his state, phoenixes appeared. He thus decided to give his subordinates bird names. For example, Fengniaoshi (meaning "Phoenix Bird") took charge of the calendar, Xuanniaoshi ("Swallow") took charge of the equinoxes, Bozhaoshi ("Butcherbird") took charge of the summer and winter solstices, Qingniaoshi ("Green Bird") took charge of the beginnings of spring and summer, and Danniaoshi ("Red Bird") took charge of the beginnings of autumn and winter. Besides these five officials, Shaohao named his officers "five Jiu" (five kinds of doves) to preside over assembling people, while the "five Zhi" (five kinds of pheasants) would preside over the handicraft industry and "nine Hu birds" would preside over agriculture. Yuan Ke argues that this story has been heavily historicized. He writes that the Shaohao story is in fact a myth and that Shaohao was a divine vulture bird who founded a bird kingdom beyond the east sea, while all his officials were actually assumed by types of birds (Yuan 1996, 174–175).

However, in later tradition, Shaohao became known as a supreme god who reigned over the west and controlled the season of autumn. According to a text in *Shanhaijing* (chapter 2), the god Shaohao, or White God, lived on a western mountain named Changliu ("Long Flow"). All the beasts there had spotted tails, and all the birds had spotted heads. The mountain was rich in jade with veins running through it. There Shaohao's function was to observe the condition of the sunset. Another text from *Huainanzi* (chapter 3) also sets Shaohao in the west and, furthermore, puts him alongside four divine emperors in an orderly pantheon distributed in five directions (east, south, west, north, and center) and five elements (wood, fire, metal, water, and earth). It states,

The East belongs to Wood. Its god is Taihao. His subordinate is Goumang. Both of them hold the compasses and control the season of spring. The South belongs to Fire. Its god is Yan Di. His subordinate is Zhuming. Both of them hold the beams of steelyards and control the season of summer. The Center belongs to Earth. Its god is Huang Di. His subordinate is Houtu. Both of them hold the ropes and control the four directions. The West belongs to Metal. Its god is Shaohao. His subordinate is Rushou. Both of them hold the carpenter's squares and control the season of autumn. The North belongs to Water. Its god is Zhuanxu. His subordinate is Xuanming. Both of them hold the sliding weights of steelyards and control the season of winter.

Some scholars believe that with the branches of the Shaohao clan migrating from east to west, the Shaohao myth was thus transmitted, diffused, and inevitably changed in the west. For this reason, Shaohao was transformed from a god who founded his bird kingdom in the east into a god who reigned over the west and autumn (Yuan 1996, 177; Yuan 1993, 162; Rao 1996, 67–68).

Shaohao has some famous relatives and subordinates. Besides Zhuanxu, mentioned above, who is Shaohao's nephew, there are also Rushou, Qiongqi, and Ban. Rushou is Shaohao's minor deity who assisted Shaohao in ruling the west and autumn. A legend recorded in *Guoyu* depicted Rushou as a deity with a human face, tiger's paws, and white fur, holding a broad axe. He followed the Supreme Divinity's order and predicted the extinction of the Guo state. In some versions, the name "Rushou" refers to a title for the official of metal (Jinzheng) instead of a certain deity. A text from *Zuozhuan* (Duke Zhao, 29th Year) states that Shaohao had four younger brothers (other versions say four sons), named Zhong, Gai, Xiu, and Xi. They understood the principles of metal, wood, and water. So Zhong was appointed as Goumang (Official of Wood), Gai was Rushou (Official of Metal), and Xiu and Xi were Xuanming (Official of Water). They all did their best to do their duty, so they were helpful in the orderly administration of Qiongsang.

Qiongqi is Shaohao's unintelligent son. He is depicted in some ancient writings as an animal shaped like a winged tiger (some versions say a dog or ox). He was able to fly and understand human language. He ate people. He was so evil that if he found two people fighting with each other, he would devour the righteous one; if he heard of someone faithful and loyal, he would bite the person's nose; if he heard of someone disobedient and evil, he would kill beasts to present to him. So he was taken as one of the Four Evils (Si Xiong) and later was exiled by the sage king Shun.

Unlike Qiongqi, another son of Shaohao, Ban, has more virtuous achievements. He is said to have invented the bow and arrow.

See also Goumang; Huang Di; Shun; Taihao; Zhuanxu
References and Further Reading
Birrell, Anne. *Chinese Mythology: An Introduction.* Baltimore and London: Johns Hopkins University Press, 1993, 207–209, 267–268.
Rao, Zongyi. "Legends about the Custom of Worshipping Birds in Ancient Eastern China: With Attention to Taihao and Shaohao" (in Chinese). In *Proceedings of the Conference on Chinese Myth and Legend.* Vol. 1, eds. Li Yiyuan and Wang Qiugui. Taibei: Center for Chinese Studies Research, 1996, 61–75.
Yuan, Ke. *Dragons and Dynasties: An Introduction to Chinese Mythology.* Selected and translated by Kim Echlin and Nie Zhixiong. New York: Penguin Books, 1993, 32–33. First published by Foreign Languages Press, Beijing, 1991–1993.
Yuan, Ke. *Myths of Ancient China: An Anthology with Annotations* (in Chinese). Beijing: Renmin Wenxue Chubanshe, [1979] 1996, 169–178.
Yuan, Ke. *A Survey of Chinese Mythology* (in Chinese). Chengdu: Bashu Shushe, 1993, 158–164.

SHENNONG

A popular culture hero who started agriculture, Chinese medicine, the market, the Zhaji Sacrificial Rite, and also invented many farm tools and musical instruments, Shennong is one of the Three Divine Sovereigns along with Fuxi and Huang Di (names may differ in different texts; some groups include the goddess Nüwa). In his name, *shen* means "divine" or "sacred," and *nong* means "farmer." Therefore, he can be called the Divine Farmer.

At the end of the Warring States era, Shennong was confused with another renowned god, Yan Di. An example of this confusion can be found in *Shiben* (*The Origin of Hereditary Families,* ca. third century BC). The two gods were mixed together to make a new prominent god named Yan Di Shennongshi (*shi* here is a respectful form of address for gods). However, this combination is comparatively loose, and it influences the Shennong myth less than it does the Yan Di myth. Since the Warring States period, Shennong and Yan Di have continued to appear separately quite often, and Shennong still usually functions as a farmer god (though he sometimes is nominally exhibited as Yan Di Shennongshi), and the content of his myths predominantly refers to the invention of agriculture and Chinese medicine. During the long developing process of his myth, he is rarely depicted as having absorbed Yan Di's main achievements, turning into a god who reigns over the south and fights with Huang Di. By contrast, Yan Di gradually takes Shennong's basic mythological functions as his own. Thus Yan Di shows up in later tradition not only as the God of the South and Spring, the half brother of Huang Di who fought against Huang Di at Banquan, but also as the God of Agriculture and Medicine by the title Yan Di Shennongshi.

As is widely known, China is a large agricultural country. It boasts a long history of agriculture and a rich farming culture. For instance, China has several gods of agriculture, such as Houji, Houtu, Shennong, and Shujun. Among them, Shennong is the most well-known.

Shennong's name and merit can be easily found in some ancient writings from the Spring and Autumn period, such as *Zhuangzi, Hanfeizi,* and *Guanzi* (which was said to have been written by a prominent politician, Guan Zhong, d. 645 BC, and later compiled by a Han scholar, Liu Xiang, ca. 77 BC–6 BC). From then on, he received much fame and respect. Numerous myths, spreading both in various written accounts and in oral tradition, describe his miraculous birth, his unique features, and his great contributions to humans. In these myths, Shennong is often portrayed as having the head of a dragon or sometimes the head of an ox. Like most gods in Chinese mythology, Shennong also is the subject of miraculous birth stories. One myth states that Shennong's mother was Shaodian's wife (here we can find elements of the Yan Di myth mixed together with the Shennong myth). Her name was Andeng (or Nüdeng in other versions). One day, when she played in Huayang, a divine dragon copulated with her at the place of Changyang. She became pregnant and later gave birth to Shennong. Shennong had a human's face and a dragon's head. He liked to farm very much, so he was called the Divine Farmer. Some versions say that when Shennong was born, nine connecting wells were suddenly and unexpectedly excavated. If one drew water from one of them, the water in the other eight wells would ripple. Others say that when Shennong was three days old he could talk; after five days he could walk; seven days later he had fully grown teeth; and after three years, he knew everything about sowing and reaping.

The greatest mythical achievements Shennong made are devoted to agriculture. He is said to have first taught people to sow grain, and for this reason he was respectfully addressed as the Divine Farmer. One version of his myth appearing in *Guanzi* (chapter 64) holds that Shennong taught people to sow and to grow grain. By this way he greatly benefited humans throughout the world. Another version in the same book (chapter 84) maintains that Shennong planted grain to the south of Mount Qi. From then on, people around the world began to understand the uses of grain and used grain for subsistence. The whole world was changed by his contribution. According to a text from *Huainanzi* (chapter 19), in prehistoric times people ate plants and drank from rivers. They gathered fruit from trees and ate wasps and worms as their meat. They suffered from sickness, poison, and pain. Hence Shennong taught people to sow the five grains (different names are given in

Shennong. Funeral stone carving of the Eastern Han dynasty, Wuliang Shrine, Jiaxiang County, Shandong Province. The inscription reads, "Shennongshi taught people to cultivate according to the land's quality and to sow grains in order to relieve the hungry people." (Feng Yunpeng and Feng Yunyuan, Research on Stone Carving, *1821)*

different explanations; this sometimes refers to rice, two kinds of millet, wheat, and beans). He also taught people to examine the land and to cultivate it according to the land's quality (dry or wet, fertile or barren, high or low, etc.). Another story recorded in *Xinyu* (*New Discourse*, written in the early Han dynasty) states that in ancient times people took flesh and blood as their food and drink, and raw animal fur as their cloth. When it came to Shennong's time, things began to change. Shennong felt that it was very hard for humans to live on reptiles and beasts. So he went out to look for better food. He tasted the fruits of hundreds of plants and grasses and recognized their sour or bitter flavors. After this process, he then taught people to take the five grains as their food.

Shennong's great contributions to agriculture are also shown in his many inventions related to farming. For example, he invented some important farm tools such as the axe, hoe, and *leisi*, a plowlike farm tool used in ancient China. He cut wood to make the plowshare, and he bent a piece of wood to make the handle of the plow. By using these tools, he taught people to open wastelands and hoe weeds. He also taught people to excavate wells and irrigate land. He invented the age-old Chinese way of storing grain seeds: he dipped the seeds in boiled horse urine to protect the seeds against being eaten by worms. He invented the calendar and *jieqi*. (According to the Chinese lunar calendar, the solar year can be divided into twenty-four seasonal divisions, referred to as *jieqi*, which indicate the change of climate and timing for agricultural activities. They are of great significance to agriculture and are still widely used in rural areas in China.)

Another of Shennong's main contributions, which clearly derives from his agricultural achievements, is that he created Chinese medicine. He tasted, or as it is variously said, he thrashed with a reddish-brown whip hundreds of herbs in order to figure out their medicinal characteristics and functions. Recordings about this are quite abundant in ancient accounts. The text cited above from *Huainanzi* further holds that Shennong tasted the flavors of hundreds of herbs and the sweetness or bitterness of the waters from rivers and wells. Then he told people what they should eat and drink, and what they should avoid. This work was sometimes dangerous. He once consumed seventy poisonous plants in one day. According to a text from *Soushenji* (*In Search of the Supernatural*, written by Gan Bao, ca. 300 CE, chapter 1), Shennong thrashed hundreds of herbs with a reddish-brown whip. Then he completely knew their flavors and properties of coldness, warmness, mildness, and toxicity. Some versions say that Shennong tasted the flavors of herbs and plants to find out their medicinal qualities, and then used them to cure diseases. Additionally, he wrote an important ancient medical book, *Shennong Bencao Jing* (*Classic of Shennong's Materia Medica*, which was attributed to Shennong but was probably written anonymously around the third century BC; it was one of the earliest Chinese medical books). Some sources even suggest the sites where Shennong tasted or thrashed the herbs. A text in *Shuyiji* (*A Record of Accounts of Marvels*, written by Ren Fang, 460?–508? CE, chapter 2) states that the tripod caldron that Shennong used to taste medicine could be found on the Shenfugang (literally meaning the "Sacred Cauldron Hill") of Taiyuan. On Mount Chengyang, there is a place where Shennong purportedly whipped the herbs. The spot came to be known as "Shennong Plain," and the mountain was sometimes called "Mount Medicinal Herb." A Taoist temple named Ziyang was built on it. For years it was popularly said that Shennong distinguished the medicinal herbs there. Another version even depicts Shennong not only as the primogenitor of Chinese traditional medicine but as a general practitioner of medicine as well. This version maintains that Shennong was the first human to carefully study the pulse conditions, discern the different characteristics of medicines, use the therapies of acupuncture and moxibustion, and write a medical book.

Besides these mythical achievements in agriculture and medicine, Shennong also gained fame for inventing many other cultural items. For example, he made the pestle, mortar, bowl, pan, pot, rice steamer, well, and kitchen range. People could then use these innovations to steep and steam rice.

Shennong is also credited with inventing the Zhaji Sacrificial Rite (later it was called the Laji Rite), which was held at the end of each year in order to thank all the gods for enabling the harvest and to pray for another good harvest in the coming year.

In another development, Shennong asked one of his subordinates to draw pictures of water routes in order to prevent rivers from blocking up. He began to measure lands and seas to set up hypsography (the study of elevation and topography). He also taught people to plant mulberry and hemp trees. People could then make clothes from cloth and silk. He made the bow and arrow, and the whole world was shocked by them. Additionally, Shennong invented some of the most important ancient Chinese musical instruments, such as *qin* (a seven-stringed plucked instrument) and *se* (a twenty-five-stringed plucked instrument). He made them to help people to be calm, to keep their childlike innocence instead of being evil. He also composed a piece of music named "Fuchi" or "Xiamou." He created the sixty-four diagrams for divination. He also started a market for trading—he told all people to come to a certain place at midday with items that they could exchange for others.

Because of Shennong's great contributions to humans, he was highly respected as one of the Three Divine Sovereigns, along with Fuxi, Nüwa, and Huang Di. In some ancient writings Shennong was heavily rationalized into a brilliant and accomplished sage king. "Shennong's time" even became a symbol of the ideal dynasty and golden era in mythical ancient Chinese history. This era was thought to be happy, peaceful, stable, and self-sufficient. According to *Zhuangzi*, the Shennong era was so fantastic that when people slept, they were very quiet; when they were awake, they were happy. They only knew their mother, and had no idea of their father. They lived alongside elk. They sowed and then ate; they weaved and then were clothed. They never thought of doing harm to others, which was the best virtue. Another text from *Shangzi* (traditionally attributed to Shang Yang, ca. 390–338 BC, but probably an essay collection by Shang Yang and some of his followers) holds that during the time of Shennong, men cultivated for food, and women weaved for clothes. Without using punishment and administration, the society was quite stable. Without using soldiers and weapons, Shennong rose up as the king.

The Shennong myth is still popularly told throughout contemporary China. Most Han Chinese know his name and his beneficial deeds of starting farming and identifying medicine. Countless myths vividly describe the tough and sometimes dangerous processes of his inventions. One myth collected in the 1980s in Ba County, Chongqing City (which formerly belonged to Sichuan Province but now is a municipality directly under the central government), says that in remote antiquity, a big flood brought immense destruction to this world. Afterwards, plants and grasses grew overabundantly. Humans had no other food than tree leaves and weeds. One day Emperor Shennong happened to find some grain seeds adhered to a dog's tail, thus protected from the flood, so he sowed them in a field. Later on one lovely day, Shennong went out to enjoy the day with his wife. When they came to the field where the seeds were planted, they found that the seeds had grown into grain chaffs. Shennong asked his wife to squeeze a little milk from her breast into the empty shells. The chaffs then grew into grains. Those chaffs that got more milk grew into plump grains, whereas those that got less milk grew into wizened grains. After the milk dried in the shells, Shennong took them as seeds and sowed them widely. Since the grain came into being from the milk of Shennong's wife, it is extremely nutritious for humans.

Modern myths are even more varied about the legendary and dangerous process by which Shennong discovered medicine. A myth collected in the 1970s in Zhejiang Province asserts that when humans first populated the earth, they did not know how to cook. They always ate raw animals and plants, so they often became sick. Shennong wanted to help them. He decided to taste everything he saw and identify what people could take as food and what they could use as drugs to cure their diseases. So he carried two bags along with him. He put those plants that could function as food into the left bag, and those plants that could function as medicine into the right bag. Shennong was very uncommon because he had a crystal stomach and he could see clearly every thing and every change in his internal organs. The first plant he tasted was a piece of green leaf. After he ate it, he found that it cleaned everything up and down in his stomach. Since it went up and down in his internal organs like it was going on a tour of inspection, Shennong named it *cha* (literally meaning "inspection"). People later incorrectly called it *cha* (meaning "tea"; the same phonetic sound, in this case *cha*, but with a different character). Shennong put tea into his left bag. Next he tasted a piece of licorice (Glycyrrhiza). He put it into his right bag. The third plant he tasted was a small green flower. It was bitter and sour. When it came into his stomach, Shennong found that it butted everywhere and his knees became swollen. He hurried to consume some tea and was detoxified. Thus he found another medicine, the Achyranthes root. In this way, Shennong tasted hundreds of herbs and was poisoned almost every day, and the tea always helped him to be detoxified. Day by day, the plants and herbs in his two bags greatly increased. There were 47,000 flowers, herbs, roots, or leaves in the left bag, and 398,000 in the right. One day Shennong tasted a yellow flower. As soon as he swallowed it, he watched his intestine break into pieces. He died before he was able to take some tea. Later this herb was popularly known as *Duanchangcao*, the Intestine-breaking Weed. Because Shennong died for humans, he won great respect in the world. He is commemorated and popularly worshiped as "the Medicine King." Today there are many temples for the Medicine King all over the country.

Besides those myths that describe the general process of Shennong tasting herbs, some myth versions further describe how Shennong discovered a special medicine. A myth collected in the 1980s in the Chengdu area of Sichuan Province attributes the origin of ginger to Shennong. It says that in the ancient past, ginger was extremely poisonous. If one touched it, one's hand would decay; if one smelled it, one's nose would rot. All people therefore hated it. Whenever they found it, they would dig it up and place it in the sun to die. Because of this, ginger was almost extinct. It fled from here to there, trying to escape being dug out of the ground. One day ginger fled to a garden. It found many plants flourishing, and an old farmer was irrigating the garden. Ginger admired those garden plants very much, so it asked a white gourd who the old farmer was. The white gourd said that it was Shennong, and it was he who dug them from the wild and then planted them in the garden and took watchful care of them. They lived there happily along with many of their family members. Ginger then complained to Shennong of his injustice for not collecting it as well. Shennong asked ginger its function. When he learned that ginger could do nothing except poison people, Shennong disliked it too. He wanted to step on ginger and exterminate it. Ginger was smart. It quickly went into the ground. As it did this, it lost all of its poison. After half a year, Shennong found a new seedling in the garden. He tasted a piece of it. It tasted a little hot. He felt pleased that he had found a new plant that could detoxify and produce heat, and could be used as both food and medicine. From then on, ginger became a companion to humans, and it was able to stay with many of its family members in the garden.

Some Shennong myths combine many of his mythical achievements and mix them into a detailed and complex story. A long folk narrative poem spread throughout Hubei Province in the Shennongjia area (*jia* means "ladder"; the name Shennongjia came from a legend that Shennong set up a rattan ladder and climbed onto a high mountain to gather herbs; later the rattan ladder turned into a vast primitive forest, which was called Shennongjia), for instance, mixes many different sources and includes long life histories of many gods, including Shennong. Popularly known by the name of Hei'anzhuan ("Story of the Chaos") and transmitted both in written transcriptions (several versions of its handwritten copies have been found through today) and in oral tradition (it is usually sung antiphonally by master singers in funeral rituals), this 3,000-line poem highly rationalizes Shennong as a significant emperor in remote Chinese history. One written version of it collected in the 1980s states that Emperor Shennong is also named Yan Di. He was the son of Shaodian and Andeng. Since he grew up on Lie Mountain, he was also called Lieshanshi. He taught people to cultivate land and rear silkworms. During his time, people suffered greatly from plagues. To cure the plagues, Shennong went into mountains and forests to look for medicines.

He tasted hundreds of herbs. He met seventy-two poisonous plants, and he neutralized these poisons himself by consuming seventy-two other plants and herbs. So he gathered these helpful herbs to cure people's diseases. However, there were thirty-six or thirty-seven poisonous plants that fled into deep forests. That is why today poisonous plants are more likely to be found in mountains and forests while good herbs are found in the plains. After he cured the plagues, he went on to seek the five grains.

Shennong climbed onto Mount Yangtou,
He looked carefully, he examined carefully,
Then he found a seed of millet.
He left it with the Chinese date tree,
And he went to open up a wasteland.
He planted the seed eight times,
Then it produced fruit.
And from then on humans were able to eat millet.
He sought for the rice seed on Mount Daliang,
The seed was hiding in grasses.
He left it with the willow tree,
And he went to open up a paddy field.
He planted the seed seven times,
Then it produced fruit.
And from then on humans were able to eat rice.
He sought for the adzuki bean seed,
And left it with a plum tree.
He planted it one time.
The adzuki bean was easy to plant and was able to grow in infertile fields.
The soybean was produced on Mount Weishi,
So it was difficult for Shennong to get its seeds.
He left one seed of it with a peach tree,
He planted it five times,
Then it produced fruit,
And later tofu was able to be made south of the Huai River.
Barley and wheat were produced on Mount Zhushi,
Shennong was pleased that he got two seeds of them.
He left them with a peach tree,
And he planted them twelve times,
Then later people were able to eat pastry food.
He sought the sesame seed on Mount Wuzhi,
He left the seed with brambles.
He planted it one time.
Then later people were able to fry dishes in sesame oil.

> Shennong planted the five grains and they all survived,
> Because they were helped by the six species of trees.
> Shennong taught people to trade,
> Then people received convenience by the way of barter.
> Shennong cut wood and made the plough to till,
> And that started agriculture. . . .
> Shennong established his capital at Chenzhou,
> Which was Chouzhou City in Henan Province.
> He was on the throne for 140 years,
> And he died at Chalin County, Changsha City in Hunan Province.

In this poem, almost all important stories about Shennong are compounded and combined into an integrated full story. Here Shennong is not only identified with Yan Di, the son of Shaodian and Andeng (or, alternatively, Nüdeng), but the last paragraph about him suggests that he is also confused with another famous god, Fuxi, who founded the capital of his mythical kingdom in ancient Chenzhou, now the Huaiyang County in Henan Province.

Shennong is a very important god in Chinese beliefs. He is popularly worshiped as the God of Agriculture or the Ancestor of Farming, and the God of Medicine or the Ancestor of Medicine. In ancient China, emperors of the central government would offer sacrifices to Shennong at the beginning of every spring. The ritual aimed to show the importance of agriculture in the national economy and, furthermore, to urge farmers to cultivate more seriously and diligently. Shennong is also respected as the divine originator of many professions and trades, such as farming, medicine, grain trade, pastry making, salt trade, and even storytelling (he is said to have composed stories and songs to amuse melancholic persons, at the same time using his herbs to cure their illnesses). There are numerous temples, mausoleums, and relics for him scattered throughout China. Many local festivals are held each year to commemorate him, sometimes by the name of "Yan Di Shennongshi." Several towns and cities contend with each other to be his hometown. Shennongjia in Hubei Province, mentioned earlier, is famous for the legend that Shennong tasted herbs there; the idea that his rattan ladder for climbing up the mountain transformed into a deep forest is also well-known. In the same province, Lishan Town in Suizhou City boasts itself as the birthplace of Yan Di Shennongshi. There are several commemorative relics in honor of him there, such as Shennong Temple, Shennong Cave, and Shennong's Nine Wells (which are said to have appeared suddenly when Shennong was born). In Gaoping County, Shanxi Province, one can find a Yan Di mausoleum and a Five Grains temple, and even a Shennong town. According to a local legend, Yan Di Shennongshi tasted herbs on Mount Yangtou in the town. On every lunar April 8, a big festival is held to commemorate Yan Di Shennong. In Taiwan, there are 130 temples that mainly worship Yan Di Shennong (Zhong 1994, 134). There Shennong is variously called King Yan, God of Five Grains, Shennong the Great Emperor, the Ancestor of Farming, the Great Emperor of Medicine, God of Earth, and God of the Field. He is also worshiped as the patron god of farmers, rice traders, doctors of Chinese medicine, and others. Since it is popularly said that Shennong was born on lunar April 26, festivals are usually held on this day in his temples to celebrate his birthday. On April 25, 1992, for example, in Xianse Temple (*Xianse* means "the Ancestor of Farming"), Sanchong City, Taibei County, people carried Shennong's statue on a truck and traveled around the whole city. Others laid sacrifices outside their gates, burned incense, and set off firecrackers when the statue on the truck passed by. The next day, the mayor of the city presided over the formal ritual of offering sacrifices (in accordance with tradition, a pig and a sheep) to Shennong. Cows and oxen are not offered as a sacrifice because they plough land and help with farming, so farmers should not slaughter them as sacrifice.

See also Fuxi; Houji; Houtu; Huang Di; Nüwa; Shujun; Yan Di

References and Further Reading

Birrell, Anne. *Chinese Mythology: An Introduction*. Baltimore and London: Johns Hopkins University Press, 1993, 47–50, 131–132.

Bonnefoy, Yves, comp. *Asian Mythologies*. Translated under the direction of Wendy Doniger. Chicago and London: University of Chicago Press, 1993, 246. Originally published as *Dictionnaire des mythologies et des religions des sociétés traditionnelles et du monde antique*. Paris: Flammarion, 1981.

Christie, Anthony. *Chinese Mythology*. Rev. ed. New York: Peter Bedrick Books, 1985, 94, 96.

Hou, Guang, and He Xianglu, comps. *Selected Myths from Sichuan Province* (in Chinese). Chengdu: Sichuan Minzu Chubanshe, 1992.

The Hubei Branch of the Chinese Folk Literature and Art Society, comp. *A Collection of Several Hei'anzhuan Versions in Shennongjia* (in Chinese). Wuhan: Zhongguo Minjian Wenyijia Xiehui Hubei Fenhui, 1986.

Tao, Yang, and Zhong Xiu, comps. *A Collection of Oral Myths in China* (in Chinese). Shanghai: Shanghai Wenyi Chubanshe, [1990] 1991, 639–643.

Walls, Jan, and Yvonne Walls, eds. and trans. *Classical Chinese Myths*. Hong Kong: Joint Publishing Co., 1984, 26–28.

Yuan, Ke, and Zhou Ming, comps. *A Source Book of Chinese Myth Texts* (in Chinese). Chengdu: Sichuansheng Shehui Kexueyuan Chubanshe, 1985, 147–151.

Zhong, Zongxian. *The Cult of Yan Di Shennong* (in Chinese). Beijing: Xueyuan Chubanshe, 1994.

SHENTU

Shentu always appears with Yulü in myths and beliefs; both are the original Gate Gods.

The earliest record about Shentu and Yulü can be found in an early text from *Shanhaijing*, which cannot be found in today's edition of *Shanhaijing*, and was cited by *Lunheng*. It describes Shentu and Yulü's power and how they become Gate Gods. Among the great seas, there was Dushuo Mountain. On the top of that mountain, a huge peach tree grew. Its branches reached 3,000 *li* (about 1,000 miles). To the northeast of its branches there was the gate of ghosts where all ghosts went in and out. Two deities, Shentu and Yulü, stayed above the gate. They had the responsibility of supervising all of the ghosts. Evil or harmful ghosts would be bound with reed rope and fed to tigers. Being inspired by that, the great mythological emperor Huang Di started and promoted a ritual that was held regularly. He taught people to paint the figures of Shentu, Yulü, and a tiger on door frames, place a statue made from peach wood beside the gate, and hang a reed rope on its top. By doing this at a specific time, all evils might be driven away from people inside the house. From then on the belief in the Gate

The Gate Gods, Shentu and Yulü, responsible for supervising the ghosts. (Courtesy of Yang Lihui)

Gods (Shentu and Yulü) spread. Similar descriptions can also be seen in *Fengsu Tongyi* (*Popular Customs and Traditions,* second century CE) and several other documents compiled in and after the Han dynasty. Many of these documents also mention that the time for doing this custom is the end of each year. These records suggest that at least in the Han dynasty, belief in the Gate Gods and the custom of painting Shentu and Yulü's pictures on door frames before the Chinese New Year had become very popular.

In later times this custom was simplified. People only painted the two deities' pictures on paper and pasted them on door frames before the Chinese New Year. The pictures would not be replaced until the next New Year. Today, in rural areas and in some urban settings, this custom is still common. However, its function has become diverse. Rather than serving to guard the house and protect the family, Gate Gods pictures are used to express happiness and celebration, to decorate, or to entertain.

After the Tang dynasty, several other mythical or legendary figures were also identified as Gate Gods. Besides the version about Shentu and Yulü, another extremely popular version is that the roles of Gate Gods were assumed by Qin Qiong and Yuchi Gong, two fierce generals in the Tang dynasty. Nowadays versions about deities who assume the role of Gate Gods are numerous. However, Shentu and Yulü continue to appear as the early Gate Gods in Chinese New Year pictures in many areas.

See also Huang Di

References and Further Reading

Li, Jianyong. "An Exploration of the Origin of Gate Gods" (in Chinese). *Guizhou Wenshi Congkan* 2 (2002): 55–57.

Yang, Lin. "The Worship of Gate Gods and Its Evolvement" (in Chinese). *Minzu Yishu* 2 (2000): 112–118.

Yuan, Ke, and Zhou Ming, comps. *A Source Book of Chinese Myth Texts* (in Chinese). Chengdu: Sichuansheng Shehui Kexueyuan Chubanshe, 1985, 105–106.

SHUJUN

Shujun is a descendent of Di Jun (Emperor Jun); he is also the God of Cultivation and a skillful craftsman who invented many vital cultural items for humans.

In different versions, Shujun's name may appear as Yijun or Shangjun. He was said to be the offspring of Di Jun, the grandson (or nephew in another version) of Houji. It was he who replaced his father and Houji to sow all sorts of grains, and he invented the technique of plowing with a cow. As one of the ministers of Huang Di, he suggested that the divine emperor should relocate Ba, the drought deity, to the north of the Red River, and hence keep central China safe from frequent drought disasters. He was thus worshiped by people as the God of Cultivation. There is also a recording that identifies Shujun as Qiaorui, a famous craftsman who invented many varieties of crafts, such as the boat, bell, and a plowlike farm tool, for people on earth.

See also Ba; Di Jun; Houji; Huang Di

References and Further Reading

Birrell, Anne. *Chinese Mythology: An Introduction.* Baltimore and London: Johns Hopkins University Press, 1993, 66, 77.

Yuan, Ke. *Myths of Ancient China: An Anthology with Annotations* (in Chinese). Beijing: Renmin Wenxue Chubanshe, [1979] 1996, 196–202, 208–214, 252–254.

SHUN

A demigod, Shun is the second of the three sage kings and the successor of Yao. He is also known as Yu Shun (Yu here is different from another demigod and sage king, Yu) and is sometimes identified as one of the Five August Emperors in the mythical history of China; he is the emperor who abdicated and gave the throne to Yu.

In early texts, stories about Shun and his two wives, Ehuang and Nüying, are recorded often. Both Ehuang and Nüying were King Yao's daughters. They were promised to Shun by King Yao. In accounts from various texts, the marriages were depicted as a result of Yao valuing Shun's virtues and abilities. In addition, through this marriage of his daughters, Yao wanted to further test Shun's ability in dealing with family affairs, which was thought of as a basic and vital ability for a person to have to govern a country. Shun proved his exceeding competence in managing family affairs. His two wives were virtuous, and their family got along very well.

As types of mythical figures, Ehuang and Nüying also showed their intelligence and divine abilities in helping Shun to overcome many difficulties and to administer the country. One of the most renowned examples is that they helped Shun to survive several murders plotted by his father and stepbrother before he succeeded to gain the crown from Yao. Shun's father, a blind man, remarried a pretty woman after Shun's mother died. He soon had a second son, Xiang, who grew to be a very arrogant man. The father only loved his second wife and child. Because he and his second wife wanted to misappropriate Shun's family possessions, and because Xiang coveted Shun's two wives, he often conspired with Xiang to kill Shun, especially after Shun married King Yao's two daughters. One day the father asked Shun to repair the roof of a barn. Before going out, Shun told this to his two wives. The wives said, "They are going to kill you. Please take off your clothes and put on the coat with the bird pattern before you go." When Shun climbed up to the roof of the barn, his father took away the ladder and set the barn on fire. But Shun flew out of the fire with his magic coat. Days later, the father asked Shun to dredge a well. Shun's wives told Shun to wear a coat with a dragon pattern. As soon as Shun went down into the well, Xiang and his father blocked the mouth of the well. However, Shun swam out of the well with his magic dragon-patterned coat. Xiang and his father also tried to kill Shun by inviting him to drink. They planned to kill Shun after he was drunk. Again, the trap was seen through by Shun's wives. They let Shun go after giving him a bath in water with dissolved magic medicine. Because of the magical medicine Shun did not get drunk throughout the whole day of drinking.

Shun, second of the three sage kings and the successor of Yao. (Wang Qi and Wang Erbin, comps., Sancaituhui, Jinchang Baohanlou Kanben, *1609. Preserved in the Library of Literature Institute, Chinese Academy of Social Sciences)*

The topic of Shun surviving his parents' and stepbrother's murder attempts is familiar in stories orally transmitted in many places, including Sichuan, Henan, Anhui, and Shanxi provinces. There are a lot of versions of this story. In each, the trick Shun's father and stepbrother plotted tends to be different from that described in others. Most of them do not mention Ehuang's and Nüying's help for Shun in pulling through every trap his father and stepbrother made. For example, a story collected in Chengdu, Sichuan Province, mentions several traps Shun's parents and Xiang made in order to kill Shun. At first they planned to kill Shun as he was asked to dredge the well. But Shun was rescued out of the well by the God of the Earth. Then they wanted to burn him as he was asked to repair the barn roof. But Shun was saved from the fire by the God of Fire. At last, they invited Shun to dinner and let him sit on a specifically prepared chair. The chair was put on a piece of bamboo mat that covered the mouth of a well. They assumed that Shun would drop down into the well and die as soon as he sat on that chair. However, when Shun sat on the chair, it was very steady. Xiang felt so curious that he lifted a corner of the mat and looked into the well stealthily. Under the mat he found that a dragon was supporting the mat with its head. This scared Xiang, and afterwards he and the parents never dared to do harm to Shun again.

Before being found by Yao, Shun was a farmer cultivating in the Li Mountains. He was so virtuous and filial, even to his parents and stepbrother who treated him badly, that many people recommended him to King Yao. Through further examination of Shun both in virtue and in ability to rule the country, King Yao recognized that Shun was worthy of receiving the throne. Thus Shun was given the crown by Yao. When he went back home as a king, he treated his father as respectfully and cautiously as before. As for his stepbrother Xiang, he conferred on him the title of duke.

It was said that after Shun took power, his wives contributed numerous ideas for keeping the country in perfect order. This was one of the main reasons why Shun became a great king.

In an account from *Shanhaijing* (chapter 12), another of Shun's wives is mentioned. This wife was named Dengbi. She gave birth to two daughters, Xiaoming ("Night Brilliant") and Zhuguang ("Torch Light"). They lived in a large marsh beside the river. Their divine aura was able to illumine a hundred square *li*. These two girls' mythical powers are taken as a reflection of Shun's divine identity.

There is a sad and moving story that describes King Shun and his wives' faithful love, which can be commonly found in both early records and orally transmitted versions. King Shun died when he made an inspection trip to the south. Receiving news of Shun's death, Ehuang and Nüying were plunged into deep sorrow. They cried and tore out their hair day after day, and their tears spattered onto the bamboo trees, which speckled those trees. From then on a kind of spotted bamboo tree appeared. They were called Xiangfei's Bamboo. *Xiangfei* literally means "Xiang Madams." According to another account, when Shun's two wives hastened to the place where Shun died, they both died from overwhelming sadness and weariness beside the Xiang River. Seeing this, the God of Heaven was touched, and he decreed that Shun should be the god of Xiang and his two wives the madams of the river.

In a text told by people in Sichuan Province in southeastern China, Shun is hailed as the hero who shot down nine of the ten suns rising together in the sky. As the ten suns, who were the sons of the God of Heaven, often came out together in the sky, plants and grass were burned. This was hard for the people, who suffered from the heat and drought. When the God of Heaven became aware of this, he ordered the god Shun to administer those suns. Shun shot down nine of those suns and therefore saved people on the earth. The God of Heaven was so distressed and angry that he drove out Shun from heaven. Shun thus descended to the earth. Because of his great merits, King Yao chose him as his successor. The most popular version of the myth of shooting suns in China is that which identifies the hero who shot the suns as Yi. In some accounts from early texts, there is also a version that depicts King Yao as the hero. But the related story of Shun is seldom found. This version is probably the result of confusing Yao and Shun, who had a lot of similar merits and a very close relationship.

See also Yao; Yi; Yu

References and Further Reading

Allan, Sarah. *The Heir and the Sage.* San Francisco: Chinese Materials Center, 1981, 55–76.

Birrell, Anne. *Chinese Mythology: An Introduction.* Baltimore and London: Johns Hopkins University Press, 1993, 74–77, 104–105, 167–169.

Bonnefoy, Yves, comp. *Asian Mythologies.* Translated under the direction of Wendy Doniger. Chicago and London: University of Chicago Press, 1993, 246–250. Originally published as *Dictionnaire des mythologies et des religions des sociétés traditionnelles et du monde antique.* Paris: Flammarion, 1981.

Chen, Yongchao. *A Study of Yao and Shun Legend* (in Chinese). Nanjing: Nanjing Shifan Daxue Chubanshe, 2000.

Hou, Guang, and He Xianglu, comps. *Selected Myths from Sichuan Province* (in Chinese). Chengdu: Sichuan Minzu Chubanshe, 1992, 298–300.

Yuan, Ke. *A Survey of Chinese Mythology* (in Chinese). Chengdu: Bashu Shushe, 1993, 206–217.

Zhang, Zhenli, and Cheng Jianjun, comps. *The Collection of Myths Transmitting in Contemporary Central Plain* (in Chinese). Zhengzhou: Zhongguo Minjian Wenyijia Xiehui Henan Fenhui, 1987, 289–300.

SKY LADDER

The mythical sky ladder connects heaven and the earth. The ladder enables gods and humans to travel between heaven and earth.

The motif of the sky ladder exists in many ethnic groups in China, such as the Han, Buyi, Miao, Yao, Qiang, Naxi, Dulong, and Kazak. The sky ladder can assume the form of a high mountain or mythical tree, and it is sometimes depicted as a rainbow, sky rope, sky tower, or cobweb. Some myth versions explain why humans or sorcerers climbed the sky ladder up to heaven, and why the sky ladders were finally destroyed and therefore humans lost their ability to ascend to heaven. A myth collected in Beichuan County, Sichuan Province, states that in remote antiquity, there was a high mountain that reached the sky. With it, men on the earth could climb up to the sky, and deities in heaven could descend to the earth. A young man climbed to heaven by going up the mountain and married one of the God of Heaven's daughters. The God of Heaven was very upset. When his daughter descended to the earth with her husband, he gave her many gifts, such as grain, pigs, and chickens, and these were the first of such things in the world. But he also cut the high mountain into two halves. From then on, humans on earth could no longer climb to heaven. The young couple became the ancestors of the Qiang people.

In another myth collected from the Yao people in Liannan County, Guangdong Province, the sky ladder was a tree. It holds that at the very beginning, the sky was very close to the earth. People on the earth could easily get to heaven by climbing the tree. One day, a handsome young man went up to heaven by the tree and fell in love with the Water Goddess. Since the goddess was so devoted to this new love and thus neglected her duty, a flood destroyed the human race on earth. With the help of the goddess's parents, the young couple re-created humans by spreading the seeds of grain and sesame on the earth. The seeds all changed into men and women. To avoid any further trouble made by humans, the supreme god (the Jade Emperor in this story) lifted up the sky. Thereafter, humans could not go up to heaven.

In myths recorded in ancient Chinese writings, sky ladders commonly appear as high mountains and huge trees. The most distinguished sky ladder is Kunlun Mountain, one of the most remarkable mythical mountains in Chinese mythology. Kunlun is said to be the earthly residence of the Supreme Divinity, and the paradise of deities and immortals, one of the pillars of the sky that keeps heaven from collapsing, and a sky ladder that linked the earth to heaven. A text from *Huainanzi* (chapter 4) clearly shows the nature of Kunlun as the sky ladder and even describes the process of climbing it to heaven. It maintains that the first tier of Kunlun Mountain was Liangfeng ("Cool Wind Mountain"). Anyone who climbed it would receive immortality. The second tier was called Xuanpu. Anyone who climbed this tier would acquire spiritual power and could control the wind and rain. And if one climbed further, one would arrive at heaven, the residence of the Supreme Divinity, and thereafter one would become a spirit. In addition to Kunlun Mountain, many other high mountains serve as sky ladders. According to a text in *Shanhaijing*, the treasure of ancient Chinese myths, there was Zhao Mountain to the east of Mount Hua and Green Water. An immortal named Bo Gao often went up to heaven and back down by this mountain (chapter 18). In another text (chapter 7), Dengbao Mountain acted as a sky ladder by which many sorcerers traveled. According to yet another text in *Shanhaijing* (chapter 16), Ling Mountain was the sky ladder with which ten sorcerers went up and down the sky. Abundant medicinal herbs grew there.

In some other versions, the sky ladder is a huge tree. The most noted tree sky ladder in ancient writings is Jianmu (literally meaning "Building Tree"). According to an account in *Huainanzi* (chapter 4), Jianmu grew in the field of Duguang. With it, the gods went up and down between heaven and earth. At midday it had no shadow; shouting to it, there was no echo. Some suggest that perhaps it was the center of the world. In another text in *Shanhaijing* (chapter 18), Jianmu was an enormous tree with a height of 800 feet. It had no branches in the middle, only twigs curled on the top and roots twisted and gnarled. Its fruit was like the seeds of hemp, and its leaves were like those of the Mang tree. Two sentences in this text are quite vague in meaning. According to Yuan Ke's analysis, they state that Taihao once went up to heaven through Jianmu, and it was made by Huang Di (Yuan 1993, 510–513).

Another well-known ancient myth relating to the sky ladder states that the Supreme Divinity had the connection between the sky and the earth cut off. Though it does not clearly mention "sky ladder," it actually tells a story about why and how the sky ladder was destroyed. A text from *Shangshu* states that Chiyou started a revolt and brought disaster to the common people. Influenced by him, people on the earth gradually were corrupted. They began to cheat and steal. However, the Miao people did not obey him at first. Chiyou thus designated five brutal punishments to deal with them. Then, little by little, the Miao people also became corrupt. They began to cheat each other within their own group, mistreat people from other groups, disobey their faith, and violate the oath between them and the Supreme Divinity. Many innocent people brought complaints against them to the Supreme Divinity. The Supreme Divinity thus ordered two of his subordinates, the deities Zhong and Li, to cut off the link between heaven and the earth. From then on, the Miao people could never ascend to heaven again, but at the same time, the deities could no longer descend to the earth.

In the oral traditions of many ethnic peoples, such as the Han, Miao, Qiang, Buyi, and Tujia, the tree of the sky ladder is commonly said to be *Coriaria Sinica maxim*. A myth told by Yang Lihui's mother (sixty-five years old at this writing, and of Han heritage; she heard this story about fifty years before in her hometown in Shehong County, Sichuan Province) in October 2004 explains why the *Coriaria Sinica maxim* tree today becomes so low and curved. In the remote past, the tree was so high that it reached heaven. One year, twelve suns showed up together in the sky. The world became so hot that the earth almost burned. At this time, a hero on the earth climbed to the sky using the tree and smashed the surplus suns with a stick, leaving only one to serve humankind. Though the world order was restored to normal again, the God of Heaven worried that humans would ascend to the sky in the future and intervene with heavenly affairs again, so he cursed,

> The *Coriaria Sinica maxim* tree,
> Will no longer grow so high any more.
> It will bend down at its waist,
> Before it reaches the height of three feet.

Since that time, the tree has grown low and curved, and, as a result, the human race can never again use it to ascend to heaven.

Some researchers argue that the sky ladder myth depicts a dichotomous world: humans on the earth and gods in heaven; the people who create and spread the sky ladder myth and a distant other land. The process of climbing the sky ladder is, in fact, a process of changing from man to god, from profane to sacred (Zhuang 2004).

See also Huang Di; Kunlun Mountain; Li; Pillars of the Sky; Taihao

References and Further Reading

Yuan, Ke. *The Classic of Mountains and Seas: A Collation and Annotation* (in Chinese). Chengdu: Bashu Shushe, 1993, 510–513.

Yuan, Ke. *A Survey of Chinese Mythology* (in Chinese). Chengdu: Bashu Shushe, 1993, 87–90.

Zhong, Nian. "A Study of the Sky Ladder." *Wenxian* 3 (1995): 104–111.

Zhuang, Meifang. "The Sky Ladder Myths" (in Chinese). Paper presented at the annual meeting of the Forum of Folk Culture Studies, Beijing, August 2004.

SUIRENSHI

Suirenshi is a famous Chinese culture hero who invented the technique of making fire by drilling on wood.

The discovery of fire is a widespread motif in worldwide mythology. In China, myths related to this motif can be found not only among Han people but also among many other ethnic groups. The stories might vary among different people; however, most of them center on a hero who first discovered the use of fire and invented the method of making fire. For example, a myth told by Zhuang people in the Guangxi Zhuang Autonomous Region in southwest China mentions that it was the great god Buluotuo who invented the method of making fire. In the ancient past, people ate only raw foods because they did not have the ability to make and use fire. One day Buluotuo saw a large tree that had been burned when it was struck by lightning. Through his observation of this natural phenomenon he discovered that he could cook food by using fire, and he taught this technique to others. People kept the fire going and used it to cook their food, until one day they lost it when it rained. Buluotuo hacked at the tree with his divine ax and got a spark, thus inventing a method for making fire.

In a story spread among the Buyi people in Guizhou Province in southwest China, the name of the hero is Leling. He discovered and taught people the method of making fire by striking together two pieces of stone.

In comparison with these two stories, a myth told by Hani people in southwest China is much more solemn and stirring. It tells of a hero, Azha, who dedicated his life to getting fire. The only source of fire at that time was in a lamp between the eyebrows of a monster. The young hero suffered through many hurdles and eventually got the fire by stealing it. However, as he was leaving to return home, the monster found him. In a fight with the monster he swallowed the fire. Azha killed the monster and returned to his hometown, and afterward he cut open his chest and took out the fire. Hani people hence received warmth and brightness, but Azha died from his struggle and his sacrifice.

The most famous fire discovery myth spread among Han people is the story of Suirenshi.

*The Fire Driller (Suirenshi) brought fire to humans in Chinese myth. (*The Dragon, Image, and Demon, *1886)*

According to a text from chapter 869 in *Taiping Yulan* (*An Imperial Reading of Texts Compiled in the Taiping Era* [977–984 CE], compiled by Li Fang, 925–996 CE), Suirenshi was a sage in ancient times. He traveled to very far places in order to find a way to change people's habit of eating raw foods. Once he traveled to the country of Suiming. In this country there was no distinction among the four seasons and between day and night. People never died here. If somebody did grow tired of living in this world, he or she would ascend to the heavens. In this place there was a huge igneous tree named the Sui tree. Its branches spanned an area of thousands of miles, and its trunk was surrounded by clouds. If one took a branch from this tree and drilled on it, there would be fire. When the sage passed by the tree, he noticed a bird like an owl pecking at the tree. Sparks appeared as it was pecking. Enlightened by the bird, the sage learned the method of making fire by drilling on a small branch of the tree. He taught this to humans when he returned, and was thus called Suirenshi. Literally *sui* means "the tool of fire making," *ren* means "human being" or "the person," and *shi* here is a respectful form of address for gods.

The recordings found in several other early texts have the same plot as the story of Suirenshi inventing a method for making fire by drilling on wood. However, in some versions orally transmitted among Han people today, the method of making fire has been changed to striking stones. The following example was collected in Shangqiu County, Henan Province: In ancient times when Suirenshi was the emperor, people still ate only raw foods. One day there was a fire in the forest that killed a lot of animals. When the fire ended, Suirenshi found many animals' bodies burned. He picked up a piece of the cooked flesh from one animal's body and tasted it. It was much more delicious than when eaten raw. He then directed other people to pick apart and eat the cooked animal flesh. Everyone enjoyed the tasty meat very much. However, the cooked meat was soon gone. Everyone expected another fire to provide cooked food again.

One day a huge bird flew to Suirenshi. It told him that it would like to carry Suirenshi to the sun to get fire. When Suirenshi arrived at the sun palace by riding the bird, he told the princess in the palace his desire. The princess bestowed on him a piece of flint. Then Suirenshi flew back to the earth on the bird's back. Because the princess did not tell him how to use the flint, Suirenshi became angry after waiting a long time for the fire to come out of the flint spontaneously. He threw away the flint in anger, and it struck a stone. Sparks appeared. Upon seeing this, Suirenshi got the idea of making fire by striking stones together. He taught this technique to others. From then on, people no longer suffered from eating only raw foods. And Suirenshi was thus worshiped as a great hero by people in later times.

References and Further Reading

Birrell, Anne. *Chinese Mythology: An Introduction.* Baltimore and London: Johns Hopkins University Press, 1993, 42–44.

Gu, Deming, comp. *Myths in Chinese Ethnic Groups* (in Chinese). Beijing: Zhongguo Minjian Wenyi Chubanshe, 1987, 71–73.

Walls, Jan, and Yvonne Walls, eds. and trans. *Classical Chinese Myths.* Hong Kong: Joint Publishing Co., 1984, 24–25.

Zhang, Zhenli. *Studies on the Transformation of Classical Myths Spreading in the Central Plain* (in Chinese). Shanghai: Shanghai Wenyi Chubanshe, 1991, 140–160.

Zhang, Zhenli, and Cheng Jianjun, comps. *The Collection of Myths Transmitting in Contemporary Central Plain* (in Chinese). Zhengzhou: Zhongguo Minjian Wenyijia Xiehui Henan Fenhui, 1987, 179–181.

TAIHAO

One of the five gods of the directions, the god of the east and the spring season, Taihao is often confused with Fuxi in later tradition. He is also known as Dahao. In his name, *tai* or *da* literally means "great" or "supreme," and *hao* means "expansive and limitless."

In an account from *Shanhaijing* (chapter 18), Taihao is associated with Jianmu, a known sky ladder. As it is described in the text, Jianmu was an enormous tree standing 800 feet in height. Its leaves were green, its trunk was purple, its flowers dark, and its fruit yellow. At the end of this text Taihao is mentioned, though the meaning is vague. The text states that "Taihao once passed by this tree." But today some scholars interpret it to mean that Taihao once went to and from heaven through Jianmu (Yuan 1993, 510–513).

In early texts, Taihao is identified as one of the five gods distributed to rule the five directions (east, south, west, north, and center) and the five elements (wood, fire, metal, water, and earth, which are elements encompassing the whole world in traditional Chinese philosophy). In different texts the names of these five gods may vary. According to a version from *Huainanzi* (chapter 3), Taihao was the god of the east, associated with the element wood. In this account, Taihao is also described as the god controlling the season of spring together with his subordinate Goumang.

During the Han dynasty, Taihao was gradually identified as another great god, Fuxi, who appeared as an independent divinity in pre-Han sources. From then on, "Taihao Fuxishi" became a unique combination that frequently appeared either in written texts or in verbal art. In many accounts they each inherit the merits and powers of the other and merge into one certain god. Fuxi not only received the honorary name of Taihao but also took Taihao's function as the god who reigned over the east and controlled the season of spring. The wood god, Goumang, became Fuxi's subordinate too. In Huaiyang County, Henan Province, for example, there is a big temple complex called the Tomb of Taihao, or, more popularly, Renzu Temple (Temple of Human Ancestors). Huaiyang is said to be the capital of King Taihao Fuxi's mythical kingdom and the hometown of Fuxi. The main god worshiped here is Taihao Fuxishi. From February 2 to March 3 according to the lunar calendar, there is a monthlong temple fair to celebrate Taihao Fuxi's birthday at the Renzu Temple complex. The fair draws thousands of pilgrims daily from nearby villages, counties, and provinces.

See also Fuxi; Goumang; Huang Di; Sky Ladder
References and Further Reading
Birrell, Anne. *Chinese Mythology: An Introduction.* Baltimore and London: Johns Hopkins University Press, 1993, 44–47.

Yang, Lihui. *The Cult of Nüwa: Myths and Beliefs in China* (in Chinese). Beijing: Zhongguo Shehui Kexue Chubanshe, 1997, 144–151.

Yuan, Ke. *The Classic of Mountains and Seas: A Collation and Annotation* (in Chinese). Chengdu: Bashu Shushe, 1993, 509–513.

Yuan, Ke, and Zhou Ming, comps. *A Source Book of Chinese Myth Texts* (in Chinese). Chengdu: Sichuansheng Shehui Kexueyuan Chubanshe, 1985, 20–21, 64–65.

TANG VALLEY

The place where the ten suns stay, rise, and bathe, the Tang Valley is also called Yang Valley in different versions.

Tang Valley is a mythical place closely related to Chinese people's beliefs about the ten suns in ancient times. People believed that each of the ten suns would be on duty one at a time in the sky, and Tang Valley is the place where they replaced each other and rose in turn. The detailed description of this imaginative explanation may be found in several parts of *Shanhaijing*. According to a text in chapter 14, the Tang Valley was located in the eastern great wilderness, in which there was a big tree named Fusang ("Leaning Mulberry"). All the ten suns rose from here in turn. Each of them was carried by a crow. As soon as one sun came back from its journey crossing the sky, another one started forth.

In chapter 10 of *Shanhaijing*, Tang Valley is described as a place where the ten suns stayed and bathed. In the water of the valley there was a large tree. On the lower branches nine of the ten suns stayed, and on the top branch was the sun that would rise next.

In an account from *Huainanzi*, Tang Valley is identified with Yang Valley. This is explained by most Chinese scholars as occurring because "Tang" and "Yang" have a similar pronunciation and shape in Chinese characters.

See also Crow of the Sun; Fusang; Xihe; Yi

References and Further Reading

Yuan, Ke. *A Survey of Chinese Mythology* (in Chinese). Chengdu: Bashu Shushe, 1993, 222–225.

Yuan, Ke, and Zhou Ming, comps. *A Source Book of Chinese Myth Texts* (in Chinese). Chengdu: Sichuansheng Shehui Kexueyuan Chubanshe, 1985, 210–212.

TEN SUNS

See Yi.

TWELVE MOONS

The mythic motif of "formerly several moons" spread in many ethnic groups in China, such as the Han, Yi, Miao, Buyi, and Lisu. It states that there were several moons in remote antiquity. The number of the moons varies from five, seven, nine, or twelve to even sixty-six among different peoples. In most cases the motif is combined with a story explaining how the surplus moons were ruined and thus only one moon was left in the sky. Sometimes the story also contains the motifs of multiple suns and destroying the surplus suns.

A creation epic of the Yi people in Guizhou Province chants that during the time of creation, the sun father and the moon mother married and then gave birth to ninety-nine suns and sixty-six moons. The suns rose up together in the day, and the moons showed up together during the night. The world became so hot that all of the trees died and the rain was exhausted. A god then shot down all the surplus suns and moons, leaving only the youngest sun and moon. But, because they became so sad, they did not rise at all. So another god fixed them in the sky. This was the beginning of the four seasons.

A myth collected from the Lisu people in Yunnan Province describes that after the brother and sister ancestors came out from a gourd that protected them from drowning in the world flood, they found that nine suns and seven moons had risen together in the sky. By using a gold bow and silver arrows they received from the dragon king, they shot down the surplus suns and moons. Then they married each other and procreated the ancestors of the Tibetan, Bai, Keqin, Han, Nu, and Lisu peoples.

In myths in the Chinese language, the renowned story about the multiple moons is that of Changxi and her twelve moon children. Changxi is said to be one of Di Jun's wives. According to a text in *Shanhaijing*, Changxi gave birth to twelve moons and was just beginning to bathe them at this time

Changxi bathing the twelve moons. Originally drawn in the 19th century. (Ma Changyi, The Classic of Mountains and Seas: Ancient Illustrations with Annotations, Shandong Huabao Chubanshe, 2001, 587)

(chapter 16). However, it is quite unclear in this text how the twelve moons worked during the night, and why they were bathed by their mother.

See also Changxi; Di Jun; Yi

References and Further Reading

Birrell, Anne. *Chinese Mythology: An Introduction.* Baltimore and London: Johns Hopkins University Press, 1993, 123–125.

Chen, Jianxian, comp. *A Collection of Prime Oral Myths of Ethnic Groups in China* (in Chinese). Wuhan: Hubei Renmin Chubanshe, 1994, 310–314.

Zhu, Guiyuan, Wu Sumin, Tao Lifan, and Zhao Guifang, comps. *A Source Book of Myths in Ethnic Minorities in China.* Vol. 1, *Creation Myths* (in Chinese). Beijing: Zhongyang Minzu Xueyuan, 1984, 167–169.

XIANGLIU

A minister of Gonggong, Xiangliu (or Xiangyou) is a monster with nine human heads and a snake's body. He was killed by the hero Yu.

The early detailed text of the Xiangliu myth can be found in *Shanhaijing* (chapter 8). It tells the story of Xiangliu's figure and powers, and gives an account of his death. Xiangliu was a minister of Gonggong, the water god who died after failing in a battle against Zhuanxu to be the Supreme Divinity. He had nine heads, each with a human face, and a snake's body that was black. With his nine heads Xiangliu ate foods from nine mountains. The places he passed by became marshes and gullies in which no animals could survive. Afterwards he was killed by Yu, one of the three sage kings (commonly known as Yao, Shun, and Yu). Xiangliu's blood stank of rot, and it poisoned the earth, making it impossible to plant grains at the place where he died. Yu wanted to remove the blood. He dug out the soil three times, but each time the blood soaked deeper into the earth. Yu then built a terrace from the excavated soil for all great gods, which was located in the area

Xiangliu, a monster with nine human heads and a snake's body. Originally drawn in the 17th century by Jiang Yinghao. (Ma Changyi, The Classic of Mountains and Seas: Ancient Illustrations with Annotations, *Jinan: Shandong Huabao Chubanshe, 2001, 466)*

to the north of Kunlun Mountain and to the east of Rouli. A similar account can be found in chapter 17 of *Shanhaijing;* in that text Xiangliu appears as Xiangyou.

Xiangliu's stories are not often told nowadays in China. However, in some areas there are still orally transmitted versions of the Xiangliu myth. One example is a text collected in 1983 from Wan County in Sichuan Province (now part of Chongqing Municipality), located in southwestern China. It tells the story that Xiangliu continued to cause floods and other kinds of harm after he was defeated by Zhurong, so he was killed by the goddess Nüwa. In this story Xiangliu is depicted as a nine-headed poisonous dragon. He not only caused flooding in the Sichuan area but also devoured humans and livestock. Being aware of this, Nüwa fought Xiangliu and finally killed him. The flooding in Sichuan was consequently controlled.

See also Gonggong; Nüwa; Yu

References and Further Reading

Birrell, Anne. *Chinese Mythology: An Introduction.* Baltimore and London: Johns Hopkins University Press, 1993, 148–152.

Walls, Jan, and Yvonne Walls, eds. and trans. *Classical Chinese Myths.* Hong Kong: Joint Publishing Co., 1984, 105–106.

Yuan, Ke. *Myths of Ancient China: An Anthology with Annotations* (in Chinese). Beijing: Renmin Wenxue Chubanshe, [1979] 1996, 315–317.

XIHE

Xihe is the mother of the ten suns and one of Di Jun's wives.

The motif of "creation of the sun" is found in many ethnic groups in China. The sun is sometimes depicted as having been created by gods, sometimes it is transformed from a divine corpse, and sometimes it is born from its parents. For example, a myth in the Buyi ethnic group holds that the god Wengga gave birth to the sky, the earth, day and night, and the sun and the moon. In the Luoba ethnic group in Tibet, the parents of the sun are the sky and the earth.

In myths in the Chinese language, the sun is commonly said to have been born by its mother Xihe and father Di Jun. However, similar to the myth of Changxi, who is the mother of the twelve moons and another wife of Di Jun, the Xihe myth is quite sparse in Chinese mythology texts in spite of Xihe's high status. Her accomplishment can mainly be found in *Shanhaijing.* A text from that book (chapter 15) states that beyond the east sea in the Gan River area was the Xihe kingdom. A lady named Xihe, wife of Di Jun, gave birth to ten suns. She was bathing the ten suns in the Gan Gulf.

Another text from the same book further describes how the ten suns work. The ten suns lived on the Fusang tree, which grew in the water of the Tang Valley.

Xihe bathing the ten suns. Originally drawn in the 19th century. (Ma Changyi, The Classic of Mountains and Seas: Ancient Illustrations with Annotations, Shandong Huabao Chubanshe, 2001, 572)

The ten suns stayed in the Fusang tree and bathed in the water there. Nine of the suns stayed on the tree's lower branches while the one that was going to rise stayed on its top branch. The ten suns rose from the Fusang tree one by one. As soon as one sun returned from crossing the sky, another sun went up. Each sun was carried by a crow (chapter 14). In another version in that book, Xihe is portrayed as the driver who steered a cart pulled by six dragons and sent her children out into the sky.

As in the Changxi myth about her bathing the twelve moons, the reason Xihe bathed the suns is unclear in these texts. Some myths spread in the Miao, Buyi, and Yi ethnic groups explain that the sun and the moon need to be washed in order to cleanse them from the dust they accumulate during their work to make them bright again. These versions may provide some help in understanding the myths about bathing the suns and the moons told among Han people.

Xihe is variously said to be the official who takes charge of the seasons and calendar. Xihe's gender seems vague in this case.

See also Changxi; Di Jun; Fusang; Tang Valley; Twelve Moons; Yi

References and Further Reading

Birrell, Anne. *Chinese Mythology: An Introduction.* Baltimore and London: Johns Hopkins University Press, 1993, 123–125.

Bonnefoy, Yves, comp. *Asian Mythologies.* Translated under the direction of Wendy Doniger. Chicago and London: University of Chicago Press, 1993, 236–237. Originally published as *Dictionnaire des mythologies et des religions des sociétés traditionnelles et du monde antique.* Paris: Flammarion, 1981.

Yuan, Ke. *Dragons and Dynasties: An Introduction to Chinese Mythology.* Selected and translated by Kim Echlin and Nie Zhixiong. New York: Penguin Books, 1993, 57–59. First published by Foreign Languages Press, Beijing, 1991–1993.

XINGTIAN

Xingtian is a notable deity who continues to fight against the supreme god even after he is beheaded. In some early texts he is also said to have served as a minister of Yan Di.

According to *Shanhaijing* (chapter 7), Xingtian fought with the supreme god to become the Supreme Divinity, and he lost the battle. The god cut off Xingtian's head and buried it on Changyang Mountain. However, Xingtian persevered. After he lost his head, he used his nipples as his eyes and his navel as his mouth and continued to brandish his shield and battle-ax. By doing this, he expressed his fierce spirit that would never submit or give up.

The solemn and stirring spirit reflected in this story has attracted and encouraged Chinese people for a long time. The hero Xingtian has become a symbol for Chinese people to express their will to resist whatever pressures and dif-

Xingtian, a notable deity who continues to fight against the supreme god even after he is beheaded. Originally drawn in the 17th century by Jiang Yinghao. (Ma Changyi, The Classic of Mountains and Seas: Ancient Illustrations with Annotations, *Shandong Huabao Chubanshe, 2001, 439)*

ficulties they face. Many writers in different eras have composed poetry and prose to express praise and admiration for Xingtian. One of the more famous examples is a poem written by Tao Yuanming (365–427 CE), a well-known poet in the Jin dynasty. This poem states that "Xingtian brandished his shield and battle-ax, his fierce spirit will live forever."

In an account from *Lushi,* a book of history compiled by Luo Mi, a scholar in the Southern Song dynasty, another of Xingtian's great deeds is mentioned. He was one of the ministers of Yan Di. In accordance with Yan Di's command, Xingtian composed music to complement the work of plowing and the harvest. The Chinese character of *xing* in this "Xingtian" is different from that in *Shanhaijing.* However, many scholars argue that they are the same figure.

See also Yan Di

References and Further Reading

Birrell, Anne. *Chinese Mythology: An Introduction.* Baltimore and London: Johns Hopkins University Press, 1993, 216–217.

Che, Baiqing. "A Study of the Rebellious Gods in Chinese Mythology" (in Chinese). *Yunnan Shifan Daxue Xuebao* (5) 1999: 67–69.

Walls, Jan, and Yvonne Walls, eds. and trans. *Classical Chinese Myths.* Hong Kong: Joint Publishing Co., 1984, 48–49.

Yuan, Ke. *The Classic of Mountains and Seas: A Collation and Annotation* (in Chinese). Chengdu: Bashu Shushe, 1993, 257–261.

XIRANG

The mythical self-growing soil, Xirang was able to grow ceaselessly by itself. If it was excavated, it grew more. The heroes Gun and Yu used it to stop the overflowing water.

See also Gun; Yu

XIWANGMU

One of the most popular goddesses in Chinese mythology and folk belief, Xiwangmu was originally a wild beastlike goddess (or god) who became the ruler of punishment, calamity, and disease, but later changed into a refined queen. She was the owner of the elixir of immortality and the divine peaches that can endow longevity on one who eats them. She also was the leader of the goddesses in the Taoist pantheon. At least as late as during the Ming dynasty she was commonly referred to as Wangmu Niangniang (*wangmu* literally means "queen mother," and *niangniang* is a respectful title for a goddess).

The Xiwangmu myth appears early in the book *Shanhaijing*, which depicts Xiwangmu as a wild and fearsome spirit whose gender is quite unclear. Many Chinese scholars maintain that Xiwangmu's image in *Shanhaijing* illustrates that she possessed both female and male features. One account (chapter 2) describes Xiwangmu as a deity of disaster, disease, and punishment. She dwelled on the Jade Mountain, which is very close to Kunlun Mountain, the earthly residence of the Supreme Divinity and a paradise for deities and immortals. She looked like a human but had a panther's tail and tiger's teeth. She was good at roaring, and wore a jade *sheng* on her head. Many Chinese scholars interpret sheng to be a hair ornament, but some argue that wearing a sheng meant "cutting off the animal's hide and wearing it" (Wang 1996, 303). Sheng can also be interpreted as a special part of a loom, which illustrates Xiwangmu's original connection with sericulture (Kominami 1993, 54).

In another text from *Shanhaijing* (chapter 12), Xiwangmu leans against a small table, wearing a jade sheng on her head. To the south of her, three green birds were fetching food for her (in some versions, a single bird—a three-legged crow—fetched her food). They were all situated north of Kunlun Mountain. Another text of the same book (chapter 16) states that Kunlun Mountain was located south of the west sea, on the shore of the Liusha, behind the Red River and in front of the Black River. The Weak River (whose water was so weak that it could not float even a feather) circled the bottom of the mountain, and a flaming mountain surrounded it. A spirit dwelled in the mountain. It was a human-headed creature with a tiger's body and white spotted tail. Xiwangmu inhabited a cave there. She wore a sheng and had tiger's teeth and a panther's tail.

From the Warring States era to the Han dynasty, Xiwangmu's image changed greatly from a wild and ferocious monsterlike deity to a cultivated queen. In a book named *Mutianzizhuan* (*A Biography of Emperor Mu*, traditionally said to have been written in the Western Zhou dynasty or the Warring States period), Xiwangmu became a polite princess when hosting Emperor Mu of Zhou at a banquet. She not only improvised poems to communicate with Emperor Mu but also sang elegantly, though, according to her own poems, she still lived with wild animals and birds. Additionally in this period, her functions increased rapidly. She was believed to control various aspects of human life such as wealth, health, fertility, and calamity, and was described as even more powerful and pervasive than the description of her in *Shanhaijing*. She became popularly known as the keeper of the elixir of immortality, which has the magic power of keeping one's vitality and preventing death. A well-known myth about the elixir is the story of Yi and Chang'e. In the early Han book *Huainanzi*, the hero Yi is said to have asked for the elixir of immortality from Xiwangmu, and

she gave it to him. But his wife Chang'e stole it, then flew to the moon and became the spirit of the moon.

In the Han dynasty, Xiwangmu is popularly depicted to have a consort named Dongwanggong, King Father of the East. There are quite a few stories about him in ancient documents. According to a text in *Shenyijing* (*The Classic of Spirits and Strange Things*, once said to have been written by a Han writer, Dongfang Shuo, 154–93 BC, but seemingly compiled later by an anonymous author), there was a bronze pillar on Kunlun Mountain. It was so big and high that it reached the sky. In fact, it was a pillar of the sky. On top of it there was a huge bird named Xiyou (literally meaning "rare"). Opening its left wing, it covered Dongwanggong; opening the right one, it covered Xiwangmu. When Xiwangmu met Dongwanggong, she had to climb onto its wing. In another account, Dongwanggong lived in a big stone house on the East Wild Mountain. He was about ten feet high, and his hair was as white as snow. He looked like a man but had a bird's face and a tiger's tail. He rode a black bear. With a Jade Maiden he often played the game of throwing chips into a pot.

Xiwangmu and Dongwanggong sitting on a bench. Above them are an immortal riding on a deer and a bird possibly fetching food for Xiwangmu. Under them is a rabbit pounding the elixir of immortality. Funeral stone carving of the Eastern Han dynasty, Nanyang City, Henan Province. (Reproduced for ABC-CLIO from Shan Xiushan, Wang Rulin and Li Chenguang, eds., A Collection of Han Pictorial Stone Carvings in Nanyang, *Henan Meishu Chubanshe, 1989, 154)*

When he threw chips into the pot, heaven sighed; when he failed, heaven laughed.

In inscriptions on bronze mirrors from this era, Xiwangmu's and Dongwang-gong's names frequently appear together. In most cases, they are described as long-lived immortals who controlled the secret of immortality. Yet people also prayed to them for wealth, safety, honor, and children. On funerary stones and brick bas-reliefs found in Henan, Shaanxi, Hebei, Jiangsu, Shandong, Hunan, Zhejiang, Sichuan, and many other provinces, Xiwangmu is sometimes shown alone, and sometimes she is accompanied by Dongwanggong. She is typically shown as a respectable goddess, sitting on a cloud or a seat made of a dragon and a tiger. She is often surrounded by Jade Rabbit, a toad, birds, or sometimes a three-legged crow, a deer, a dragon, a nine-tailed fox, and immortal servants with wings. The rabbit (sometimes the immortal servants also) usually is pounding the elixir in a mortar in front of Xiwangmu and Dongwanggong.

During the Wei and Jin dynasties, with the flourishing of Taoism, Xi-wangmu was further immortalized and became a leader of the female immor-tals. She also is widely known as the owner of the divine saucer peach, a fruit that has the magic power of endowing longevity. In a book written in this pe-riod, *Hanwudi Neizhuan,* or *The Biography of Emperor Wu of Han,* Xiwangmu is depicted as a beautiful and graceful female immortal dressed up in Taoist style. Thousands of immortals accompanied her, and even her two serving maid-ens were extremely beautiful. She gave four saucer peaches to the emperor (who reigned from 156 to 87 BC). Since the peaches tasted so good, the emperor kept the pits, hoping to plant them when he came back to the central land. But Xi-wangmu told him that this kind of peach needed to be harvested for 3,000 years before yielding ripe peaches. The emperor felt disappointed and gave up. In some other Taoist books in this period, Xiwangmu is given a more honorable origin and became the daughter of the highest god in Taoism, Yuanshi Tianzun.

After the Tang and Song dynasties, Xiwangmu becomes more common in folk tradition. She often appears in a later-formed pantheon (far from orderly and stable) as the consort of Yu Di, the Jade Emperor, the highest ruler of heaven and gods. One of their daughters is the famous Weaving Maiden. In legends she is said to secretly descend to the world and marry a cowboy. Her mother felt quite an-noyed so she pulled out her hairpin and made a line in the air. The line then turned into the Milky Way that divided the lovers on the two sides of the shore. From then on, on every lunar July 7, the lovers were allowed to meet each other. Magpies would fly over to make the bridge for them. In the renowned mythic novel *Xiyouji (Journey to the West,* written by Wu Cheng'en, ca. 1500–1582), which found many of its sources in folk tradition, Xiwangmu is addressed as

Wangmu Niangniang, the bearer of peaches that gave immortality to whoever ate them. She often invited other immortals and gods to the Saucer Peach Banquet. The peaches she used for the banquet were classified into three sorts: the first one ripened every 3,000 years and could make the person who ate it healthy; the second one ripened every 6,000 years and could bring the one who ate it a long life; the third one ripened every 9,000 years and could make the one who ate it as long-lived as heaven and the earth. In the novel, the Monkey King ate many of the best peaches and disturbed the banquet because he was not invited.

Today, the wild and ferocious Xiwangmu can hardly be found in Chinese mythology. Compared to Nüwa, Fuxi, Pangu, and many other ancient gods and goddesses in mythology, modern myths about Wangmu Niangniang are not rich in detail. Wangmu Niangniang usually appears in the stories as a minor character, a divine predictor, an adviser, a helper, an intervener, and so on. Perhaps this is because her original mythological behaviors are slim and pale in comparison to the deeds of others.

A myth collected in the 1980s in Gao County, Yibin District, Sichuan Province, portrays Wangmu Niangniang as the consort of Yu Di and the mother of the sun and the moon. It states that the sun and the moon were siblings. Their parents were Yu Di and Wangmu. In the beginning, the sun and the moon worked together, one shining in the east and west while the other shined in the south and north. Later, because of the sun's sexual harassment of his sister the moon, she confronted him in front of Yu Di. Their father was so angry that he decided to kill his son. At this time Wangmu arrived. She cried and suggested that Yu Di not do so. Finally, Yu Di accepted a minor god's idea and separated the siblings. From then on, the sun worked in the daytime, and the moon came out only during the nighttime.

Occasionally Wangmu Niangniang plays a crucial role in a myth. A myth collected in 1986 in a village of Zhongning County, Ningxia Province, northwest China, attributes the contribution of repairing the broken sky and the earth to Wangmu Niangniang and Lishan Laomu (who sometimes is identified as Nüwa). It holds that Wangmu Niangniang was Lishan Laomu's younger sister. Both of them were good helpers of their elder brother Fuxi. One year, Gonggong fought Zhurong and destroyed the sky pillar Mount Buzhou. The sky then tilted toward the northwest, the earth was damaged at the southeast, and floodwater overflowed everywhere. The two sisters felt sympathetic to humans and decided to repair the damaged sky and earth. They gathered and melted stones of five different colors to patch the sky at the site of Mount Li (now in Shaanxi Province). The firelight they made was absorbed by the sun. Thus it could illuminate the world with sunlight. The fire also melted ice on the earth, so it became a hot spring. The sisters cooperated to accomplish the huge project. Wangmu Niangniang took care of the fire while Lishan Laomu kneaded the stone paste and made numerous stone cakes. She then stuck them in the broken sky. To prevent the stone cakes from falling down from the sky, Lishan Laomu cut the legs off a huge tortoise and set them up to support the four extremities of the sky. Wangmu Niangniang then used the ashes to fill in the flaws on the earth. After their arduous labor, the world was restored again. After they died, people built a temple at Mount Li to commemorate their tremendous accomplishment.

Xiwangmu or Wangmu Niangniang has long played an important role in folk beliefs. In 3 BC, for example, under the disordered social circumstances of the end of the Western Han, numerous people became involved in a movement of worshiping Xiwangmu. They sang and danced to amuse the goddess. Believing that the goddess would come to the world soon and that only those persons having Xiwangmu's special chips would be able to live, swarms of frightened people traveled around the country and passed the chips (a piece of straw or dried hemp) to others. The movement lasted several months and spread to twenty-six prefectures and shocked the capital. Wang Zijin, a modern Chinese historian, argues that the movement illustrates the Han people's strong folk belief in Xiwangmu's power of controlling longevity and also the deep fear of her western origin (Wang 1999, 114–122). In contemporary China, Wangmu Niangniang is much more popular than Nüwa, Fuxi, and Pangu in popular religion. Temples to her can be found almost all over the area populated by Han people. In Jingchuan County, Gansu Province, there is a Wangmu palace. The building's history can be traced to 1,000 years ago, though the current structure was partially rebuilt in 1992. Now the gods worshiped in the temple complex include Wangmu Niangniang, Dongwanggong, the Three Divine Sovereigns, the Five August Emperors, and even Emperor Mu of Zhou and Emperor Wu of Han. On every lunar March 3 and July 18, residents from local towns join those from faraway cities such as Lanzhou, Yinchuan, Xianyang, Xi'an—and even Taiwan—at the palace to worship Wangmu Niangniang, Dongwanggong, and other gods (according to a field report based on two fieldwork studies in 1999 and 2001, many common pilgrims do not know the name "Xiwangmu"). They pray to receive rain during drought, to rid their farms of locusts, to find a wife, to get a child (especially a son), to recover from an illness, and to receive a long life, as well as for luck in entering college, being wealthy, finding a job, regaining what has been lost, and so forth. Many pilgrims believe that Wangmu Niangniang is very powerful and mighty. She can protect her pilgrims' land from locusts when other land next to it is full of locusts (Zhao 2002, 97–108). On the Tai Mountain in Shandong Province can be found a temple complex named Wangmu Pool. Most of it was built during the Qing dynasty. Every lunar March 3, a Saucer Peach Festival is held to celebrate Wangmu Niangniang's birthday. Pilgrims often try to throw coins into the basins in the center of the pool, believing that they will get the goddess's blessing if they get them in. Some of them like to bring spring water back home, believing the divine water can keep them healthy. According to a report based on two fieldwork studies done in 2000 and 2001, the sacrifices pilgrims offer to the goddess include wine, cigarettes, imitation RMB (renminbi, Chinese currency)—usually with a "10 billion" face value—and even imitation U.S. dollars (Zhao 2002, 109–119).

See also Chang'e; Elixir of Immortality; Feng Bo; Xihe; Xiwangmu; Yao

References and Further Reading

Birrell, Anne. *Chinese Mythology: An Introduction.* Baltimore and London: Johns Hopkins University Press, 1993, 171–176.

Christie, Anthony. *Chinese Mythology.* Rev. ed. New York: Peter Bedrick Books, 1985, 80–81.

Editorial Committee for the Folk Literature Collections in Ningxia Province, comp. *The Collection of Stories in Ningxia Province* (in Chinese). Yinchuan, 1994.

Fracasso, Riccardo. "Holy Mother of Ancient China: A New Approach to the His-wang-mu Problem." *T'oung Pao* 74 (1988): 1–46.

Hou, Guang, and He Xianglu, comps. *Selected Myths from Sichuan Province* (in Chinese). Chengdu: Sichuan Minzu Chubanshe, 1992, 41–42.

Kominami, Ichirou. *Chinese Myths, Legends, and Ancient Novels* (in Chinese). Trans. Sun Changwu. Beijing: Zhonghua Shuju, 1993, 1–128.

Rainey, Lee. "The Queen Mother of the West: An Ancient Chinese Mother Goddess?" In *Sages and Filial Sons: Mythology and Archeology in Ancient China*, eds. Julia Ching and R. W. L. Guisso. Hong Kong: Chinese University Press, 1991, 81–100.

Walls, Jan, and Yvonne Walls, eds. and trans. *Classical Chinese Myths.* Hong Kong: Joint Publishing Co., 1984, 14–15.

Wang, Xiaolian. "Xiwangmu and the Emperor Mu of Zhou" (in Chinese). In *Proceedings of the Conference on Chinese Myth and Legend.* Vol. 1, eds. Li Yiyuan and Wang Qiugui. Taibei: Center for Chinese Studies Research, 1996, 299–318.

Wang, Zijin. "The Folk Belief on Xiwangmu in Han Dynasty" (in Chinese). *Shijie Zongjiao Yanjiu* 2 (1999): 114–122.

Yuan, Ke, and Zhou Ming, comps. *A Source Book of Chinese Myth Texts* (in Chinese). Chengdu: Sichuansheng Shehui Kexueyuan, 1985, 226–232.

Zhao, Zongfu. "The Belief of Xiwangmu: A Study of the Origin and Early Transformations" (in Chinese). PhD diss., Beijing Normal University, 2002.

YAN DI

God of the south, summer, and fire, Yan Di is one of the Five August Emperors (names differ in different texts) who ruled over the five directions and five elements; he is the half brother of Huang Di. He engaged in an extensive war against Huang Di and lost. In later tradition Yan Di was often confused with Shennong, the Divine Farmer. Afterward he was further respected jointly with Huang Di as the common ancestor of all Chinese people. Literally *yan* means "flame," and *di* means "emperor."

According to an account from *Shiji,* Yan Di was the son of Shaodian. He was born after his mother, Nüdeng, was touched by a divine dragon and became pregnant. Shaodian was also said to be the father of Huang Di, the Yellow Emperor. In this explanation, Yan Di and Huang Di were brothers. This relationship is demonstrated in another account from *Xinshu* (*New Documents,* written by a Han dynasty writer, Jia Yi, 201–168 BC). It states that Yan Di was Huang Di's half brother. The same text describes the war between Yan Di and Huang Di. At the beginning of their time, each of the two brothers controlled half of the world. Huang Di ruled his kingdom based on benevolence and morality, but Yan Di did not follow these principles. This finally caused a war between them at the open plain of Zhuolu (which now belongs to modern Hebei Province). The battle was fierce and brutal. It ended in the failure of Yan Di. Huang Di then executed Yan Di and took over his land. The world therefore became peaceful.

The war between Yan Di and his brother is one of the most noteworthy deeds that Yan Di did; it is also one of the most well-known stories in Chinese mythology. Versions of this myth can easily be found in both written texts and oral traditions. However, as for the end of Yan Di, the explanation is quite different in various accounts. Versions recorded in early texts such as the one cited above from *Xinshu* state that Yan Di was killed by Huang Di. But in stories told by people today, the event is the opposite. For example, a narrative collected in the 1980s in Xinzheng County, Henan Province, says that after being defeated, Yan Di accepted Huang Di's good intentions and became an ally to him. They became sworn brothers, and their clans were united into one large country. This version is a good rationalization for the reason both Yan Di and Huang Di have been identified as common ancestors of Chinese people for a long time.

In early texts, Yan Di is also known as one of the Five August Emperors, gods that were distributed according to the five directions (east, south, west, north, and center) and the five elements (wood, fire, metal, water, and earth). Their names may be different in various stories. According to a popular account, Yan Di was the god of the south and the element of fire. He and his subordinate Zhuming managed the beams of steelyards and controlled the season of summer.

Yan Di, god of the south, summer, and fire. (From Wang Qi and Wang Erbin, comps., Sancaituhui, *Jinchang Bao-hanlou Kanben, 1609. Preserved in the Library of Literature Institute, Chinese Academy of Social Sciences)*

As an exalted god, Yan Di had many distinguished descendents who are also famous figures in Chinese mythology. One example is his daughter Nü Wa (literally *nü* means "female," and *wa* means "child"). She drowned while playing in the sea. But she was so unyielding to death that she turned into Jingwei, a mythical bird, and indomitably tried to fill up the sea with pebbles. Another of Yan Di's daughters, Yao Ji, is also well-known for her transformation after dying. She changed into a mythical grass that could make the person who ate it attract other people, causing them to fall in love with that person. Besides these uncommon daughters, the two eminent deities Chiyou (the god of war) and Zhurong (the god of the fire and of the south in some myth versions) are also said to be Yan Di's descendents.

In later tradition, Yan Di was confused with another great god, Shennong, the Divine Farmer. He takes Shennong's basic mythological functions as his own. Therefore, in myths recorded or told by people in later times, Yan Di not only appears as the God of the South and Summer, the half brother of Huang Di who fought against Huang Di at Zhuolu, but also as the God of Agriculture and Medicine, and is given the title "Yan Di Shennong Shi" (*shi* here is a respectful form of address for gods.)

See also Chiyou; Huang Di; Jingwei; Shennong; Yao Grass; Zhurong
References and Further Reading

Birrell, Anne. *Chinese Mythology: An Introduction.* Baltimore and London: Johns Hopkins University Press, 1993, 131–132, 214–215.

Bonnefoy, Yves, comp. *Asian Mythologies.* Translated under the direction of Wendy Doniger. Chicago and London: University of Chicago Press, 1993, 239–241. Originally published as *Dictionnaire des mythologies et des religions des sociétés traditionnelles et du monde antique.* Paris: Flammarion, 1981.

Yuan, Ke. *A Survey of Chinese Mythology* (in Chinese). Chengdu: Bashu Shushe, 1993, 111–118, 130–133.

Zhong, Zongxian. *The Cult of Yan Di Shennong* (in Chinese). Beijing: Xueyuan Chubanshe, 1994.

YAO

A demigod, Yao was the first of the three sage kings. He is famous for initiating the system of abdicating and handing over the crown to a worthy person, and he is the king who ordered the hero Yi to shoot down nine of the ten suns that appeared together in the sky (in some versions he is identified as the hero who shot down those nine suns). He also is known as one of the Five August Emperors in the mythical history of China.

Yao was said to be one of the sagest sovereigns in the remote antiquity of Chinese history. In numerous Confucian writings, he is praised as an exemplary model for emperors in later eras. His virtues include diligence, thrift, and loving his people. He ruled his country by using his virtues and benevolence to influence people instead of using penalties to punish them. Under his rule, society went along in perfect order. Because of that, Confucians identified the era of Yao and several following eras as a golden age in Chinese history. Yao was worshiped together with his successor, Shun, and later Yu as the three sage kings.

Several texts record stories of Yao, Shun, and Yu. The most renowned is that Yao abdicated and handed over his power to Shun. From then on a political system of abdication in favor of a worthy person was started.

In a text from *Shiji,* Yao is described as a son of Di Ku, a god and one of the Five August Emperors in mythical history. As a benevolent and wise sovereign, he had taught people the knowledge of sowing different crops according to different seasons, ordered Gun and his son Yu to stop the flood successively, and had defeated Gonggong and put down all kinds of turbulence throughout the country. With his administering, people were living in happiness and safety.

The most mythical stories of Yao recorded in early documents are those about his birth and about shooting ten suns rising together in the sky. It was said that Yao was born after his mother copulated with a red dragon. His mother, named Qingdu, was the daughter of a great god. When she grew up, her body was often surrounded by yellow clouds. She did not get married until she was twenty years old. One day, as she was beside a river, with a sudden blast, a red dragon flew to her and had sex with her. She then became pregnant and gave birth to Yao after fourteen months.

The myth of shooting down the extra suns that come out together in the sky is very well-known in China. The most common version of this story tells

Yao, the first of the three sage kings, who is famous for initiating the system of abdicating and handing over the crown to a worthy person. He is also known as one of the Five August Emperors in the mythical history of China. (Instructional Resources Corporation)

that the hero Yi shot down nine suns according to Yao's order. But there is also an account in early texts that identifies Yao as the hero who shot the ten suns, which is not popular today. Some scholars believe that in early times there were two versions of the myth of shooting ten suns, and both were popular among the people. In later times because the one telling of Yi became dominant, the other one passed into silence.

Some early records also describe Yao as a culture hero who invented the famous Chinese game of *weiqi* (or Go, a game played with black and white pieces on a square board of 361 intersections formed by nineteen vertical lines and nineteen horizontal lines). This is often related to his eldest son, Danzhu, who was described as a playboy who did not inherit any of his father's merits. In order to exert a favorable influence on him, Yao invented the game of weiqi. He made the board out of mulberry wood and the pieces with rhinoceros and elephant bones, and then taught the art of weiqi to his son. Danzhu was smart enough in learning the game. He even became the best player. However, Danzhu was finally banished to Danshui because he was still a vicious person. One version even mentions that he was executed by Yao.

The Yao myth is still told by people in many areas of China today. For example, a story orally transmitted in Henan Province tells of the conflict between Yao and Danzhu. In this telling, Danzhu was the only son of King Yao. Differing from his father, he was a very snippy and vicious person. He lived in extreme extravagance and often bullied and oppressed ordinary people. Seeing his son be so cruel to people, Yao decided to hand over his throne to a virtuous person, Shun, instead of Danzhu. Danzhu was so angry at hearing this that he decided to murder Yao before he gave the crown to Shun. One day he invited Yao to a new palace where he had prepared a trap to murder his father. According to Danzhu's plan, as soon as Yao went into the palace, he would close and lock the gate, and then have it plugged up with clay. Yao would definitely be killed inside. But Yao was so wise that he saw through Danzhu's trick. He ordered Danzhu to lead the way into the palace. As soon as Danzhu stepped through the gate, Yao closed the gate and locked it. Eventually Danzhu dug a grave for himself.

A story collected from Shanxi Province in northern China describes one of Yao's mythical helpers, a divine goat. When Yao was the king, in the Yangxie area a goat with a single horn was born among a shepherd's goats. This goat was very wise in judging right or wrong. Whenever it saw two persons in a quarrel or a fight, it would butt the one who was in the wrong. The shepherd was surprised at this, so he reported this to Gaotao, one of Yao's ministers. Gaotao then told it to King Yao, and suggested the king see it himself. When they got to Yangxie and saw the goat, Gaotao told Yao that the goat was divine and had appeared as an auspicious sign to the wonderful societies ruled by great sage kings. According to Gaotao, the goat had only appeared one time before, during Huang Di's reign. Yao was moved by the gift from the supreme god. He bought the divine goat, and it served Yao's court as a judge of people's character (faithfulness or treachery, and innocence or guilt).

See also Di Ku; Gonggong; Gun; Huang Di; Shun; Yi; Yu

References and Further Reading

Allan, Sarah. *The Heir and the Sage.* San Francisco: Chinese Materials Center, 1981, 27–54.

Birrell, Anne. *Chinese Mythology: An Introduction.* Baltimore and London: Johns Hopkins University Press, 1993, 138–143, 193–195, 238–240.

Bonnefoy, Yves, comp. *Asian Mythologies.* Translated under the direction of Wendy Doniger. Chicago and London: University of Chicago Press, 1993, 246–250. Originally published as *Dictionnaire des mythologies et des religions des sociétés traditionnelles et du monde antique.* Paris: Flammarion, 1981.

Chen, Yongchao. *A Study of Yao and Shun Legends* (in Chinese). Nanjing: Nanjing Shifan Daxue Chubanshe, 2000.

Yuan, Ke. *A Survey of Chinese Mythology* (in Chinese). Chengdu: Bashu Shushe, 1993, 198–206, 248–251.

Zhang, Zhenli, and Cheng Jianjun, comps. *The Collection of Myths Transmitting in Contemporary Central Plain* (in Chinese). Zhengzhou: Zhongguo Minjian Wenyijia Xiehui Henan Fenhui, 1987, 284–288.

YAO GRASS

Yao Grass is a mythical grass that transformed from the body of Yan Di's daughter Yao Ji after she died. It had special effects on people who ate it, causing them to be charming and attractive to others.

According to *Shanhaijing* (chapter 5), Yan Di's daughter died on Guyao Mountain. Her body transformed into Yao Grass. Its leaves were very luxuriant, its flowers were yellow, and its fruits looked like those of the dodder plant. It had a specific magical power that could make the person who ate it attract other people and cause people to fall in love with them.

The same chapter of *Shanhaijing* states that Yao Grass grew at Taishi Mountain, appearing like the medicinal plant *atractylodes* with white flowers and black fruit. Anyone who used it would never be confused. However, this type of Yao Grass is different from that which Yan Di's daughter transformed into.

See also Yan Di

References and Further Reading

Yuan, Ke. *Myths of Ancient China: An Anthology with Annotations* (in Chinese). Beijing: Renmin Wenxue Chubanshe, [1979] 1996, 91–98.

YI

Yi is Chang'e's husband, a great divine archer and a famous culture hero who shoots down nine surplus suns and also wipes out different kinds of monsters. In later tradition, he is often confused with another archer, Houyi.

Among Yi's various accomplishments, the most known is that he eliminates the nine surplus suns disturbing the cosmic order and returns it to normal. Though he is the most popular hero related to this mythological achievement, he finds many counterparts in myths of other ethnic groups in China.

The myth motif of "formerly several suns" is quite popular among the Han, Hani, Lahu, Luoba, Lisu, Naxi, Qiang, Tujia, Miao, Yao, Dong, Yi, Zhuang, Li, Buyi, Gelao, Mongol, Hezhe, and many other ethnic groups. It illustrates that there was more than one sun appearing in the sky in remote antiquity. The number of the suns may be two, three, seven, nine, ten, or twelve, according to different versions. Usually, the motif appears with another one of "eliminating the surplus suns," and they serve as an etiological myth to explain why there is only one sun today. It usually tells that in ancient ages, several suns appeared in the sky. The weather became extremely hot, the earth was burned, and the crops all died. Humans suffered greatly from the disaster. Then a hero showed up. He shot down (sometimes biting down or knocking down with a bamboo pole in different versions) the surplus suns and left only one for the normal use of this world. In some cases, these motifs about suns show up symmetrically together with the ones of "formerly several moons" and "eliminating the surplus moons."

In ancient written texts in the Chinese language, the number of the multiple suns is usually ten. In some texts of *Shanhaijing,* the goddess Xihe gave birth to ten suns and bathed them in the Gan Gulf. The ten suns lived on the Fusang tree. When one sun finished its work and came back home, another sun would go out in its place. They were all carried by crows (chapters 14 and 15). According to this picture, the ten suns worked in orderly fashion. However, in some other versions, instead of taking duty one by one in order, the ten suns somehow rose up together and thus brought great disaster to the world. The hero who showed up at this time and cleared up the disaster is Yi. The early poem "Tianwen" clearly mentions Yi's story by asking: "Why did Yi shoot down the suns? Why did the crows shed their feathers?" Wang Yi (ca. second century CE), the commentator of "Tianwen," cites a paragraph from *Huainanzi* to explain these questions, stating that at the time of the sage king Yao, the ten suns rose together and burned up the woods and grass. Yao then ordered the hero Yi to shoot down the ten suns in the sky, and Yi shot down nine of them. The nine crows settling on these suns died, and their feathers fell out.

In addition to shooting down the suns, Yi accomplishes other remarkable deeds, such as wiping out various monsters doing harm to people. A text of *Huainanzi* depicts that at the time of Yao, ten suns rose up together in the sky. They burnt crops and killed the grasses and woods, so that humans could not find food. Many ferocious monsters, such as Zhayu (a monster with a dragon's head and leopard's body), Zaochi (whose teeth are as sharp as chisels), Jiuying (a monster with nine heads), Dafeng (an enormous bird), Fengxi (a large wild boar), and Xiushe (a huge snake), all took advantage of this time to devour humans. Yao ordered Yi to eliminate the monsters, and Yi complied. People were so pleased that they respected Yao as their king ("the Son of the Heaven"). Afterward the world became inhabitable and people began to communicate with each other (chapter 8). In some other myths, Yi also punishes the damaging river god, He Bo, and the wind god, Feng Bo. He Bo drowned men, so Yi shot him and blinded his left eye. Feng Bo destroyed people's houses, so Yi shot him in his knees. In another version, Yi stopped Feng Bo from damaging houses by shooting him at the Qinqiu Marsh. Yi is also variously said to have killed Feng Bo.

Another famous Yi myth relates to his wife Chang'e. According to a text in *Huainanzi* (chapter 6), Yi asked for the elixir of immortality from Xiwangmu, the Queen Mother of the West. He got it, but later Chang'e stole it from him and consumed it. Then she flew to the moon. Yi was very disappointed but could not recover the elixir. In some versions, Chang'e is said to transform into a toad after she escapes to the moon. This is usually interpreted as a punishment for her behavior of stealing the precious elixir and abandoning her husband.

Like many Chinese gods and spirits, Yi eventually died. A popular story attributes Yi's death to his apprentice Fengmeng. Fengmeng learned the shooting art from Yi and gradually became an expert. When he realized that Yi was the only obstacle preventing him from being the best archer in the world, he killed Yi by surprise. In some versions, he used a big peach tree branch to strike Yi down. So, from then on, ghosts all fear peach trees, and for this reason the latter are widely used in rituals. After his death, Yi was worshiped as Zongbu, a god who takes charge of averting disasters.

In many versions, especially in many living myths today, Yi is often identified as Houyi. Some scholars argue that because the Yi myth became divergent during its long transmission, Yi is addressed as Houyi sometimes in later tradition and Yi and Houyi are actually the same person (Hu 1994, 1–17). Others believe that the two are originally two separate great archers but are confused in later traditions (Yuan 1996, 267–272).

The Yi story continues to be popularly transmitted in contemporary China. Compared to his various accomplishments in ancient written recordings, the modern Yi myth usually shows more interest in his shooting down the suns and his wife's escaping to the moon. A myth collected in the 1980s in Ba County, Chongqing Municipality, formerly Sichuan Province, states that when humans just came to this world, there were ten suns in the sky. Sometimes they showed up together, sometimes they appeared in turn. Because of this, there was no night in this world, only day. The suns burnt the earth into cracks, and men died of thirst and hunger. At that time, a man named Houyi appeared. He had great strength, and he decided to shoot down the suns in the sky. His bow was made of tiger's bone, and his arrows were made of dragon's tendons. Using his magic bow and arrows, he shot down nine suns in one breath. The last sun was so scared that it ran away and hid. The world was then cast into a long night. Humans could not live in this environment either, so they asked Houyi not to shoot the last remaining sun. Though Houyi did not shoot it, the last sun still did not dare to appear. So people shouted to it: "Come out, please!" But the sun did not reveal itself. The people in turn sent a magpie, a crow, and a night owl to shout to the sun as an invitation, but the sun still did not rise. Finally, the cock sincerely shouted to the sun: "Oh Brother, Brother [pronounced *gege* in Chinese], come out please!" The sun was touched, so it finally rose. From then on, every morning, the cock shouts to the sun: "Gege, Gege." Hearing its voice, the sun gradually shows up and brings brightness to the world.

In another myth collected in the 1980s in Henan Province, the ten suns are described as the grandsons of the God of Heaven. Every morning they came out together to play, which caused serious calamity: the crops withered and rivers dried up. To banish the disaster, Houyi shot down nine of them. When he was going to shoot the last one, the sun disappeared. The world became so dark that nothing could be seen. Then an earthworm told Houyi that the sun was hiding on the earth, under a lush purslane. But Houyi could not find it because of the darkness. Later, since humans could not live without the sun, they invited the sun to rise again. When the sun rose up to the sky, to pay a debt of gratitude to the purslane for protecting it from being discovered by Houyi, the sun would never bask the purslane to death. But as soon as the earthworm showed itself, it would be basked to death.

Another group of Yi myths orally transmitted in contemporary China connects Houyi with Chang'e. A version that attributes the origin of the Mid-Autumn Festival to their love story goes like this: In the remote past, there was a hero named Yi who was excellent at shooting. One year, the ten suns rose in the sky together and brought great disaster to people. Yi shot down nine of them and was given the elixir of immortality as a reward. Yi did not want to be immortal without his wife Chang'e with him, so he did not consume it. One day, on the fifteenth of August in the lunar calendar, when Yi went out hunting, his apprentice, Fengmeng, broke into Yi's house and forced Chang'e to give the elixir to him. Chang'e refused to do so. To protect it from being stolen, she swallowed it and flew into the sky. Since she loved her husband very much and hoped to live nearby, she chose the moon for her residence. When Yi came back and learned what had happened, he felt so sad that he displayed the fruits and cakes Chang'e liked in the yard and gave sacrifices to his wife. People were sympathetic to Chang'e, so they participated in these sacrifices with Yi. From then on, on every August 15 in the lunar calendar, people eat moon cakes and round fruits to commemorate Chang'e.

See also Chang'e; Elixir of Immortality; Feng Bo; Kunlun Mountain; Xihe; Xiwangmu; Yao

References and Further Reading

Birrell, Anne. *Chinese Mythology: An Introduction.* Baltimore and London: Johns Hopkins University Press, 1993, 138–145.

Bodde, Derk. "Myths of Ancient China." In *Mythologies of the Ancient World,* ed. Samuel Noah Kramer. Garden City, NY: Anchor Books, 1961, 394–398.

Bonnefoy, Yves, comp. *Asian Mythologies.* Translated under the direction of Wendy Doniger. Chicago and London: University of Chicago Press, 1993, 236–237. Originally published as *Dictionnaire des mythologies et des religions des sociétés traditionnelles et du monde antique.* Paris: Flammarion, 1981.

Guan, Donggui. "A Study of the Ten Suns Myth in Ancient China." In *Selected Essays on Chinese Mythology Studies* (in Chinese), ed. Ma Changyi. Beijing: Zhongguo Guangbo Dianshi Chubanshe, 1994, 93–118.

Hou, Guang, and He Xianglu, comps. *Selected Myths from Sichuan Province* (in Chinese). Chengdu: Sichuan Minzu Chubanshe, 1992, 111–112.

Hu, Nianyi. "A Study of the Houyi Myth." In *Selected Essays on Chinese Mythology Studies* (in Chinese), ed. Ma Changyi. Beijing: Zhongguo Guangbo Dianshi Chubanshe, 1994, 1–17.

Walls, Jan, and Yvonne Walls, eds. and trans. *Classical Chinese Myths*. Hong Kong: Joint Publishing Co., 1984, 65–76.

Yuan, Ke. *Dragons and Dynasties: An Introduction to Chinese Mythology*. Selected and translated by Kim Echlin and Nie Zhixiong. New York: Penguin Books, 1993, 73–91. First published by Foreign Languages Press, Beijing, 1991.

Yuan, Ke. *Myths of Ancient China: An Anthology with Annotations* (in Chinese). Beijing: People's Literature, [1979] 1996, 260–288.

Zhang, Zhenli, and Cheng Jianjun, comps. *The Collection of Myths Transmitting in the Contemporary Central Plain* (in Chinese). Zhengzhou: Zhongguo Minjian Wenyijia Xiehui Henan Fenhui, 1987, 190–191.

YINGLONG

A divine winged dragon who helped Huang Di to overcome Chiyou in a battle, Yinglong is also identified as the god of rain in some texts. *Yinglong* literally means "Responding Dragon."

Several texts about Yinglong are scattered in different sections of *Shanhaijing*. According to Jin dynasty scholar Guo Pu (276–324 CE), who wrote a commentary on *Shanhaijing*, Yinglong was a type of dragon who had wings. As a story in *Shanhaijing* (chapter 17) illustrates, Yinglong made a great contribution to Huang Di in winning the battle against Chiyou. When Chiyou started a war to challenge Huang Di, Huang Di commanded Yinglong to launch an attack against Chiyou in the wilderness of the central plain. Yinglong began by storing all of the water in order to flood and submerge his rivals. Chiyou responded with the same tactic. He asked the gods Feng Bo and Yu Shi to release a gale and a cloudburst in aid of his attacks. Huang Di then asked the drought goddess Ba to descend down from the heavens and cause a drought. With her help, the rain was stopped. In this way, through the use of a drought, Huang Di killed Chiyou.

In another version of the myth found in the same chapter of *Shanhaijing*, the person who killed Chiyou is said to be Yinglong, and it is written that later Yinglong also killed Kuafu. Afterwards he moved to the south to settle down. Because of his arrival in the south and inhabitance there, the south was abundant with rain.

In a text from chapter 14 of *Shanhaijing*, Yinglong is described as a god who had the power of controlling the rain. He dwelled in the remote south after he killed Chiyou and Kuafu. Since he could not ascend to the heavens, there was no longer a deity to release the rain, and drought occurred frequently on the earth. Whenever and wherever a drought appeared, if the people there made a statue of Yinglong with clay and held a ritual, it would rain. This myth has shaped a complicated praying-for-rain ritual that was practiced in later times.

See also Ba; Chiyou; Dragon; Feng Bo; Huang Di; Kuafu; Yu Shi

References and Further Reading

Birrell, Anne. *Chinese Mythology: An Introduction.* Baltimore and London: Johns Hopkins University Press, 1993, 132–134, 148.

Christie, Anthony. *Chinese Mythology.* Rev. ed. New York: Peter Bedrick Books, 1985, 96.

Yuan, Ke. *The Classic of Mountains and Seas: A Collation and Annotation* (in Chinese). Chengdu: Bashu Shushe, 1993, 413–415, 490–494.

YOUCHAOSHI

A celebrated culture hero, Youchaoshi was the inventor of the house (or "nest") in which people could live. Literally, *you* means "have," *chao* means "nest," and *shi* here is a respectful form of address. Thus, Youchaoshi literally means "the person who invented the nest." He is also known as Youchao or Da Chao (*da* means "great").

Records about Youchaoshi in early texts are not very detailed. According to several similar accounts scattered in different classical documents, Youchaoshi was a sage who invented the nest for people to live in. In the remote past, the world was home to many beasts and birds, many more than there were human beings. People suffered from the animals' disturbances. Then a wise man invented a wooden nest for people to dwell in. People were happy to be safe from harm by different animals, so they chose the wise man as their king. The man was called Youchaoshi.

A myth collected in the 1980s in Ba County, Chongqing Municipality, southwest China, gives a detailed description of the story about Youchaoshi's invention of the house. In ancient times, people had neither clothes to wear nor houses to live in. When it snowed, many people died from frostbite. A man named Youchaoshi worried about this. He was determined to figure out an idea to help people get away from the harmful cold. One day when he napped on the branch of a tree, he dreamed that he flew up to heaven. With a god's indication, he located the god of construction. He asked the god how people could keep from dying in the winter. Though Youchaoshi repeatedly asked for the god's help, the god refused to contribute any ideas, with the excuse that he did not care about the affairs of the earth. At last the god pushed Youchaoshi down on his hands, and he dropped down to the earth. As Youchaoshi awoke from this dream, he thought of the buildings in heaven and wished they could be made on the earth. He was so frustrated that he pawed at a huge tree. Immediately a furrow appeared in the trunk of the tree that was large enough to accommodate four or five people. Youchaoshi recognized that the god of construction had transmitted a divine power to him in pushing him down on his hands. He then set about fashioning many furrows in trees for people to live. Afterwards, the human population grew larger and larger, whereas large trees became fewer and fewer. Remembering that the buildings he had seen in heaven were made of wood, Youchaoshi tried to construct one by putting small trees onto the branches of large trees. With his efforts, he eventually invented the first house in the shape of a nest.

References and Further Reading

Christie, Anthony. *Chinese Mythology*. Rev. ed. New York: Peter Bedrick Books, 1985, 87.

Hou, Guang, and He Xianglu, comps. *Selected Myths from Sichuan Province* (in Chinese). Chengdu: Sichuan Minzu Chubanshe, 1992, 255–256.

Yuan, Ke, and Zhou Ming, comps. *A Source Book of Chinese Myth Texts* (in Chinese). Chengdu: Sichuansheng Shehui Kexueyuan, 1985, 28.

YOUDU

Youdu is the capital of the other world that is located below the surface of the earth. It is also the name of a place where the sun sets.

You in Chinese means "dark," and *du* means "capital." According to Chinese people's beliefs, when human beings die, their souls will go to the underground world that is reigned over by the god Houtu. Youdu is the capital of this world. Because it is a very dark place, it is named Youdu, the Dark Capital.

Another version about Youdu describes it as the place where the sun sets. When the sun reaches Youdu it sets, and therefore the whole world is in darkness.

See also Houtu

References and Further Reading

Yuan, Ke, and Zhou Ming, comps. *A Source Book of Chinese Myth Texts* (in Chinese). Chengdu: Sichuansheng Shehui Kexueyuan Chubanshe, 1985, 32, 50.

YU

Yu is a demigod miraculously born from the belly of Gun's corpse, a hero famous for controlling the world flood, and the successor of Shun. He is the third of the three sage kings; the founder of the first civilized state, Xia; and is sometimes identified as a descendent of Zhuanxu and Huang Di. His name often appears as Da Yu in verbal art (*da* literally means "great").

According to a renowned account recorded in many early texts, Yu was born from the belly of his father's corpse. Yu's father, Gun, was executed by Zhurong (names vary in different versions) for stealing Xirang, the self-growing soil, from the Supreme Divinity in order to stop the flood, though Gun failed in his mission. However, for three years after Gun died, his corpse was not tampered with. When his belly was opened with a sword, Yu emerged out of it.

None of the early records mention how and by whom the belly of Gun's corpse was opened. A reasonable explanation for this vagueness might be found in a detailed description from a story orally transmitted in the Huai River valley. It states that after Gun was executed, his spirit was so unyielding that he conceived a new life in his belly. Learning this news, the Supreme Divinity sent one of his subordinates to inspect it. The subordinate found that Gun's corpse had vitality as if he was still alive. He hacked at Gun's belly with a precious sword the Supreme Divinity granted him. Then the baby Yu was born, riding a dragon from the opened belly.

The greatest deed that Yu performed was that he stopped the world flood. A version tells that Yu was commanded by the Supreme Divinity to spread Xirang to control the floodwaters and stabilize the world. In another popular version, Yu was recommended to King Yao by Shun to fight against the flood. However it is recounted, being born of Gun's indomitable spirit, Yu continued his father's unfinished work as he grew.

It is said that in dealing with this difficult task, Yu suffered and struggled for thirteen years. He devoted himself thoroughly to the mission of stopping the flood, so that he

Yu. Funeral stone carving in the Eastern Han dynasty, Wuliang Shrine, Jiaxiang County, Shandong Province. The inscription reads, "Yu of the Xia was good at examining lands and water, and knew the cosmic principle. He built dams according to seasons. After retiring, he invented the method of cultivating the quietness in one's soul." (Feng Yunpeng and Feng Yunyuan, Research on Stone Carving, *1821)*

did not visit his home even once during this long term. According to a famous story, even when he had three opportunities to pass by his home, he did not go into his house. This virtue of selflessness and strong-mindedness won him great respect from people in later times.

As a wise and astute hero, he sought assistance from different mythical helpers and performed many miracles in battling the flood. Differing from the method of only barricading against the overflowing water with soil his father had used, Yu mainly applied a strategy to channel the floodwater into the sea together with building barricades. Evidence for this can be found in an account in "Tianwen." It states in a questioning style, "The whirlpool was so deep, how could Yu fill it in with mud? How did Yinglong (Responding Dragon) drag on the earth with his tail so that the flood was channeled into the sea?" A similar depiction may be found in another text from *Shiyiji* (*Researches into Lost Records*, ca. fourth century). It mentions that when Yu was on his mission of stopping the flood, Yinglong dragged its tail to channel the water in front of him, while a huge black turtle carrying green mud followed him.

Many stories mention Yu getting help from different gods. One of the popular versions is that he was given a detailed map for controlling flood by He Bo, the god of the Yellow River (*he* literally means "river," and *bo* means "master" or "god"). It was said that He Bo used to be a human being named Fengyi (sometimes Pingyi or Bingyi; names differ in some versions). He was drowned while ferrying the Yellow River. The Supreme Divinity had compassion for him, so that he appointed Fengyi to be the god of the river. When Yu started his mission of flood control with an investigation of the situation at the Yellow River, a god with a white human face and a fish trunk emerged from the water. He told Yu that he was He Bo, and he gave a map of the locations of rivers to Yu. Then he dove into the river again. With this map, Yu got the big picture concerning the situation of world flooding and made reasonable methods to deal with it, which helped him greatly in stopping the flood.

In order to control the flood, Yu defeated and controlled many different monsters that brought disasters to men. One example is that he executed Xiangliu, a nine-headed monster that, wherever it passed, turned land into marshes and gullies in which no animals could survive. Another example is that he controlled Wuzhiqi, the monster in the Huai River. When Yu traveled to Tongbai Mountain on his mission of flood control, several times he encountered gales and thunder made by the monster Wuzhiqi and its mythical followers, which prevented him from starting his work here. Yu became angry. He assembled all the gods and ordered Kui to clear all of the evils. Gods from Tongbai and other mountains who used to follow Wuzhiqi were scared, so they yielded to Yu. Yu put some of them into jail and hence enticed Wuzhiqi, spirit of the Huai River, to appear. It appeared as a monkey with a green trunk, white head, yellow eyes, and white paws. Its neck reached nearly 100 feet when stretched, and its strength was as powerful as that of nine elephants. The monster was good at talking, very smart and quick to act. After failing several times in choosing a person among his subordinate gods to control the monster, Yu finally found that Gengchen was the right choice, capable of controlling Wuzhiqi. Gengchen drove away all kinds of demons that came to disturb his work. He tied Wuzhiqi's neck with a thick and sturdy chain, pierced its nose with a golden bell, and kept it at the foot of Gui Mountain. From then on the Huai River was under control.

Because he could not only defeat and execute demons or gods who disobeyed his orders but also govern all the gods, Yu was identified by some scholars as the Supreme Divinity. This assumption might be supported by the stories about his banishing Gonggong, the water god, and killing Fangfeng, a god and giant who arrived late to his assembly of gods.

Except for his mythical power, Yu is also praised in various texts for his extraordinary braveness. For example, an account recorded in different early texts depicts that Yu, as a human being, once overcame a dragon. One time in his travels to inspect the south, when Yu was ferried across the Yangzi River, a yellow dragon suddenly appeared on the boat. All the passengers in the boat were terrified except for Yu. Yu said to the dragon with a laugh, "On behalf of the heavens, I'm doing my best to save all the people. For me, I am just temporarily staying in the world, and will be going back home to die. How could you scare me?" During his talk, he looked at the dragon as if he was facing a small worm. The dragon thus fled.

Among the Yu myths, stories about Yu and his wife, a lady from Tushan, are very rich in detail. It is said that Yu did not marry until he was thirty years old, when he passed by Tushan on his travels to control the flood. According to an account from early texts, Yu was afraid that he would transgress the moral rite of passage that required a man to marry by the age of thirty; he therefore prayed for an omen to signify his marriage. Immediately after this, a white fox with nine tails appeared to him. Yu explained this as an omen that he would marry a girl from the Tushan clan. He thus made his marriage with Tushanshi, the girl from Tushan (shi here is an address for a married woman).

Some versions tell that on the fifth day after he got married, Yu left his wife and continued his work of controlling the flood. Nevertheless, a lot of stories mention that Yu was working with his wife's help. The most well-known is that about Yu changing into a bear. When Yu was starting to excavate through a mountain in order to channel the flood to the sea, he told Tushanshi, "Please send me food whenever you hear the drum." Then he went to the mountain and changed into a bear to cut off the mountains and rocks. While working, he stepped on the drum by error. Hearing the drum, Tushanshi brought food to her husband. Yu was unaware of his wife's presence, and he continued to work as a bear. Tushanshi was ashamed of seeing that her husband had changed into a beast, so she fled. At the foot of the mountain, she began to change into a stone. This happened right at the time when she was going to give birth to a baby. When Yu finally found his wife, she had already become a rock. He asked the transformation of his wife to give him back the baby. The rock then split at the side facing the north. From the opening Yu's son, Qi, was born (*qi* literally means "open"). Qi later inherited his father's throne and became the first emperor of Xia, the first civilized state in China.

By working hard for thirteen years, Yu eventually stopped the flood. As a result, the world became dry, and people became settled again. Because of his great contribution to the world and because of his virtues, Yu was chosen by King Shun as the successor to his crown.

In addition to controlling the flood, Yu accomplished many other impressive deeds that were influential in Chinese mythology and history. The most famous one is that he had the earth measured. According to an account from *Shanhaijing* (chapter 9), Yu ordered his subordinate Shuhai to measure the earth from the extreme area of the east to that of the west. He then got the information about the distance between these two extremes. It was 500,109,800 *bu* (*bu* literally means "pace"; according to one version, one bu is about eight feet). In different texts, the details about Yu having the earth measured vary. For instance, in a text from chapter 4 of *Huainanzi*, Yu is said to have both the distance between the east and the west and that between the two poles measured, and the figure is different from that noted in *Shanhaijing*. However, this work is believed to have greatly helped Yu in controlling the flood and ruling the country.

Another of Yu's mythical deeds is that he cast the Nine Cauldrons after succeeding to Shun's throne. Those cauldrons had the divine function to teach people to distinguish between faithfulness and treachery, and to keep evils and demons from harming people, so they were treated as national treasures. In later tradition, though these cauldrons were scattered and disappeared, they were identified as the symbol of the supreme imperial power. It was believed that whoever wanted to be the emperor should possess the Nine Cauldrons.

As a hero who devoted himself to saving people, who made a great contribution to the world, and who showed great spirit in making every effort to complete a task no matter how arduous, Yu has been respected not only as a paragon of sovereigns in later times but also as an exemplary model to encourage people to actively handle difficult situations and to strive for a better life. Besides being a major mythological figure, Yu also has had widespread influence in Chinese culture and society. For example, in Taoism, the most popular traditional religion in China, there is a renowned ritual dance named the Yu Pace. It is believed to be a powerful magic dance. In important rituals Taoists will perform it while imitating being lame. This dance is said to originate from Yu. One version associates this with Yu's work of controlling the flood. Because he had been keeping at this work for so long, he got rheumatism in one leg and became lame. To commemorate him, people in later times created the ritual dance by imitating his walk, and named it after Yu. Another version says this dance was created by Yu himself by imitating a divine bird's act. When he assembled all the gods, he often danced with this pace.

Furthermore, in many places all over the country, such as Shandong, Henan, Shanxi, Shaanxi, Zhejiang, and Sichuan provinces, one can find many temples to King Yu built in different times. In Hequ County, Shanxi Province, for instance, there is a King Yu temple, built in the Qing dynasty. Every July 15 according to the lunar calendar, people will hold a grand ritual to worship Yu. In the evening, there will be a lantern festival. In Shaoxing City, Zhejiang Province, there is the Tomb of Yu, where Yu is said to be buried (the legendary location of Yu's tomb varies from one version to the next). Beside the tomb, an old King Yu temple has been rebuilt and redecorated many times. Originally this temple was built in the Southern and Northern dynasties (420–589 CE), but it was demolished in later times. Repeatedly, the temple was reconstructed after being destroyed. The temple in existence today was reconstructed in 1934; it is still maintained and kept in good condition. Both the tomb and the temple served as the place where sovereigns in different dynasties offered sacrifices to King Yu. According to early records, the first emperor of the Qin dynasty came here to worship King Yu. This started a rite for emperors in later times to worship King Yu at the Tomb of Yu in Shaoxing. At present, this place is still attractive to Chinese leaders and a lot of ordinary people.

Another place famous for temples of Yu is Beichuan County in Sichuan Province. This is one of the places where Yu is said to have been born. In this county, from the Tang dynasty (618–907) through the present, several temples and memorials for Yu were built. The most impressive one is the Da Yu Memorial. It is an ancient-style building built in 1991 with the support of the local government. Inside, pictures about Da Yu's legendary remains, rubbings of related inscriptions, books and articles studying Yu, and various artworks are presented. As the first memorial to Da Yu in China, it can be taken as a typical symbol for Chinese people nowadays to express their highest respect to the great Yu.

See also Fangfeng; Floods, The; Gonggong; Gun; Huang Di; Shun; Xiangliu; Yao; Yinglong

References and Further Reading

Allan, Sarah. *The Heir and the Sage.* San Francisco: Chinese Materials Center, 1981, 55–76.

Birrell, Anne. *Chinese Mythology: An Introduction.* Baltimore and London: Johns Hopkins University Press, 1993, 81–83, 121–123, 146–159.

Bonnefoy, Yves, comp. *Asian Mythologies.* Translated under the direction of Wendy Doniger. Chicago and London: University of Chicago Press, 1993, 241–244, 246–260. Originally published as *Dictionnaire des mythologies et des religions des sociétés traditionnelles et du monde antique.* Paris: Flammarion, 1981.

Christie, Anthony. *Chinese Mythology.* Rev. ed. New York: Peter Bedrick Books, 1985, 92–96.

Tao, Yang, and Zhong Xiu, comps. *A Collection of Oral Myths in China* (in Chinese). Shanghai: Shanghai Wenyi Chubanshe, [1990] 1991, 526–531, 538–539.

Walls, Jan, and Yvonne Walls, eds. and trans. *Classical Chinese Myths.* Hong Kong: Joint Publishing Co., 1984, 94–109.

Xie, Xinpeng. "The History of Da Yu's Worship" (in Chinese). Web site of Zhongguo Xianqinshi, http://www.zgxqs.org/ztwh/dyyj.

Yuan, Ke. *A Survey of Chinese Mythology* (in Chinese). Chengdu: Bashu Shushe, 1993, 248–277.

Yuan, Ke. *Myths of Ancient China: An Anthology with Annotations* (in Chinese). Beijing: Renmin Wenxue, [1979] 1996, 289–321.

Zhang, Zhenli, and Cheng Jianjun, comps. *The Collection of Myths Transmitting in Contemporary Central Plain (in Chinese). Zhengzhou: Zhongguo Minjian Wenyijia Xiehui Henan Fenhui, 1987, 301–368.*

YU SHI

The rain god Yu Shi was one of the great aides of Chiyou in the battle against Huang Di. In his name *yu* means "rain" and *shi* means "master."

Yu Shi usually appears in Chinese myth and popular religions together with the wind god Feng Bo. The most famous story about him is from *Shanhaijing* (chapter 17). This text tells how Yu Shi and Feng Bo helped Chiyou in his fight against Huang Di. When Huang Di's subordinate Yinglong attacked Chiyou by storing all water, Chiyou asked Feng Bo and Yu Shi to release a storm. Huang Di sent a request to the drought goddess Ba to descend from heaven and stop the storm. Because of the subsequent drought caused by Ba, Chiyou lost the battle. However, Yu Shi and Feng Bo are remembered and written about for the impressive powers they showed in the war, and the text in *Shanhaijing* recounts these divine powers.

Another account about Yu Shi appears in *Hanfeizi.* It depicts Yu Shi, Feng Bo, and even Chiyou as subordinate gods of Huang Di. When Huang Di assembled the deities and ghosts on Mount Tai, he was surrounded by many retinues. Elephants and dragons pulled the cart for him, the divine bird Bifang accompanied him, Chiyou led the way, Feng Bo cleaned the road, Yu Shi created sprinkles of rain along the way, tigers and wolves ran ahead, and deities and ghosts followed him. The descriptions in this text are quite contrary to those in the above text from *Shanhaijing* that presents these gods as enemies of Huang Di. Chinese scholars have been trying to find an explanation for this paradox; however, no convincing conclusions have been made.

Among the Han people and some ethnic groups such as the Maonan people in southwest China, Yu Shi is still active (as is Feng Bo) in popular religion today. In rituals held to pray for rain, Yu Shi is often worshiped as one of the important gods of rain. However, the Yu Shi in this context holds a higher divine position than the deity who had a close but subordinate relation to Huang Di in the battle between Huang Di and Chiyou. This suggests that Yu Shi may be identified with other deities in different areas and ethnic groups.

See also Ba; Chiyou; Feng Bo; Huang Di; Yinglong

References and Further Reading

Christie, Anthony. *Chinese Mythology.* Rev. ed. New York: Peter Bedrick Books, 1985, 72–73.

Liu, Chenghuai. *Myths in Ancient China* (in Chinese). Shanghai: Shanghai Wenyi Chubanshe, 1988, 126–135.

Wei, Qiutong, and Tan Yazhou. "On the Myths of the Maonan People" (in Chinese). *Chizhou Shizhuan Xuebao* 1 (1996): 61–66.

YULÜ

One of the earliest Gate Gods, Yulü always appears with Shentu in myths and popular religion.

See also Shentu

YUQIANG

Yuqiang is a descendent of Huang Di. He is the god of the north sea and the god of wind. He appears as Yujing in some versions.

In several sections of *Shanhaijing*, Yuqiang's pedigree, appearance, and power are described in detail. In a text from chapter 14, Yuqiang is identified as Yuhao's son. Yuhao was born by Huang Di, the Yellow Emperor. He lived in the east sea, and his son Yuqiang lived in the north sea. They both were sea gods. Two other accounts from *Shanhaijing* (chapters 8 and 17) depict Yuqiang as a god that had a human face and a bird's body. He pierced his ears with a pair of dark snakes, and he often stepped on two dark (or red, in a record in chapter 17) snakes that served as his bearers. This kind of feature corresponds to his mythical power. From his human face and bird's body, some scholars assume that Yuqiang was also the wind god. He was actually a god who took charge of affairs both about the sea and the wind. This may be substantiated by various accounts in *Huainanzi* and *Lüshi Chunqiu* (*Annals of Master Lü*, third century BC). They all mention that the northwest wind came from Yuqiang.

In *Liezi*, another story is recorded that tells how Yuqiang helped the God of Heaven rearrange the natural order. In the remote area east of the Bohai Sea, there was a bottomless deep into which all water from every river and other source flowed. In this deep there stood the five highest mountains. Each mountain was 30,000 *li* (about 10,000 miles) in height and circumference, and the distance between two mountains was 70,000 li (about 23,000 miles). On the top of these mountains were fantastic scenery and many mythical animals and fruits. Many gods and demigods lived there. They could fly from one mountain to another in one day and night. However, because these mountains did not have roots, they often floated with the waves and were never still. The gods and demigods living there worried about this and complained to the God of Heaven. Yuqiang was in turn asked to deal with the situation. Yuqiang arranged for fifteen huge sea turtles to carry the mountains on their heads. The turtles were divided into three groups. Each group should take a turn in carrying the mountains for 60,000 years. From then on the mountains were fixed. It is obvious that this story has been strongly influenced by the ideas of Taoism; however, it clearly reflects Yuqiang's mythical power and important role among all gods.

See also Huang Di

References and Further Reading

Birrell, Anne. *Chinese Mythology: An Introduction.* Baltimore and London: Johns Hopkins University Press, 1993, 185–186.

Christie, Anthony. *Chinese Mythology.* Rev. ed. New York: Peter Bedrick Books, 1985, 71–72.

Yang, Kuan. "The Pictures of Gods for Four Seasons and the Creation Myths in the Silk Paintings of Chu" (in Chinese). *Wenxue Yichan* 4 (1997): 4–12.

ZHONG

Zhong is noted as the god who cut off the connection between the sky and the earth with another god, Li.

See also Li

ZHUANXU

A descendent of Huang Di, Zhuanxu was the God of the North and one of the Five August Emperors in the mythical history of China. He ordered Zhong and Li to separate heaven from the earth. He is also known as Gaoyang.

According to a text from *Shanhaijing* (chapter 18), Zhuanxu was one of Huang Di's great-grandsons. He was the son of Hanliu, a grandson of Huang Di and Leizu. A text from *Shiji* (chapter 1) states that Zhuanxu is the offspring of Huang Di and Leizu. However, in that version Zhuanxu is also known as Huang Di's grandson. This may be taken as textual evidence of the confusing and contradictory elements that often appear in Chinese myths.

In other early texts Zhuanxu's various mythical powers and great deeds are mentioned. Some texts depict him as a god who had two dragons as his bearers, some say that it was he who had arranged the positions of the sun and stars, and some state that he was the god who defeated Gonggong's challenge for power and executed him. Among these, the most well-known versions are the myths about separating the sky and the earth and those about his identity as the God of the North.

The myth of separating the sky and the earth can be found in many early written texts in the Chinese language. The details of the story vary in different accounts, but they each state that it was Zhuanxu who ordered his subordinates Zhong and Li to cut off the link between the sky and the earth, which from then on prevented people from ascending to the sky and also prohibited the deities from descending to the earth.

A text from *Huainanzi* (chapter 3) identifies Zhuanxu and another four gods, Huang Di, Yan Di, Houtu, and Shaohao, as the five great gods corresponding to the five basic directions (east, south, west, north, and center) and the five basic elements (wood, fire, metal, water, and earth). Zhuanxu was the god who ruled the north, which is associated with water. With the help of his subordinate Xuanming, he also ruled the sliding weights of steelyards and controlled the season of winter. In the mythical history of China, the five great gods were historicized and explained as the Five August Emperors in ancient times. There are several versions about the names of these divine sovereigns, and Zhuanxu is included in every version.

After he died, Zhuanxu was said to be buried at Wuyu Mountain with his nine concubines (*Shanhaijing*, chapters 8 and 17). He had many offspring, some of whom were very famous. For example, Zhong and Li, the two deities who separated the sky and the earth, are introduced as Zhuanxu's grandsons in some versions. Another example is Pengzu, known as the great-grandson of Zhuanxu in one text. He is famous in myths and legends for having the longest human life, living

800 years. Zhuanxu also had many offspring who did not inherit their progenitor's virtues, such as the three of his sons who died and became pestilent ghosts. One of them became the ghost who distributes diseases, another became a monster, and the third became the ghost who scares and harms infants and children.

Nowadays, the Zhuanxu myth is not often told, but Zhuanxu is still worshiped in many places as one of the primogenitors of human beings. In Henan, Hebei, and Shandong provinces there are many different places claiming to be Zhuanxu's hometown or the place where his tomb is located. Based on these kinds of "historical remains," each of these places has developed local rituals or customs for Zhuanxu worship. In Neihuang County, Henan Province, for instance, there is a place where people believe Zhuanxu was buried; a tomb was subsequently built for him. Every March 18 in the lunar calendar, a big festival is held here to celebrate Zhuanxu's birthday. On this date in 2003, supported and directed by the local government, the county even had a public worship service for Zhuanxu. It was said that the number of pilgrims and participants from mainland China and areas overseas reached 300,000.

See also Huang Di; Leizu; Li; Yan Di

References and Further Reading

Birrell, Anne. *Chinese Mythology: An Introduction.* Baltimore and London: Johns Hopkins University Press, 1993, 91–97.

Bonnefoy, Yves, comp. *Asian Mythologies.* Translated under the direction of Wendy Doniger. Chicago and London: University of Chicago Press, 1993, 246–247. Originally published as *Dictionnaire des mythologies et des religions des sociétés traditionnelles et du monde antique.* Paris: Flammarion, 1981.

Christie, Anthony. *Chinese Mythology.* Rev. ed. New York: Peter Bedrick Books, 1985, 58–60.

Li, Hucheng. "A Large-Scale Public Worship Service for Zhuanxu and Di Ku Was Held in Neihuang" (in Chinese). *Henan Daily,* Apr. 20, 2003.

Yang, Kuan. "The Pictures of Gods for Four Seasons and the Creation Myths in the Silk Paintings of Chu" (in Chinese). *Wenxue Yichan* 4 (1997): 4–12.

Yuan, Ke. *A Survey of Chinese Mythology* (in Chinese). Chengdu: Bashu Shushe, 1993, 165–175.

ZHULONG

Zhulong is a powerful deity who appears to be part dragon and originates the day and night, the seasons, and the wind. In his name *zhu* means "torch" and *long* means "dragon." He appears as Zhuyin ("Torch Shadow") in other versions.

According to *Shanhaijing* (chapter 17), Zhulong lived on Zhangwei Mountain located north of the Red River, beyond the northwest sea. He was a deity

Zhulong, part dragon, who originates the day and night, the seasons, and the wind. Originally drawn in the 17th century by Jiang Yinghao. (Ma Changyi, The Classic of Mountains and Seas: Ancient Illustrations with Annotations, *Shandong Huabao Chubanshe, 2001)*

with a human face and a snake's trunk. His body was completely red and was 1,000 *li* (about 300 miles) in length. He had vertical eyes in two straight seams. When his eyes opened there was daylight, and when they closed it became night. He never ate, slept, or breathed, and he only swallowed the wind and the rain. This deity could light the darkness to extreme depths under the earth, thus he was called Zhulong ("Torch Dragon").

In a similar account from *Shanhaijing* (chapter 8), Zhulong appears as Zhuyin. In addition to the features and powers mentioned in the version cited above, this text describes Zhuyin as a deity who composed the seasons. When he blew hard it was winter, and when he exhaled hotly it was summer. He neither drank, ate, nor breathed, but when he did breathe in and out his breath would make the wind.

The Zhulong myth has interested many scholars, and many different interpretations of this myth have been put forward. Among them the most controversial hypotheses are those that suggest the myth is a fantastic reflection of actual phenomena that had been seen by ancient people before they composed this myth. For example, some scholars assume that this myth is in fact a reflection of a kind of natural spectacle; some argue that it is a description of an active volcano; some identify it with the northern polar lights. These perspectives that trace the origin of a myth based on modern scientific discoveries have stirred

Chinese mythology scholarship for several years. But a commonly accepted conclusion has not been reached yet, and it may never be reached.

See also Dragon; Pangu

References and Further Reading

Birrell, Anne. *Chinese Mythology: An Introduction.* Baltimore and London: Johns Hopkins University Press, 1993, 68–69, 232.

Han, Xiangchu. "A Query about the Idea of Equating the Zhulong Myth with Polar Lights" (in Chinese). *Huanan Shifan Daxue Xuebao* 5 (2003): 42–46.

Zhou, Shuchun. "An Interpretation to Zhulong" (in Chinese). *Zhongguo Lishi Dili Luncong* 3 (1998): 171–175.

ZHURONG

A descendent of Yan Di (or Huang Di in various texts), Zhurong was the god of fire and of the south.

According to *Shanhaijing* (chapter 18), Zhurong was the fifth generation of Yan Di's offspring, and he also had many renowned descendants. Yan Di's wife Tingyao, a lady from the Red River, gave birth to Yanju; Yanju bore Jiebing; Jiebing gave birth to Xiqi; and Xiqi bore Zhurong. Zhurong was consigned to the Jiang River, and he fathered Gonggong, the famous water god. Gonggong in turn fathered Shuqi, whose head was square and flat. It was Shuqi who reoccupied his grandfather's territory along the Jiang River. Gonggong also sired Houtu, the earth deity. Houtu bore Shaming, and Shaming begat the twelve months of the year.

However, in another text from the same chapter of *Shanhaijing* (chapter 16), Zhurong is identified as the descendent of Zhuanxu. Zhuanxu was an offspring of Huang Di (*Shanhaijing,* chapter 18). Therefore, according to this version, Zhurong was the descendent of Huang Di. The reason for this inconsistency appearing in *Shanhaijing,* as some scholars explain, is rooted in the argument that Huang Di and Yan Di originally came from the same clan.

In *Shanhaijing* (chapter 6) there is a text that describes Zhurong's appearance. He was a deity with a human face and a beast's body. He rode on two dragons, an extraordinary feature that is symbolic of his great powers. As another account from *Shanhaijing* (chapter 18) states, in accordance with the Supreme Divinity, Zhurong killed Gun, who stole Xirang from the Supreme Divinity to prevent the flood.

In texts from *Huainanzi* and *Mozi* (written mainly by the philosopher Mo Di, ca. 468–376 BC), as well as other early documents, Zhurong is depicted as a god who ruled the south and controlled fire. This identity as the deity of fire and the south continued and later became more popular in Chinese beliefs. Today *Zhurong* has even become an alternate word for *fire* in many written texts.

In a version of the Gonggong myth, Zhurong is said to be the god who fought with Gonggong and defeated him. After his failure, Gonggong became so angry that he butted into Mount Buzhou and destroyed this sky pillar. Therefore, in some versions of this story, the great goddess Nüwa used colorful stones to patch the sky, and cut off the tortoise legs to support the heaven. In addition to Zhurong, Gonggong's rivals might variously be Di Ku, Zhuanxu, or Shennong, very great gods in Chinese mythology. This is a reflection of Zhurong's high status in both myth and popular religion.

See also Buzhou, Mount; Gonggong; Gun; Huang Di; Pillars of the Sky; Yan Di

References and Further Reading

Christie, Anthony. *Chinese Mythology.* Rev. ed. New York: Peter Bedrick Books, 1985, 58–60.

Walls, Jan, and Yvonne Walls, eds. and trans. *Classical Chinese Myths.* Hong Kong: Joint Publishing Co., 1984, 94–97.

Yuan, Ke, and Zhou Ming, comps. *A Source Book of Chinese Myth Texts* (in Chinese). Chengdu: Sichuansheng Shehui Kexueyuan Chubanshe, 1985, 39–40.

4

PRINT AND NONPRINT RESOURCES

PRINT RESOURCES

There are numerous books and articles presenting and discussing Chinese mythology, history, and culture in English or in Chinese. The following are a selection of them that might be useful for readers to further study these topics.

General Works on Chinese History and Culture

Bai, Shouyi, chief ed. *Zhongguo Tongshi* [A General History of China]. 12 vols., 22 books. In Chinese. Shanghai: Shanghai Renmin Chubanshe, 1989–1999.

> As the largest-scale research project about the general history of China ever to be undertaken, this series traces Chinese history from 1.8 million years ago until 1949, when the People's Republic of China was established. With more than 500 historians' and archaeologists' participation, the series reflects new achievements in research that Chinese scholars have made in historical studies in the past twenty years.

Ebrey, Patricia Buckley. *The Cambridge Illustrated History of China.* Cambridge: Cambridge University Press, 1999.

> An excellent introduction to the 8,000-year history of Chinese civilization. With more than 200 valuable images, this book vividly and extensively presents the transformation of Chinese society and the developments of Chinese economy, technology, art, attitudes toward women, national policies, migration, and many other facets. Remarkably, it pays much attention to how those transformations and developments influence ordinary Chinese people's lives.

Fairbank, John K., and Edwin O. Reischauer. *China: Tradition and Transformation.* Rev. ed. Boston: Houghton Mifflin Co., 1989.

This book provides a concise but thorough description of Chinese history from the prehistoric period through the post-Mao era. From eminent American sinologists' standpoint, this book not only portrays the tremendous changes Chinese traditions have undergone over the past 3,000 years but also puts forward insightful perspectives on China's contemporary revolution.

Hu, Sheng, chief ed. *Zhonghua Wenming Shihua* [A Narrative History of Chinese Civilization]. 100 vols. In Chinese. Beijing: Zhongguo Dabaike Chubanshe, 1998–2003.
   Chiefly edited by a renowned scholar and written by many experts, this encyclopedia-like series comprehensively displays various aspects of Chinese civilization, such as economy, politics, military, philosophy, history, literature, art, scientific technology, cuisine, clothing, traffic, architecture, rituals, and customs. This series is quite readable and thus accessible to common readers.

Huang, Ray. *China: A Macro History.* New York: M. E. Sharpe, 1988.
   Fascinating to average readers and scholars, both Westerners and Chinese, this book examines the full sweep of Chinese history from Neolithic times to the present. Written by a distinguished Chinese American historian, the book provides many provocative and insightful interpretations of Chinese history from a macro perspective.

Xiao, Ke, chief ed. *Zhonghua Wenhua Tongzhi* [A General Record of Chinese Culture]. 101 vols. In Chinese. Shanghai: Shanghai Renmin Chubanshe, 1998–1999.
   With more than 200 experts' contributions, this massive project aims to comprehensively and systematically reveal the developing history of Chinese culture. It exhibits the components of Chinese culture, historical evolution, and key features and contributions of different local cultures and ethnic cultures. The subjects covered include ancient history, local cultures, ethnic cultures, institutions and rules, education and etiquette, scholarships, science and technology, art and literature, religion and customs, and the cultural exchanges between China and other civilizations in the world.

Books and Articles on Chinese Mythology and Relevant Culture

Birrell, Anne. *Chinese Mythology: An Introduction.* Baltimore and London: Johns Hopkins University Press, 1993.

A very useful book that introduces the most important myths in ancient China. It provides concise and insightful interpretations and reliable accounts that are translated from primary sources in ancient Chinese writings into English. There is a very comprehensive bibliography arranged in three parts: classical Chinese texts; Chinese, Japanese, and Western works related to Chinese mythology; and research works on comparative mythology. In its foreword, renowned scholar on Chinese mythology Yuan Ke discusses the main reasons why people are under the false impression that China lacks a systematic and remarkable mythology.

Bodde, Derk. "Myths of Ancient China." In *Mythologies of the Ancient World*, ed. Samuel Noah Kramer. Chicago: Quadrangle Books, 1961, 369–408.

A short but serious work that is still very useful today. Bodde discusses three problems related to data that scholars of the East and West usually confront when studying myths of ancient China: those of euhemerization, of fragmentation and language, and of chronology. He goes on to examine five examples of creation myths: myths of Pangu, Nüwa, the separation of heaven and earth, the sun(s), and the flood. In his conclusion, Bodde summarizes several features of Chinese mythology.

Bonnefoy, Yves, comp. *Asian Mythologies*. Translated under the direction of Wendy Doniger. Chicago and London: University of Chicago Press, 1993. Originally published as *Dictionnaire des mythologies et des religions des sociétés traditionnelles et du monde antique*. Paris: Flammarion, 1981.

Among discussions of myths in East Asia and inner Asia, abundant Chinese myths are extensively examined in various subjects in part four of this volume. Chapters include "Chinese Cosmogony"; "Sky and Earth, Sun and Moon, Stars, Mountains and Rivers, and the Cardinal Points in Ancient China"; "Ancient Chinese Goddesses and Grandmothers"; "Mythical Rulers in China: The Three Huang and Five Di"; "The Great Flood in Chinese Mythology"; "Myths and Legends about the Barbarians on the Periphery of China and the Land of Chu"; and "Chinese Demons." The book contains illustrations, including black-and-white line drawings and photographs of ancient bronze and funerary ledgers.

Chen, Jianxian, comp. *Ren Shen Gong Wu* [A Collection of Prime Oral Myths of Ethnic Groups in China]. In Chinese. Wuhan: Hubei Renmin Chubanshe, 1994.

This book presents 108 myths from thirty-six ethnic groups in China. Three-fourths of them come from the national project San Tao Jicheng, the largest collection of living myths from oral tradition in modern China. The compiler, an outstanding Chinese mythologist in China today, successively arranges them according to themes such as "The Origin of Humans," "Humans and Surroundings," "Human Life," "Human's End-result," and "Myths in Series."

Christie, Anthony. *Chinese Mythology.* Rev. ed. New York: Peter Bedrick Books, 1985.

This book begins with the Chinese setting, the early history and cultures, and main sources of Chinese myths. It then presents primary myths such as the myths of Pangu, Nüwa and Fuxi, Gun and Yu, Shennong, Huang Di, and Chiyou, which appear under subject headings such as "The Creation of the World," "Earth, Water, and Air," "The Useful Arts," and "Peasant Myths." Numerous beautiful illustrations are provided, many of which can rarely be seen in mainland China.

Eberhard, Wolfram. *The Local Cultures of South and East China.* Translated by Alide Eberhard. Leiden, the Netherlands: E. J. Brill, 1968.

This book is a revised version of the second volume of the author's *Lokalkulturen im alten China* translated into English. Though some conclusions seem outdated, this influential book written by a prominent sociologist and sinologist provides many interesting and inspiring ideas about the local cultures of the south and the east in ancient China. Among its rich information about ritual, festival, belief, dance, art, and story, abundant myths such as those of Panhu, Yi, Shennong, and the dragon are also discussed.

Hou, Guang, and He Xianglu, comps. *Sichuan Shenhua Xuan* [Selected Myths from Sichuan Province]. In Chinese. Chengdu: Sichuan Minzu Chubanshe, 1992.

As one fruit of the San Tao Jicheng project, this book contains more than 120 living myths and various versions spread among ten ethnic groups in Sichuan Province in the 1980s. The myths are distributed under seven subjects: "Creation of the Cosmos," "Celestial Phenomena," "Animals and Plants," "Totem Ancestors," "Flood and the Procreation of Humans," "Emergence of Culture," and "Gods and Divine Heroes."

Karlgren, Bernhard. "Legends and Cults in Ancient China." *Bulletin of the Museum of Far Eastern Antiquities* 18 (1946): 199–365.

Karlgren was a scholar of Chinese myths who wrote historical analyses of myth writings. He was critical of early Chinese scholars' method of historicization, or the placement of Chinese mythical events into a consistent whole that can be explained by history. Most Han dynasty and other early authors modified the old traditions in order to make them consistent with the doctrines of their philosophical school. Karlgren called for a rigorous and systematic categorization of recordings in order to place them within their historical and political contexts. He suggested that the texts of classical China should be chronologically separated into those that date back to pre-Han times (before third century BC) and those that were only fabricated during the early or late Han period (206 BC–AD 220).

Liu, Tieliang, and Dong Xiaoping, eds. *Zhongguo Ge Minzu Shenhua* [Fairy Tales of Chinese Nationalities]. 20 vols. (in Chinese) Tianjin: Xinlei Chubanshe, 1991.
 Edited and compiled by experts, this picture-story-book series aims to introduce to children many of China's well-known myths, along with some fairy tales, that are spread among the fifty-six ethnic groups of China. The volumes are beautifully illustrated and provide explanations in both Chinese and English.

Lu, Yilu. *Hongshui Shenhua* [Flood Myth: Centered on the South Ethnic Groups and the Aborigines of Taiwan in China]. In Chinese. Taibei: Liren Shuju, 2002.
 The first book focusing on the Chinese flood myth. The author compares numerous flood myths spread among ethnic groups in the south, Taiwan, and the Central Plain area of China.

Lü, Wei. "Shenhua Shi" [History of Chinese Myths]. In Chinese. In *Zhonghua Minjian Wenxue Shi* [History of Chinese Folk Literature], eds. Qi Lianxiu and Cheng Qiang. Shijiazhuang: Hebei Jiaoyu Chubanshe, 1999, 1–103.
 A helpful work for understanding the historical processes by which ancient Chinese myths undergo considerable transformations.

Ma, Changyi. *Gu Ben Shanhaijing Tu Shuo* [The Classic of Mountains and Seas: Ancient Illustrations with Annotations]. In Chinese. Jinan: Shandong Huabao Chubanshe, 2001.
 Ma Changyi, a prolific Chinese mythologist, selected 1,000 illustrations from nine *Shanhaijing* versions produced in the Ming and Qing dynasties and compares these valuable drawings with the written texts. Contrary to the commonly adopted method of analyzing the written texts of *Shanhaijing*, the author tries to understand *Shanhaijing* as part of an integrated tradition, which begins in early Chinese history and tells the stories by combining both written text and drawings. These ancient line drawings are very impressive.

Ma, Changyi, ed. *Zhongguo Shenhuaxue Wenlun Xuancui* [Selected Essays on Chinese Mythology]. 2 vols. In Chinese. Beijing: Zhongguo Guangbo Dianshi Chubanshe, 1994.

> These volumes contain ninety-eight essays written from 1903 to 1991. Many of them were quite influential during the century-long history of Chinese myth studies. The editor attempts to outline the development of modern Chinese mythology and to provide a useful reference book for students of mythology.

Maspero, Henri. *Shujing Zhong de Shenhua* [Myths in Shu Jing]. Translated by Feng Yuanjun. Beiping: Shangwu Yinshuguan, 1939. Originally published as "Légends mythologiques dans le Chou Jing," *Journal Asiatique* 204 (1924): 1–100.

> The French sinologist Maspero argues that Chinese scholars always historicize Chinese myths by using euhemerism and then interpret myths as real history, understanding gods as humans. He analyzes three examples from *Shang Shu* (*Ancient History*, also called *Shu Jing*, *The Classic of History*, traditionally said to have been compiled by Confucius, 551–479 BC, but later mixed with some other texts) that relate to the myths of Xihe, the flood, and the separation of heaven and earth.

Meng, Huiying. *Huotai Shenhua* [Living Myths: Studies of Myths in Chinese Ethnic Minorities]. In Chinese. Nanjing: Nankai Daxue Chubanshe, 1990.

> An inspirational book about living myths in Chinese ethnic minorities. The author argues that typical living myths rely on rituals and other special occasions on which myths are told in heightened performances. Two chapters about myth tellers and the rituals in which myths are told provide perceptive discussions of living myth traditions.

Walls, Jan, and Yvonne Walls, eds. and trans. *Classical Chinese Myths*. Hong Kong: Joint Publishing Co., 1984.

> An interesting story book for ordinary readers. The authors vividly retell forty popular classical Chinese myths. The introduction explores in detail the universal and unique features of all forty myths presented. Two useful lists of mythic motifs and origin motifs are provided as appendices.

Wang, Xiaolian. *Zhongguo de Shenhua Shijie* [The Chinese Mythological World: A Study of the Creation Myths and Relevant Beliefs in Ethnic Groups of China]. 2 vols. In Chinese. Taibei: Shibao Chuban Gongsi, 1987.

> This book broadly discusses various myths in ethnic groups in the northeast, southwest, and the Central Plain area of China. Abundant important

Chinese myths, such as those of the wolf ancestor, Zhumeng, Panhu, Fuxi and Nüwa, Kunlun, Kuafu, and many others, are thoroughly explored. Many arguments are very persuasive. The appendix is a long essay that discusses the two forerunners of modern Chinese mythology, Gu Jiegang and Yang Kuan.

Yang, Lihui. *Nüwa de Shenhua Yu Xinyang* [The Cult of Nüwa: Myths and Beliefs in China]. In Chinese. Beijing: Chinese Social Sciences Publishing House, 1997.

This book explores Nüwa's nature and her myth's transformation over the past 2,000 years by using nearly 400 myth versions collected from oral tradition in recent years. The author examines the cult of Nüwa in ancient times and in contemporary China. Chapter 4 contains three field reports from the author's fieldwork in Henan and Hebei provinces in 1993.

Yuan, Ke. *Dragons and Dynasties: An Introduction to Chinese Mythology*. Selected and translated by Kim Echlin and Nie Zhixiong. New York: Penguin Books, 1993. First published by Foreign Languages Press, Beijing, 1991.

Written by the distinguished Chinese mythologist Yuan Ke, selected and translated by Canadian and Chinese scholars, and arranged for Western readers. This volume concisely presents principal ancient Chinese myths in six chapters: "The Gods of Creation," "The Gods Descend to Earth," "War of the Gods," "Divine Heroes," "Three Dynasties," and "Other Favorite Tales."

Yuan, Ke. *Shanhaijing Jiaozhu* [The Classic of Mountains and Seas: A Collation and Annotation]. In Chinese. Chengdu: Bashu Shushe, 1993.

The best collation and annotation book on *Shanhaijing,* the treasure house of ancient Chinese myths. Yuan Ke provides many insightful perspectives in the annotations.

Yuan, Ke. *Gu Shenhua Xuanshi* [Myths of Ancient China: An Anthology with Annotations]. In Chinese. Beijing: Renmin Wenxue Chubanshe, [1979] 1996.

One of the best sourcebooks for studying myths in ancient China. Yuan Ke selects most primary ancient texts from numerous writings and compiles them in an orderly way by listing them under different gods' and goddesses' names. He annotates many ancient words, phrases, and accounts that are often hard to understand even for a trained student of Chinese mythology. After each paragraph, he interprets the relevant myths with rich data, which come mainly from ancient written documents but sometimes from modern oral tradition of the Han and other ethnic groups, as well as from archeological findings.

Yuan, Ke. *Zhongguo Gudai Shenhua* [Myths in Ancient China]. In Chinese. Beijing: Huaxia Shushe, 2004.
> A popular book on ancient Chinese myths, especially welcomed by amateurs and beginners. Yuan Ke collects scattered and fragmented ancient myths from diverse sources and rewrites them into a logical and integrated system. The book was originally published in 1950. The new edition is expanded with many black-and-white line drawings and photographs.

Yuan, Ke. *Zhongguo Shenhua Da Cidian* [A Comprehensive Dictionary of Chinese Mythology]. In Chinese. Chengdu: Sichuan Cishu Chubanshe, 1998.
> The most comprehensive dictionary of Chinese mythology through today. The book is made up of two parts. The first part includes numerous entries based on ancient written documents. The entries broadly refer to eight subject areas: gods and goddesses, immortals, and demons; unusual men and heroes; mythical animals, plants, and apparatus; sky; earth; books and series relating to Chinese myths; mythical events; and others. The second part presents myths and mythical stories collected from oral traditions in the fifty-six ethnic groups in China. Yuan Ke collects them from various magazines, books, and collections, and then summarizes their basic plots.

Zhang, Zhenli, and Cheng Jianjun, comps. *Zhongyuan Shenhua Zhuanti Ziliao* [The Collection of Myths Transmitting in Contemporary Central Plain]. In Chinese. Zhengzhou: Zhongguo Minjian Wenyijia Xiehui Henan Fenhui, 1987.
> This useful sourcebook contains more than 100 living myths Zhang Zhenli and his research team collected from Han people in the Central Plain area (mainly Henan Province) of China from 1983 to 1987. Relevant ancient written accounts and descriptions of related modern customs based on fieldwork studies are also provided.

NONPRINT RESOURCES

Videos

The Legend of Nezha
> This interesting fifty-two-volume animated cartoon tells legendary stories of a little hero named Nezha. Volumes 20 and 21 present stories relating to

the three-legged crow and Kuafu pursuing the sun. The powerful goddess and gods Nüwa, Pangu, Zhurong, and Gonggong are also woven into the cartoon film. Available from http://www.dangdang.com.

Nüwa Mends the Sky
Made in 1985 by the Shanghai Animation Film Studio (Shanghai Meishu Dianying Zhipianchang), this animated cartoon film tells the famous stories of Nüwa creating humans by molding mud, and mending the broken sky. The film won a prize in 1986 at the International Children's Film Festival held in France. Also available from http://www.dianyingke.cn/20040311/mfq/mfdyktc3j04.htm.

Zhonghua Wuqian Nian [The Five-Thousand Years of China: History and Story] This animated cartoon series intends to display the long Chinese history and the development process during the past 5,000 years of Chinese civilization. The first ten volumes tell famous Chinese myths about Jingwei, Pangu, Nüwa, Kuafu, Shennong, Suirenshi, Yao and Shun, Cangjie, Yi and Chang'e, Huang Di, Yan Di, and Chiyou. Produced in cooperation with the Tianhuo and Xin Zixun Companies, Taiwan. Partially available from http://www.dianyingke. cn/20040311/mfq/mfdyktc3j04.htm, a Web site run by the research project team named "Film Experimental Course," supported by National Audio-Video Teaching Aid Center under the Ministry of Education, China.

Web Sites

Plentiful information about Chinese mythology can be easily found on various Web sites, but most of them are run by amateurs and often provide confusing and misleading knowledge. The following Web sites might be, comparatively, more reliable.

The China Experience: China Culture Index
http://www.chinavista.com/experience/index.html
Run by Xindeco Business Information Company, this site widely and rather comprehensively introduces Chinese culture regarding festivals, folk customs, food and drink, clothing, transportation, arts and crafts, performing arts, architecture, script and calligraphy, literature, and people. Under the catalog of "Literature" are two links: "Chinese Myths and Fantasies," which discusses the history and features of Chinese mythology as well as the style and art of ancient writing; and "Selected Chinese Myths and Fantasies,"

which explores some principal ancient Chinese myths. The sources from ancient writings are declared along with some annotations.

Chinese Folk Literature: Myths and Legends

poetic.ayinfo.cn/sccs/shenhua/

A Chinese Web site popular among Chinese students of folklore and mythology. Though some arguments about myth seem outdated today, it contains many excellent essays written by Chinese folklorists about abundant well-known Chinese myths. It also introduces numerous remarkable legends, folktales, folk songs, and proverbs. Examples from ethnic minorities are also listed.

Chinese Mythology

http://en.wikipedia.org/wiki/Chinese_mythology

A helpful Web site in English that displays Chinese mythology in four sections: "Important Mythologies and Deities," "Mythical Creatures," "Mythical Places," and "Literary Sources of Chinese Mythology." For each mythical name, traditional Chinese, simplified Chinese, and Pinyin are all provided. The site also provides links about Chinese astrology, religion, martial arts, and Chinese mythology in Chinese. However, some entries and sources are less selective.

Chinese Mythology

http://www.pantheon.org/areas/mythology/asia/chinese/articles.html

The Encyclopedia Mythica is an online encyclopedia on mythology, folklore, and legends. It contains entries on gods and goddesses, heroes, legendary creatures, and beings from all over the world. The entries are arranged alphabetically. The section on "Chinese Mythology" contains more than 160 entries. The names of deities and places are transcribed according to the Pinyin system of romanization. Still, some entries and sources are indiscriminative.

Chinese Myths in Remote Antiquity

http://www.chiculture.net/0401/html/

This is a good Chinese Web site run by the Academy of Chinese Studies (Zhongguo Wenhua Yanjiuyuan). The site provides rich information about ancient Chinese mythology in five sections. Section 1 introduces various academic arguments about some fundamental questions relating to myth. Section 2 discusses *Shanhaijing*. Section 3 contains many famous classical Chinese myths. Section 4 focuses on several important gods and goddesses. Section 5 is a game that aims to help players remember mythical figures. Many illustrations are presented.

GLOSSARY

Ba   The drought deity; the daughter of Huang Di. She can bring severe drought to the world by withholding water and rain. Also known as Nüba or Hanba.

Boyi   Domesticator of beasts and birds; a capable helper of the hero Yu in controlling the great flood and taming all kinds of animals in the world. Also appears as Yi in different versions.

Buzhou, Mount   A famous sky pillar; one of the mythical mountains holding up the sky; damaged by Gonggong in a war.

Cancong   The founder of the ancient Shu kingdom in mythical history; a mythological hero who taught the techniques of sericulture to humans in local mythology.

Cangjie   A culture hero who invented Chinese characters.

Chang'e   The goddess of the moon. She stole the elixir of immortality from her husband, the great hero Yi, and flew to the moon.

Changxi   Mother of the twelve moons; one of Di Jun's wives.

Chiyou   Offspring of Yan Di; the god of war; the inventor of military weapons. He rebelled against Huang Di but failed in the war and was killed.

Chuci   *The Songs of Chu*; major repository of Chinese ancient myths; ancient poem collection from the end of the Warring States era and the early Western Han era. It was written mainly by Qu Yuan (ca. 340–278 BC), who was the earliest celebrated poet in ancient China, as well as several other poets.

Cords of the Earth   Cords tied to the earth to prevent it from collapsing. Commonly known as Di Wei in Chinese mythology.

Crow of the Sun   A mythical bird functioning as the spirit of the sun or, in some versions, the bearer of the sun across the sky. Sometimes it is said to be three-legged.

Culture hero   Deity to whom are attributed the early achievements of civilization, such as the discovery of fire; the invention of tools or writing; the origin of agriculture, fishing, and hunting; the domestication of animals; the development of medicine; and the founding of ceremonies, rituals, and customs. Also acts as the mythic hero who dispels and eliminates the evil gods and monsters, clears up the chaos, and establishes the general order of social life on the earth.

Di Jun   One of the supreme gods in ancient times; companion to Xihe, mother of the suns; also companion to Changxi, mother of the moons. Many of his descendants are famous culture heroes or demigods.

Di Ku   Also called Gaoxin; grandson of Huang Di; one of the Five August Emperors in the mythical history of China. During his reign he oversaw the composition of many Chinese traditional songs and the invention of several musical instruments. By his order, his two sons who fought every day became star gods.

Dragon   One of the most important mythical creatures in Chinese mythology; the controller of the rain, the river, the sea, and all other kinds of water; symbol of divine power and energy; great helper of heroes; bearer of gods or demigods. In the Imperial era it was identified as the symbol of imperial power.

Elixir of Immortality   Magic drug that can bring longevity and immortality to the one taking it.

Fangfeng   A god and giant, killed by Yu for arriving late to the assembly of the gods.

Feng Bo   The wind god; helped Chiyou in a battle against Huang Di. In one version he was shot by the archer Yi. Also known as Feng Shi.

Five August Emperors   Legendary sovereigns in mythical ancient Chinese history; names differ in different texts, but often refer to Huang Di, Zhuanxu, Di Ku, Yao, and Shun; sometimes said to be Taihao Fuxishi, Yan Di Shennongshi, Huang Di, Shaohao, and Zhuanxu; also variously depicted as the five sovereigns distributed to rule over the five directions and the five elements.

Flood   A worldwide mythical theme; the flood in ancient times imperiled the world; heroes or heroines tried to stop the flood and save the world from the disaster. Afterward human ancestors tried to re-create human races, and eventually a new cosmic order was built and a new civilization appeared.

Fusang   A world-tree in the east where the ten suns stay, bathe, and rise. Also known as Fumu.

Fuxi   Culture hero; human ancestor; one of the most powerful primeval gods in Chinese mythology. May also be called Paoxi or Baoxi in ancient literature. In later tradition he is often said to be Nüwa's brother and husband and is confused with Taihao. He invented many important cultural items and established the marriage rule in remote antiquity. Also known as a human ancestor who procreated humans by marrying his sister.

Gonggong   The water god, having a man's head with red hair and a serpent's body, who caused a flood disaster and bumped into Mount Buzhou, giving rise to cosmic disorder. Also known as Kanghui in ancient texts.

Goumang   The wood god and the inventor of the *luo* (a net for catching birds); assistant of Fuxi in reigning over the east and the season of spring. In some versions, "Goumang" is a title for the officer of wood.

Gun   A popular culture hero. He stole Xirang, the self-growing soil, from the Supreme Divinity in order to stop the flood, but failed in his mission and was killed by the God of Fire, Zhurong, at Mount Yushan. His corpse turned into a yellow bear and dove into the pool of Yuyuan. His son Yu was miraculously born from the belly of his corpse and continued to fight the flood until he succeeded.

He Bo   The god of the Yellow River who helped Yu stop the flood by providing him a map of the rivers' situations. In some versions, he was shot by the hero Yi because he drowned men.

Houji   Important culture hero who brought varieties of grain to people and taught them cultivating and harvesting; widely known as the God of Agriculture. He was miraculously born by Jiang Yuan, the first consort of the god Di Ku, and later became the ancestor of the Zhou people. Also named Qi.

Houtu   The Deity of the Earth; descendant of Yan Di, son of Gonggong, grandfather of Kuafu, and the assistant god of Huang Di who assisted Huang Di in reigning over the central part of the world. Also described as the ruler of the netherworld. Houtu's gender was ambiguous in early accounts but later was changed to female in writings and popular religion.

Huainanzi   Major repository of Chinese ancient myths; a book written and compiled at the beginning of the Western Han dynasty (ca. 139 BC) by Liu An, the king of Huainan, and many of his aides; preserves many ancient myths, legends, and historical accounts.

Huang Di   Also named Xuanyuan. The most important of the Five August Emperors; the half brother of Yan Di, and the forebear of some ethnic groups and many notable deities. He defeated Yan Di, Chiyou, and other deities and became the most powerful ruler of the central part of ancient China in mythical history. In later tradition he was highly respected as a common ancestor of all Chinese people. Also a great culture hero who invented almost all of the necessary items in ancient times.

Hundun   An obscure mythical figure in Chinese mythology; variously said to be the god of the central region who had not a single aperture but later was killed by two meddling gods by chiseling openings on his body. Also described as a bad and ferocious deity in some other writings.

Jiandi   Ancestress of the Shang people; the second wife of Di Ku. She ingested a swallow's egg and miraculously gave birth to Qi, the founder of the Shang people.

Jiang Yuan   Ancestress of the Zhou people; the first consort of Di Ku and the mother of Houji. She stepped into a huge footprint in a field and miraculously gave birth to Houji, the God of Agriculture and the founder of the Zhou people.

Jianmu   One of the most famous sky ladders in Chinese myth, which enabled gods and humans to travel between heaven and earth.

Jingwei   A mythical bird that metamorphosed from Yan Di's daughter, who drowned in the eastern sea, and thus indomitably tried to fill up the sea with pebbles.

Kuafu   The grandson of Houtu; the mythical hero who chased the sun to compete with it in a race but died of thirst in the end. His stick then transformed into a forest of peach trees.

Kui   A one-legged mythical monster; killed by Huang Di. Its hide was used by Huang Di to make a drum for defeating Chiyou.

Kunlun Mountain   One of the most remarkable mythical mountains in Chinese mythology; the earthly residence of the Supreme Divinity; paradise of deities and immortals; one of the pillars of the sky that prevented the heaven from collapsing; a sky ladder that linked the earth to heaven.

Leizu   The first wife of Huang Di, the grandmother of Zhuanxu. She started sericulture, the cultivation of silkworms and production of silk, and was worshiped as the Sericulture Goddess after she died.

Li   The Governor of Fire; offspring of Zhuanxu. He cut off the connection between heaven and the earth with another deity, Zhong.

Linglun   The culture hero who invented music and many musical instruments.

Living Myth   A myth orally transmitted in modern China in various contexts.

Nüwa   Great Mother of humans; culture heroine; one of the most important and powerful primeval goddesses in Chinese mythology. She repaired the broken sky and created human beings by molding them from yellow earth. In other versions she married her brother and propagated humans.

Pangu   The creator of the world; the first divine human, who was miraculously born within the cosmic egg. It was he who separated heaven and earth, and when he died, his body transformed into the universe.

Pillars of the Sky   Huge pillars that supported heaven and prevented it from collapsing or swinging; sometimes used to separate heaven from the earth.

Qi   The founder of the Shang people; the son of Di Ku. He was miraculously born by Jiandi after she ingested a swallow's egg and then became pregnant.

Sericulture   The cultivation of silkworms and production of silk.

Shanhaijing   *The Classic of Mountains and Seas;* an important book in ancient Chinese mythology studies and a major repository of Chinese ancient myths; describes various mountains and seas, products of the mountains such as plants or medicines, myths, witchcraft, and religion of ancient China; also records the geography, history, medicine, custom, and ethnicities in ancient times.

Shaohao   One of the most notable supreme gods in Chinese mythology. He founded his capital in the east, but later was known as the god who reigns over the west and controls the season of autumn. Also known as Jintianshi, Zhi, Zhuxuan, and Baidi.

Shennong   A popular culture hero who started agriculture, Chinese medicine, the market, and the Zhaji Sacrificial Rite, and also invented many farm tools and musical instruments; one of the Three Divine Sovereigns. He was confused with Yan Di in later tradition.

Shentu   Always appears with Yulü in myths and popular religion; both are the original Gate Gods.

Shiji   *Historical Records;* the first general history book of China, written by an exemplary historian, Sima Qian (ca. 145–ca. 86 BC); presents a number of myths, together with various legends, folktales, and popular customs.

Shujun   Descendent of Di Jun; the God of Cultivation; skillful craftsman who invented many vital cultural items for humans.

Shun A demigod; the second of the three sage kings; successor of Yao; also identified as one of the Five August Emperors in the mythical history of China in some versions; the one who abdicated and gave the throne to Yu.

Sky Ladder Mythical ladder that connected heaven and the earth; enabled gods and humans to travel between heaven and earth.

Suirenshi A famous Chinese culture hero who invented the technique of making fire by drilling on wood.

Taihao One of the five gods of the directions; the god of the east and the spring season. He is often confused with Fuxi in later tradition. Also known as Dahao.

Tang Valley The place where the ten suns stay, rise, and bathe. Also called Yang Valley in different versions.

Ten Suns A popular motif in myths in the Chinese language; formerly ten suns that lived on the Fusang tree and rose one by one. In some versions they appeared together in the sky, and nine of them were shot down by the hero Yi.

Three Divine Sovereigns Mythical rulers in ancient Chinese history; names differ in different texts; sometimes said to be Fuxi, Nüwa, and Shennong; sometimes refer to Fuxi, Suirenshi, and Shennong; or variously said to be the Heaven God, the Earth God, and the Human God.

Three Sage Kings Legendary emperors in remote antiquity; traditionally said to be Yao, Shun, and Yu.

"Tianwen" "Questions of Heaven," a poem of *Chuci (Songs of Chu)*; asks 172 questions related to popularly spread myths, legends, and pieces of history.

Twelve Moons Born and bathed by Changxi.

Xiangliu Minister of Gonggong; a monster with nine human heads and a snake's trunk who was killed by the hero Yu.

Xihe Mother of the ten suns; one of Di Jun's wives.

Xingtian A notable deity who continued to fight against the supreme god even after he was beheaded. In some early texts he is also said to be a minister of Yan Di.

Xirang A mythical soil that was able to grow ceaselessly by itself; used by the heroes Gun and Yu to stop the overflowing floodwaters.

Xiwangmu One of the most popular goddesses in Chinese mythology and folk religion; originally a wild beastlike goddess (or god); the ruler of punishment, calamity, and disease; later changed into a cultivated queen, the owner of the elixir of immortality and the divine saucer peach that could endow longevity on the one who ate it. Later she was known as the leader of the goddesses of the Taoist pantheon. Now widely known as Wangmu Niangniang.

Yan Di God of the south, summer, and fire, one of the Five August Emperors who ruled over the five directions and five elements; half brother of Huang Di. He had an extensive war with Huang Di but lost. In later tradition he was often confused with Shennong. He was further respected as the common ancestor, together with Huang Di, of all Chinese people.

Yao   A demigod; the first of the three sage kings; famous for initiating the system of abdicating and handing over the crown to a worthy person; the king who ordered the hero Yi to shoot down nine of the ten suns that appeared together in the sky; in some versions identified as the hero who shot down those nine suns; also known in one account as one of the Five August Emperors in the mythical history of China.

Yao Grass   A mythical grass transformed from the body of Yan Di's daughter after she died. It could make people who ate it charming and attractive.

Yi   Chang'e's husband; a great divine archer and a famous culture hero who shot down the nine surplus suns, and also wiped out various kinds of monsters. In later tradition, he was often confused with another archer, Houyi.

Yinglong   A divine winged dragon that helped Huang Di to overcome Chiyou; also identified as the god of rain in some versions.

Youchaoshi   A culture hero; inventor of the nest for people to live in. Also known as Youchao or Da Chao.

Youdu   The capital of the other world that is located below the surface of the earth. Also the name of a place where the sun sets.

Yu   A demigod miraculously born from the belly of Gun's corpse; a hero famous for controlling the world flood; successor of Shun; the third of the three sage kings; the founder of the first civilized state, the Xia; identified as a descendent of Zhuanxu and Huang Di in some versions. Often appears as Da Yu in verbal art.

Yu Shi   The rain god; one of the great helpers of Chiyou in the battle against Huang Di.

Yulü   Always appears with Shentu in myths and popular religion; both are the original Gate Gods.

Yuqiang   Descendent of Huang Di; the god of the north sea and the wind. Also appears as Yujing in some versions.

Zhong   A god who cut off the connection between heaven and the earth with another god, Li.

Zhuanxu   Descendent of Huang Di; the god of the north; one of the Five August Emperors in the mythical history of China; also known as Gaoyang. It was he who ordered Zhong and Li to separate heaven and the earth.

Zhulong   A powerful deity who appears to be part dragon and originates the day and night, seasons and wind. Also appears as Zhuyin.

Zhurong   Descendent of Yan Di (or Huang Di in various texts); god of fire; god of the south. In one version he is said to be the god who fought with Gonggong and defeated him.

INDEX

Note: bolded page numbers indicate a more substantive discussion.

ABOUT THE AUTHORS

Lihui Yang, Ph.D., is professor of folklore and mythology at the College of Chinese Language and Literature at Beijing Normal University, Beijing, China. Her published works include *The Cult of Nüwa: Myths and Beliefs in China* (1997) and *Rethinking on the Source Area of the Cult of Nüwa* (1999). She has won some of the most prestigious research and teaching awards in her discipline given in China.

Deming An, Ph.D., is associate professor of folklore at the Institute of Literature, Chinese Academy of Social Sciences, Beijing, China. His published works include *Averting Natural Disaster: A Study of Agricultural Rituals from Farming Villages in Tianshui, Gansu Province* (2003) and *Going Back to Hometown: A Folklorist's Field Experiences in Familiar Place* (2004).

Jessica Anderson Turner is a Ph.D. candidate in the Department of Folklore and Ethnomusicology at Indiana University, Bloomington, Indiana. She was a 2003–2004 Fulbright Fellow and conducted research on revivals of tradition and music in China's developing tourism industry.